STORRS LECTURES ON JURISPRUDENCE
YALE LAW SCHOOL, 1963

THE
MORALITY
OF
LAW

Revised edition

BY LON L. FULLER

NEW HAVEN AND LONDON, YALE UNIVERSITY PRESS

ISBN: 0–300–00472–9 (cloth), 0–300–01070–2 (paper)
Library of Congress catalog number: 72–93579

Designed by Sally Hargrove Sullivan,
set in Times Roman type,
and printed in the United States of America by
BookCrafters, Inc.,
Fredericksburg, Virginia.

26   25   24   23   22

PREFACE TO

THE SECOND EDITION

In this new edition of *The Morality of Law* the first four chapters have been reprinted from the type as it was originally set, with only a minor correction or two. The only change of substance consists, therefore, in the addition of a fifth and final chapter entitled "A Reply to Critics."

The fact that the first four chapters remain virtually unchanged does not imply complete satisfaction with either the form or the substance of the presentation achieved in them. It means simply that I have not proceeded far enough in my rethinking of the problems involved to undertake any substantial reformulation of the views I first expressed in lectures delivered in 1963. It means also that basically I stand by the positions taken in those lectures.

I hope that the new fifth chapter will not be viewed simply as an exercise in polemics. For many decades legal philosophy in the English-speaking world has been largely dominated by the tradition of Austin, Gray, Holmes, and Kelsen. The central place their general view of law has occupied does not mean that it has ever been received with entire satisfaction; even its adherents have often displayed discomfort with some of its implications. In the new concluding chapter of this book I have achieved, I think, a better articulation of my own dissatisfactions with analytical legal positivism than I had ever achieved before. For this I am deeply indebted to my critics, and particularly to H. L. A. Hart, Ronald Dworkin, and Marshall Cohen. Their strictures have not always been softly phrased, but by the same token they have not been blunted by the self-protective obscurities often found in polemic attacks. By laying bare the basic premises of their thought, they have helped me to do the same with mine.

Since the first edition of this book has been found of some value by scholars whose primary interests lie in legal sociology and anthropology, it might be well to offer a suggestion to those first approaching the book from the standpoint of similar interests. My suggestion is that they begin by reading Chapters II and V in that order, skipping for the time being the others. This mode of approaching the book will serve the dual purpose of suggesting whatever of value it may have for their special concerns, at the same time offering some notion of the basic differences in viewpoint that divide legal scholars in the task of defining their own subject.

In closing I want to express a word of appreciation for the contribution made to this book (and to my peace of mind) by Martha Anne Ellis, my secretary, and Ruth D. Kaufman of the Yale University Press. Their diligence and perception have largely lifted from my concern the time-consuming and anxiety-producing details that always accompany the conversion of a manuscript into final printed form.

May 1, 1969   L.L.F.

PREFACE TO

THE FIRST EDITION

This book is based on lectures given at the Yale Law School in April 1963 as a part of the William L. Storrs Lecture Series. Though the present volume expands the original text several times over, I have preserved the lecture form as congenial to the subject matter and as permitting the informal and often argumentative presentation I preferred. The result is a certain incongruity between form and substance; even the polite patience of a Yale audience would hardly have enabled it to sit through my second "lecture" as it now appears.

As an appendix I have added something that I wrote long before I undertook these lectures. It is called The Problem of the Grudge Informer. It may be found useful to read and think about this problem before turning to my second chapter. The problem was originally conceived to serve as a basis for discussion in my course in jurisprudence. During the past few years it has also been used as a kind of introduction to the problems of jurisprudence in a course taken by all first-year students in the Harvard Law School.

In making my acknowledgments first thanks must go to the Yale Law School, not only for the welcome spur of its invitation, but for granting an extension of time so that I might more nearly meet its demands. I must also express my gratitude to the Rockefeller Foundation for helping me to gain access, during the school year 1960–61, to that rarest commodity in American academic life: leisure. By leisure I mean, of course, the chance to read and reflect without the pressure of any immediate commitment to being, or pretending to be, useful. Quite simply, without the aid of the Foundation I would not have been able to accept Yale's invitation. My indebtedness to colleagues runs to so many for such diverse forms of aid that it is impossible to acknowledge it adequately. None of them, it should be said, had any chance to rescue the final text from those last-minute infelicities to which stubborn authors are prone. During the early stages of the undertaking, however, their contributions were of so essential a nature that in my eyes this book is as much theirs as mine. Finally, in acknowledging the very real contribution of my wife, Marjorie, I shall borrow a conceit from another writer: she may not know what it means, but she knows what it meant.

L. L. F.

CONTENTS

Preface to the Second Edition   v

Preface to the First Edition   vii

I. THE TWO MORALITIES   3
   The Moralities of Duty and of Aspiration   5
   The Moral Scale   9
   The Vocabulary of Morals and the Two Moralities   13
   Marginal Utility and the Morality of Aspiration   15
   Reciprocity and the Morality of Duty   19
   Locating the Pointer on the Moral Scale   27
   Rewards and Penalties   30

II. THE MORALITY THAT MAKES LAW POSSIBLE   33
   Eight Ways to Fail to Make Law   33
   The Consequences of Failure   38
   The Aspiration toward Perfection in Legality   41
   Legality and Economic Calculation   44
   The Generality of Law   46
   Promulgation   49
   Retroactive Laws   51
   The Clarity of Laws   63
   Contradictions in the Laws   65
   Laws Requiring the Impossible   70

Constancy of the Law through Time 79
Congruence between Official Action and Declared Rule 81
Legality as a Practical Art 91

III. THE CONCEPT OF LAW 95
Legal Morality and Natural Law 96
Legal Morality and the Concept of Positive Law 106
The Concept of Science 118
Objections to the View of Law Taken Here 122
Hart's *The Concept of Law* 133
Law as a Purposeful Enterprise and Law as a
    Manifested Fact of Social Power 145

IV. THE SUBSTANTIVE AIMS OF LAW 152
The Neutrality of the Law's Internal Morality
    toward Substantive Aims 153
Legality as a Condition of Efficacy 155
Legality and Justice 157
Legal Morality and Laws Aiming at Alleged Evils
    That Cannot Be Defined 159
The View of Man Implicit in Legal Morality 162
The Problem of the Limits of Effective Legal Action 168
Legal Morality and the Allocation of Economic
    Resources 170
Legal Morality and the Problem of Institutional Design 177
Institutional Design as a Problem of Economizing 178
The Problem of Defining the Moral Community 181
The Minimum Content of a Substantive Natural Law 184

V. A REPLY TO CRITICS 187
The Structure of Analytical Legal Positivism 191
Is Some Minimum Respect for the Principles of
    Legality Essential to the Existence of a Legal System? 197

Do the Principles of Legality Constitute an "Internal
    Morality of Law"?   200
Some Implications of the Debate   224

APPENDIX: THE PROBLEM OF THE
    GRUDGE INFORMER   245
Index   255

THE MORALITY OF LAW

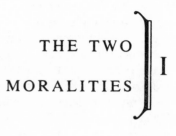

THE TWO MORALITIES

I

Sin, *v.i.* *1. To depart voluntarily from the path of duty prescribed by God to man.*—Webster's New International Dictionary

Die Sünde ist ein Versinken in das Nichts.[1]

The content of these chapters has been chiefly shaped by a dissatisfaction with the existing literature concerning the relation between law and morality. This literature seems to me to be deficient in two important respects. The first of these relates to a failure to clarify the meaning of morality itself. Definitions of law we have, in almost unwanted abundance. But when law is

1. This quotation may be purely imaginary. I *think* I recall it from something I read long ago. Friends learned in theology have been unable to identify its source. They inform me that its thought is Augustinian and that there is a closely parallel passage in Karl Barth: "Die Sünde ist ein Versinken in das Bodenlose." However, "das Bodenlose" implies a loss of limits or boundaries and therefore suggests a transgression of duty. What I have sought is an expression of the concept of sin as viewed by a morality of aspiration—sin as a failure in the effort to achieve a realization of the human quality itself.

3

compared with morality, it seems to be assumed that everyone knows what the second term of the comparison embraces. Thomas Reed Powell used to say that if you can think about something that is related to something else without thinking about the thing to which it is related, then you have the legal mind. In the present case, it has seemed to me, the legal mind generally exhausts itself in thinking about law and is content to leave unexamined the thing to which law is being related and from which it is being distinguished.

In my first chapter an effort is made to redress this balance. This is done chiefly by emphasizing a distinction between what I call the morality of aspiration and the morality of duty. A failure to make this distinction has, I think, been the cause of much obscurity in discussions of the relation between law and morals.

The other major dissatisfaction underlying these lectures arises from a neglect of what the title of my second chapter calls, "The Morality That Makes Law Possible." Insofar as the existing literature deals with the chief subject of this second chapter—which I call "the internal morality of law"—it is usually to dismiss it with a few remarks about "legal justice," this conception of justice being equated with a purely formal requirement that like cases be given like treatment. There is little recognition that the problem thus adumbrated is only one aspect of a much larger problem, that of clarifying the directions of human effort essential to maintain any system of law, even one whose ultimate objectives may be regarded as mistaken or evil.

The third and fourth chapters constitute a further development and application of the analysis presented in the first two. The third, entitled "The Concept of Law," attempts to bring this analysis into relation with the various schools of legal philosophy generally. The fourth, "The Substantive Aims of Law," seeks to demonstrate how a proper respect for the internal morality of law limits the kinds of substantive aims that may be achieved through legal rules. The chapter closes with an examination of the extent to which something like a substantive "natural law" may be derived from the morality of aspiration.

The Moralities of Duty and of Aspiration

Let me now turn without further delay to the distinction between the morality of aspiration and the morality of duty. This distinction is itself by no means new.[2] I believe, however, that its full implications have generally not been seen, and that in particular they have not been sufficiently developed in discussions of the relations of law and morals.

The morality of aspiration is most plainly exemplified in Greek philosophy. It is the morality of the Good Life, of excellence, of the fullest realization of human powers. In a morality of aspiration there may be overtones of a notion approaching that of duty. But these overtones are usually muted, as they are in Plato and Aristotle. Those thinkers recognized, of course, that a man might fail to realize his fullest capabilities. As a citizen or as an official, he might be found wanting. But in such a case he was condemned for failure, not for being recreant to duty; for shortcoming, not for wrongdoing. Generally with the Greeks instead of ideas of right and wrong, of moral claim and moral duty, we have rather the conception of proper and fitting conduct, conduct such as beseems a human being functioning at his best.[3]

Where the morality of aspiration starts at the top of human achievement, the morality of duty starts at the bottom. It lays down the basic rules without which an ordered society is impossible, or without which an ordered society directed toward certain

2. See, for example, A. D. Lindsay, *The Two Moralities* (1940); A. Macbeath, *Experiments in Living* (1952), pp. 55–56 et passim; W. D. Lamont, *The Principles of Moral Judgement* (1946); and by the same author, *The Value Judgement* (1955); H. L. A. Hart, *The Concept of Law* (1961), pp. 176–80; J. M. Findlay, *Values and Intentions* (1961); Richard B. Brandt, *Ethical Theory* (1959), esp. pp. 356–68. In none of these works does the nomenclature I have adopted in these lectures appear. Lindsay, for example, contrasts the morality of "my station and its duties" with the morality of the challenge to perfection. Findlay's book is especially valuable for its treatment of the "hortatory" abuses of the concept of duty.

3. Cf. "the Greeks never worked out anything resembling the modern notion of a legal right." Jones, *The Law and Legal Theory of the Greeks* (1956), p. 151.

specific goals must fail of its mark. It is the morality of the Old Testament and the Ten Commandments. It speaks in terms of "thou shalt not," and, less frequently, of "thou shalt." It does not condemn men for failing to embrace opportunities for the fullest realization of their powers. Instead, it condemns them for failing to respect the basic requirements of social living.

In his *Theory of Moral Sentiments,* Adam Smith employs a figure that is useful in drawing a distinction between the two moralities I am here describing.[4] The morality of duty "may be compared to the rules of grammar"; the morality of aspiration "to the rules which critics lay down for the attainment of what is sublime and elegant in composition." The rules of grammar prescribe what is requisite to preserve language as an instrument of communication, just as the rules of a morality of duty prescribe what is necessary for social living. Like the principles of a morality of aspiration, the principles of good writing, "are loose, vague, and indeterminate, and present us rather with a general idea of the perfection we ought to aim at, than afford us any certain and infallible directions of acquiring it."

It will be well at this point to take some form of human conduct and ask how the two moralities might proceed to pass judgment on it. I have chosen the example of gambling. In using this term I do not have in mind anything like a friendly game of penny ante, but gambling for high stakes—what in the translation of Bentham's *The Theory of Legislation* is called by the picturesque term, "deep play."[5]

How would the morality of duty view gambling thus defined? Characteristically it would postulate a kind of hypothetical moral

4. *The Theory of Moral Sentiments, 1,* 442. The distinction taken by Smith is not between a morality of duty and a morality of aspiration, but between justice and "the other virtues." There is plainly, however, a close affinity between the notion of justice and that of moral duty, though the duty of dealing justly with others probably covers a narrower area than that embraced by moral duties generally.

5. See the note to page 106 of Hildreth's translation as reprinted in the International Library of Psychology, *Philosophy and Scientific Method* (1931).

legislator who would be charged with the responsibility of deciding whether gambling was so harmful that we ought to consider
that there is a general moral duty, incumbent on all, to refrain
from engaging in it. Such a legislator might observe that gambling
is a waste of time and energy, that it seems to act like a drug on
those who become addicted to it, that it has many undesirable
consequences, such as causing the gambler to neglect his family
and his duties toward society generally.

If our hypothetical moral legislator had gone to the school
of Jeremy Bentham and the later marginal utility economists, he
might find good reasons for declaring gambling intrinsically harmful and not merely harmful because of its indirect consequences.
If a man's whole fortune consists of a thousand dollars and he
wagers five hundred of it on what is called an even bet, he has
not in fact entered a transaction in which possible gains and
losses are evenly balanced. If he loses, each dollar he pays out
cuts more deeply into his well-being. If he wins, the five hundred
he gains represents less utility to him than the five hundred he
would have paid out had he lost. We thus reach the interesting
conclusion that two men may come together voluntarily and
without any intent to harm one another and yet enter a transaction which is to the disadvantage of both—judged, of course,
by the state of affairs just before the dice are actually thrown.

Weighing all these considerations, the moralist of duty might
well come to the conclusion that men ought not to engage in
gambling for high stakes, that they have a duty to shun "deep
play."

How is such a moral judgment related to the question whether
gambling ought to be prohibited by law? The answer is, very
directly. Our hypothetical legislator of morals could shift his role
to that of lawmaker without any drastic change in his methods of
judgment. As a lawmaker he will face certain questions that as a
moralist he could conveniently leave to casuistry. He will have
to decide what to do about games of skill or games in which the
outcome is determined partly by skill and partly by chance. As
a statutory draftsman he will confront the difficulty of distin-

guishing between gambling for small stakes as an innocent amusement and gambling in its more desperate and harmful forms. If no formula comes readily to hand for this purpose, he may be tempted to draft his statute so as to include every kind of gambling, leaving it to the prosecutor to distinguish the innocent from the truly harmful. Before embracing this expedient, often described euphemistically as "selective enforcement," our moralist turned lawmaker will have to reflect on the dangerous consequences that would attend a widened application of that principle, already a pervasive part of the actual machinery of law enforcement. Many other considerations of this nature he would have to take into account in drafting and proposing his statute. But at no point would there be any sharp break with the methods he followed in deciding whether to condemn gambling as immoral.

Let us now view gambling as it might appear to the morality of aspiration. From this point of view we are concerned not so much with the specific harms that may flow from gambling, but with the question whether it is an activity worthy of man's capacities. We would recognize that in human affairs risk attends all creative effort and that it is right and good that a man engaged in creative acts should not only accept the risks of his role, but rejoice in them. The gambler, on the other hand, cultivates risk for its own sake. Unable to face the broader responsibilities of the human role, he discovers a way of enjoying one of its satisfactions without accepting the burdens that usually accompany it. Gambling for high stakes becomes, in effect, a kind of fetishism. The analogy to certain deviations in the sex instinct is readily apparent and has in fact been exploited to the full in an extensive psychiatric literature on obsessive gambling.[6]

The final judgment that the morality of aspiration might thus pass on gambling would not be an accusation, but an expression of disdain. For such a morality, gambling would not be the violation of a duty, but a form of conduct unbefitting a being with human capacities.

6. See the bibliography listed in Edmund Bergler, *The Psychology of Gambling* (1957), note 1, pp. 79–82.

What bearing would the judgment thus passed have on the law? The answer is that it would have no direct bearing at all. There is no way by which the law can compel a man to live up to the excellences of which he is capable. For workable standards of judgment the law must turn to its blood cousin, the morality of duty. There, if anywhere, it will find help in deciding whether gambling ought to be legally prohibited.

But what the morality of aspiration loses in direct relevance for the law, it gains in the pervasiveness of its implications. In one aspect our whole legal system represents a complex of rules designed to rescue man from the blind play of chance and to put him safely on the road to purposeful and creative activity. When in transacting affairs with another a man pays money under a mistake of fact, the law of quasi contract compels a return. The law of contracts declares void agreements entered under a mutual misapprehension of the relevant facts. Under the law of torts a man may become active without having to answer for injuries that are the fortuitous by-product of his actions, except where he enters upon some enterprise causing foreseeable risks that may be reckoned as an actuarial cost of his undertaking and thus subjected to rational calculation in advance. In the early stages of the law, none of these principles was recognized. Their acceptance today represents the fruit of a centuries-old struggle to reduce the role of the irrational in human affairs.

But there is no way open to us by which we can compel a man to live the life of reason. We can only seek to exclude from his life the grosser and more obvious manifestations of chance and irrationality. We can create the conditions essential for a rational human existence. These are the necessary, but not the sufficient condititons for the achievement of that end.

The Moral Scale

As we consider the whole range of moral issues, we may conveniently imagine a kind of scale or yardstick which begins at the bottom with the most obvious demands of social living and extends upward to the highest reaches of human aspiration. Somewhere along this scale there is an invisible pointer that marks the dividing line where the pressure of duty leaves off and the challenge of excellence begins. The whole field of moral argument is dominated by a great undeclared war over the location of this pointer. There are those who struggle to push it upward; others work to pull it down. Those whom we regard as being unpleasantly—or at least, inconveniently—moralistic are forever trying to inch the pointer upward so as to expand the area of duty. Instead of inviting us to join them in realizing a pattern of life they consider worthy of human nature, they try to bludgeon us into a belief we are duty bound to embrace this pattern. All of us have probably been subjected to some variation of this technique at one time or another. Too long an exposure to it may leave in the victim a lifelong distaste for the whole notion of moral duty.

I have just spoken of an imaginary pointer that marks the line dividing duty from aspiration. The task of finding the proper resting place for this pointer has, I think, been needlessly complicated by a confusion of thought that runs back at least as far as Plato. I have in mind an argument along these lines: In order to judge what is bad in human conduct, we must know what is perfectly good. Every action must be appraised in the light of its contribution to the perfect life. Without a picture of the ideal of human existence before us, we can have no standard, either for imposing duties or for opening new avenues for the expression of human capabilities. Those who accept this line of reasoning will reject as either meaningless or insoluble the problem of correctly locating the line where duty leaves off and aspiration begins. In their view it is obvious that the morality of aspiration is the foundation of all morality. Since the morality of duty must inevitably incorporate standards borrowed from the morality of aspiration, there is neither occasion nor warrant for drawing a clear line between the two moralities.

Curiously, the view that all moral judgments must rest on some conception of perfection has historically been employed to reach diametrically opposed conclusions concerning the objectivity of moral judgments. One side argues as follows: It is a fact of experience that we can know and agree on what is bad. It must follow that we have in the back of our minds some shared picture of what is perfectly good. The task of moral philosophy is therefore to bring to articulation something we already know and agree upon. This is the route taken by the Platonic Socrates. The opposing party reasons as follows: It is obvious that men do not agree on what is perfectly good. But since meaningful judgments as to what is bad are impossible without an agreement on what is perfectly good—an agreement that plainly does not exist —it must follow that our apparent agreement on what is bad is an illusion, born perhaps of social conditioning, habituation, and shared prejudice.

Both conclusions rest on the assumption that we cannot know the bad without knowing the perfectly good, or, in other words, that moral duties cannot be rationally discerned without first embracing a comprehensive morality of aspiration. This assumption is contradicted by the most elementary human experience. The moral injunction "thou shalt not kill" implies no picture of the perfect life. It rests on the prosaic truth that if men kill one another off no conceivable morality of aspiration can be realized. In no field of human endeavor is it true that our judgments as to what is undesirable must be secretly directed by some half-perceived utopia. In the field of linguistics, for example, none of us pretends to know what a perfect language would be like. This does not prevent us from struggling against certain corruptions of usage which plainly tend to destroy useful distinctions.

In the whole field of human purpose—including not only human actions but artifacts of every kind—we find a pervasive refutation for the notion that we cannot know what is unsuited to an end without knowing what is perfectly suited to achieve it. In selecting instruments for our purposes we can and do make out everywhere with imperfectly defined conceptions of what it is we are trying to achieve. No ordinary human tool, for example, is perfectly suited to any particular task. It is designed rather to accomplish an indefinite range of tasks reasonably well. A car-

11

penter's hammer serves adequately over a large but indefinite range of uses, revealing its deficiencies only when we try to use it to drive very small tacks or heavy tent stakes. If a working companion asks me for a hammer, or the nearest thing to it available to me, I know at once, without knowing precisely what operation he is undertaking, that many tools will be useless to him. I do not pass him a screwdriver or a length of rope. I can, in short, know the bad on the basis of very imperfect notions of what would be good to perfection. So I believe it is with social rules and institutions. We can, for example, know what is plainly unjust without committing ourselves to declare with finality what perfect justice would be like.

None of the arguments just advanced is intended to imply that there is no difficulty in drawing the line that separates the morality of duty from that of aspiration. Deciding where duty ought to leave off is one of the most difficult tasks of social philosophy. Into its solution a large element of judgment must enter and individual differences of opinion are inevitable. What is being argued here is that we should face the difficulties of this problem and not run away from them under the pretext that no answer is possible until we have constructed a comprehensive morality of aspiration. We know enough to create the conditions that will permit a man to lift himself upward. It is certainly better to do this than to try to pin him to the wall with a final articulation of his highest good.

This is perhaps the point to forestall one further misunderstanding. It has been suggested that the morality of duty relates to man's life in society, while the morality of aspiration is a matter between a man and himself, or between him and his God.[7] This is true only in the sense that as we move up the ladder from obvious duty to highest aspiration individual differences in capacity and understanding become increasingly im-

7. The valuable analysis of W. D. Lamont seems to me to be marred by his assumption that the morality of duty has to do with social relations, while the morality of value is concerned with individual preference ratings. See *The Value Judgement* (1955).

portant. But this does not mean that the social bond is ever broken in that ascent. The classic statement of the morality of aspiration was that of the Greek philosophers. They took it for granted that man as a political animal had to find the good life in a life shared with others. If we were cut off from our social inheritance of language, thought, and art, none of us could aspire to anything much above a purely animal existence. One of the highest responsibilities of the morality of aspiration is to preserve and enrich this social inheritance.

The Vocabulary of Morals and the Two Moralities

One reason the distinction between the morality of duty and that of aspiration does not take a firmer hold in modern thought lies, I believe, in the fact that our moral vocabulary itself straddles this distinction and obscures it. Take, for example, the term "value judgment." The concept of value is congenial to a morality of aspiration. Had we chosen some other companion for it, and spoken, say, of "the perception of value," we would have had an expression thoroughly at home in a system of thought directed toward the achievement of human excellence. But instead we coupled "value" with the term "judgment," an expression which suggests not a striving toward perfection, but a conclusion about obligations. Thus a subjectivism appropriate to the higher reaches of human aspiration spreads itself through the whole language of moral discourse and we are easily led to the absurd conclusion that obligations obviously essential for social living rest on some essentially ineffable preference.

The much debated question of the relation between fact and value would, I believe, be clarified if the disputants took pains to keep in mind the distinction between the moralities of duty and of aspiration. When we are passing a judgment of moral duty, it seems absurd to say that such a duty can in some way flow directly from knowledge of a situation of fact. We may understand the facts from top to bottom, and yet there will still seem to intervene an act of legislative judgment before we conclude that a duty

13

ought to exist. This act of legislative judgment may not be difficult, but in principle it is always there.

It is quite otherwise with the morality of aspiration, which in
this respect shows its close affinity with aesthetics. When we seek
to comprehend some new form of artistic expression, our effort—
if it is well informed—will direct itself at once to the purpose
pursued by the artist. We ask ourselves, "What is he trying to do?
What does he seek to convey?" When we have answered these
questions, we may like or dislike the work in question. But no
distinct step intervenes between our understanding and our approval or disapproval. If we disapprove, but remain distrustful of
our judgment, we do not ask ourselves whether we have applied
the wrong standard of approval, but whether we have after all
truly understood what the artist was trying to do. Indeed, I. A.
Richards has shown the havoc wrought in students' judgments of
literary value when they concern themselves not with the writer's
objective, but with the application of standards by which they
suppose literature should be judged to be good or bad.[8] Similarly,
Norman T. Newton has demonstrated how aesthetic judgments
of architecture can be distorted by the effort to find some verbal
formula that will seem to justify the judgment passed.[9]

These last remarks are not intended to deny the quality of
rationality to the morality of aspiration. Rather they are intended
to assert that the discursive kind of justification that characterizes
judgments of duty is out of place in the morality of aspiration.
This point is illustrated, I believe, in the Platonic Socrates.

Socrates identified virtue with knowledge. He assumed that
if men truly understood the good they would desire it and seek to
attain it. This view has often been considered as being either
puzzling or absurd—depending on the modesty of the critic. If
Socrates were teaching a morality of duty, the criticisms of him
would certainly have been justified. But his was a morality of
aspiration. He sought to make men see and understand the good
life so that they would strive to attain it. His argument would not

8. *Practical Criticism—A Study of Literary Judgment* (1949).
9. *An Approach to Design* (1951).

14

have been clarified, but confused, if he had said, "First, I shall demonstrate what the good life is like so that you may understand it and discern what kind of man you would become if you led it. Then I shall advance reasons why you ought to lead such a life."

The Socratic identification of virtue with knowledge itself illustrates the uneasy way our ethical vocabulary has of migrating back and forth between the two moralities. With us the word "virtue" has become thoroughly identified with the morality of duty. For moderns the word has largely lost its original sense of power, efficacy, skill, and courage, a set of connotations that once put it plainly within the morality of aspiration. The word "sin" has undergone a similar migration. With us to sin is to violate a duty. Yet the words translated in the Bible as "sin" contained originally the metaphor of "missing the mark." Something of this original figure remained among the early Christians, for they listed among the deadly sins, not only Avarice and Unchastity, but also what Sidgwick calls "the rather singular sins" of Gloominess and Languid Indifference.[10]

Marginal Utility and the Morality of Aspiration

I have suggested that if we look for affinities among the human studies, the morality of duty finds its closest cousin in the law, while the morality of aspiration stands in intimate kinship with aesthetics. I now propose an inquiry that may seem a little bizarre, that of determining the relationship between the two moralities and the modes of judgment characteristic of economic science.

A difficulty encountered at the outset lies in the fact that no general agreement exists among economists about the definition of their subject. Though economics has the deserved reputation of being the most advanced of all the social sciences, the world still awaits a final answer to the question, "What is it about?" Most economic treatises are content to introduce the reader to their subject with a more or less impressionistic listing of the

10. *Outlines of the History of Ethics* (1949), p. 129.

kinds of problems that are the special concern of the economist. Beyond that the reader is left to decide for himself just what it is he is studying.[11]

There are, however, a few serious attempts to come to grips with the problem of properly defining economic science.[12] In these, two general views emerge. One is that economics has to do with relationships of exchange. The other is that the heart of economics lies in the principle of marginal utility, the principle by which we make the most effective allocation of the resources at our command in achieving whatever objectives we have set for ourselves. The standard figure employed for distinguishing between these views is, of course, that of Robinson Crusoe. Until the arrival of Friday, at least, there was no one with whom Crusoe could exchange anything, except in the metaphorical sense in which one may be said to trade one's solitary labor against the fruits of nature. If economics is identified with exchanges between human beings, then Crusoe had no economic problems. On the other hand, he did have to decide how to make the most effective application of the scarce resources at his command, including his own time and energy. If at a given moment he were cultivating a field, he might have to ask himself whether if he shifted his efforts to fishing he might expect a greater return from his first hour as a fisherman than he would from another hour as a farmer. In this

11. Paul A. Samuelson's treatise, *Economics—An Introductory Analysis*, is said to be one of the most widely used college textbooks ever written. In the second edition (1951, pp. 14–16) there appeared a discussion of the "Boundaries and Limits to Economics," in which the view was advanced that economics is concerned exclusively with means and has no competence to deal with ends. In the fifth edition (1961) this attempt to delimit the competence of the subject has disappeared and in its place there is simply a listing of the kinds of subjects with which economics deals (pp. 5–6). An interesting demonstration that economic science is characterized by a particular kind of end, and is incompetent to answer questions when that end is excluded from consideration, will be found in R. F. Harrod, *Scope and Method of Economics* (1938), reprinted in Clemence, *Readings in Economic Analysis, 1* (1950), 1–30.

12. The most widely read treatment of the subject is that of Lionel Robbins, *An Essay on the Nature and Significance of Economic Science* (2d ed. 1935).

sense Crusoe not only had economic problems, but very serious ones.

Now there is, I believe, a striking parallel between these two conceptions of economics and the two views of morality that are the subject of this chapter. The economics of exchange has a close affinity with the morality of duty. The economics of marginal utility is, as it were, the economic counterpart of the morality of aspiration. Let me begin with this second relationship.

The morality of aspiration has to do with our efforts to make the best use of our short lives. Marginal utility economics deals with our efforts to make the best use of our limited economic resources. The two are not only alike in what they seek to do, but also in their limitations. It is said that the morality of aspiration necessarily implies some conception of the highest good of man, though it fails to tell us what this is. Exactly the same criticism, with the same force, can be directed against the marginal utility principle. The consumer is viewed by marginal utility economics as seeking to equalize the return for each dollar he spends. When he has spent so many dollars for books that the return from this particular expenditure begins to diminish perceptibly, he may shift his expenditures to some other direction, say, for a richer and more satisfying diet. In this shift—in the very idea that one *can* compare and equalize expenditures for radically different things —there seems to be implied some ultimate criterion that stands above books, food, clothing, and all the other things and services for which men may spend their money. The marginal utility economist cannot describe what this criterion is, though, unlike the moralist of aspiration, he has a word to cover his ignorance. That word is, of course, "utility." When the utility derived from a dollar's worth of Commodity A declines to a point where it is lower than the utility derived from a dollar's worth of Commodity B, the consumer shifts his expenditure toward the second kind of good. It is with this word "utility" that the economist draws a veil over his failure to discern some economic good that stands above all particular goods and serves to guide choice among them. The economist's default remains, however, in essence the same as that of the moralist who purports to show men the way to the Good Life, without defining what the highest aim of life is or should be.[13]

Bentham's attempt to substitute for the goal of excellence that of pleasure was in effect simply to introduce into morality the same covert default that is inveterate in economics. It is impossible to maintain the assertion that all human striving is directed toward pleasure unless we are willing to expand the notion of pleasure to the point where it becomes, like utility in economics, an empty container for every kind of human want or striving. If, following Mill, we try to be more selective about what goes into the container, we end, not with the greatest happiness principle, but something like the Greek conception of excellence.

In default of some highest moral or economic good, we resort ultimately, both in the morality of aspiration and in marginal utility economics, to the notion of balance—not too much, not too little. This notion is not so trite as it seems. It is a characteristic of normal human beings that they pursue a plurality of ends; an obsessive concern for some single end can in fact be taken as a symptom of mental disease. In one passage Aquinas seems to make the curious argument that the existence of an ultimate end for human life is revealed in the circumstance that we do in fact shift from one particular end to another, for if there were no standard by which this shift could be guided we would go on forever striving in one direction. Since this is impossible and absurd

13. It may be objected that the comparison in the text confuses description with prescription. Unlike the moral philosopher, the economist, it may be said, is indifferent to the question what the consumer *ought* to want; he merely describes a process of evaluation and finds the term "utility" useful in this description. But this view dodges the difficulties involved in trying to describe in wholly non-evaluative terms a process that is itself evaluative. (These difficulties were the occasion for an exchange between myself and Professor Ernest Nagel; see 3 *Natural Law Forum* 68–104 [1958]; 4 id. 26–43 [1959].) The economist may not care what the consumer wants, but he cannot be indifferent to the process by which the consumer reaches his decision as to what he wants. If he is to understand that process, the economist must be capable of participating in it vicariously and have an understanding of its terms.

18

it follows that we would not act at all, in any direction, if we were not guided by some highest end.[14] Whatever one may think of this paradoxical reasoning, there is nothing banal about Aristotle's conception of the just mean. This mean is not to be confused with the modern notion of "the middle way." For moderns the middle way is the easy way, involving a minimum of commitment. For Aristotle the mean was the hard way, the way from which the slothful and unskilled were most likely to fall. In this respect it made the same demands on insight and intelligence that sound economic management does.

Reciprocity and the Morality of Duty

So much for the relation between the morality of aspiration and a view of economic science that sees it as being concerned essentially with prudent management. Let me now turn to the affinity I have asserted to exist between the morality of duty and the economics of exchange.

It is obvious that duties, both moral and legal, can arise out of an exchange, say, an exchange of promises or the exchange of a promise for a present act. A territory exists, therefore, that is shared in common by the concepts of exchange and duty. On the other hand, it would certainly be perverse to attempt to construe all duties as arising out of an explicit exchange. We can assert, for example, that the citizen has a moral duty to vote, and to inform himself sufficiently to vote intelligently, without implying that this duty rests on a bargain between him and his government or between him and his fellow citizens.

To establish the affinity between duty and exchange we require a third member, a mediating principle. This is to be found, I think, in the relationship of reciprocity. Exchange is, after all, only a particular expression of this more general, and often more subtle, relationship. The literature of the morality of duty is in fact filled with references to something like the principle of reciprocity.

14. *Summa Contra Gentiles,* III, ch. II.

Even in the midst of the exalted appeals of the Sermon on the Mount there is a repeated note of sober reciprocity. "Judge not, that ye be not judged. For with what judgment ye judge, ye shall be judged; and with what measure ye mete, it shall be measured to you again . . . Therefore all things whatsoever ye would that men should do to you, do ye even so to them: for this is the law and the prophets."[15]

Teachings like these—and they are to be found in all moralities of duty—do not, of course, imply that every duty arises out of a face-to-face relationship of bargain. This becomes apparent if we rephrase the Golden Rule to read something like this: "So soon as I have received from you assurance that you will treat me as you yourself would wish to be treated, then I shall be ready in turn to accord a like treatment to you." This is not the language of morality, nor even of friendly commerce, but of cautious and even hostile trade. To adopt its thought as a general principle would be to dissolve the social bond altogether.

What the Golden Rule seeks to convey is not that society is composed of a network of explicit bargains, but that it is held together by a pervasive bond of reciprocity. Traces of this conception are to be found in every morality of duty, from those heavily tinctured by an appeal to self-interest to those that rest on the lofty demands of the Categorical Imperative. Whenever an appeal to duty seeks to justify itself, it does so always in terms of something like the principle of reciprocity. So in urging a reluctant voter to the polls it is almost certain that at some point we shall ask him, "How would you like it if everyone acted as you propose to do?"

It may be objected that these remarks relate to the rhetoric of duty rather than to its sociology. It is natural that a moralist trying to push men toward an unpleasant duty should include in his

15. Matthew 7:1 and 12. Cf. Deuteronomy 7:11–12, "Thou shalt therefore keep the commandments, and the statutes, and the judgments, which I command thee this day, to do them. Wherefore it shall come to pass, if ye hearken to these judgments, and keep, and do them, that the LORD thy God shall keep unto thee the covenant and the mercy which he sware unto thy fathers."

argument some appeal to self-interest. It is also natural that any-one trying to get men to accept an unwelcome compulsion—a compulsion that is in fact external—should seek to give to it the appearance of being voluntarily assumed, just as the harsh fact of political power has historically been obscured by the fiction of an original compact.

This argument underestimates, I believe, the extent to which the principle of reciprocity has roots not only in our professions but in our practices as well. The rephrasing of the Golden Rule I presented a short while ago was an obvious perversion of its intent. I do not think its meaning would be distorted, however, if we were to add a qualification reading somewhat as follows: "So soon as it becomes perfectly clear that you have no intention whatever of treating me as you yourself would wish to be treated, then I shall consider myself as relieved from the obligation to treat you as I would wish to be treated." Here the element of reciprocity is displaced by several removes from the duty itself; it represents a kind of "fail-safe" point. Men are certain to be of different minds as to just when this point is reached. But there are obvious cases where no dispute is possible. So when I urge on a fellow citizen that he has a duty to go to the polls, my appeal will certainly lose its force if he knows quite well there is no likelihood that his ballot will be counted.

The duty to vote is not absolute, but depends upon the fulfill-ment of certain expectations concerning the actions of others. This would be true even of a citizen who might vote knowing his ballot would not be counted where his object was to make a test case of certain election abuses. If all the world remains indifferent and unmoved by his action—does not come forward with some reaction to it—then it remains utterly pointless.

In this broad sense there is a notion of reciprocity implicit in the very notion of duty—at least in the case of every duty that runs toward society or toward another responsible human being. One can imagine a social bond that knows nothing of duties. Such a bond might exist between a couple deeply in love, or among a small band of men united by some emergency—making, let us say, a last stand against an encircling enemy. In such a situation there would be no thought of measuring contributions. The appropriate organizing principle would be "one for all and all for one." But so soon as contributions are designated and measured—which means so soon as there are duties—there must be some standard—however rough and approximate it may be—by which the kind and the extent of the expected contribution is determined. This standard must be derived from the pattern of a social fabric that unites strands of individual action. A sufficient rupture in this fabric must—if we are to judge the matter with any rationality at all—release men from those duties that had as their only reason for being, maintaining a pattern of social interaction that has now been destroyed.

In the argument just presented there is implicit the notion of a sort of anonymous collaboration among men by which their activities are channeled through the institutions and procedures of an organized society. This conception seems a long way from that of a simple exchange of economic values. But we should recall that even the direct and explicit relationship of reciprocity is by no means confined to anything like a horse trade. Suppose, for example, that two men exchange promises to give equal sums to the same charity. Here the usual self-serving motives of exchange are absent, as is also the notion of performances running between the parties to the exchange. Yet in this case we certainly have a relation of reciprocity and, assuming no rights of the charity have intervened, the repudiation of his promise by one of the parties ought in fairness to excuse the other. The duties of both arise from and depend upon a relation of reciprocity that is not different in kind from that which unites the members of a society in more complex ways.

If it is true that duties generally can be traced to the principle of reciprocity, it is also true that the reciprocity out of which a given duty arises can be visible, as it were, in varying degrees. At times it is obvious to those affected by it; at others it traces a more subtle and obscure course through the institutions and practices of society. This suggests the question: Under what circumstances does a duty, legal or moral, become most understandable and most acceptable to those affected by it? I think we may discern three conditions for the optimum efficacy of the notion of duty. *First,* the relationship of reciprocity out of which the duty arises must result from a voluntary agreement between the parties immediately affected; they themselves "create" the duty. *Second,* the reciprocal performances of the parties must in some sense be equal in value. Though the notion of voluntary assumption itself makes a strong appeal to the sense of justice, that appeal is reinforced when the element of equivalence is added to it. We cannot here speak of an exact identity, for it makes no sense at all to exchange, say, a book or idea in return for exactly the same book or idea. The bond of reciprocity unites men, not simply *in spite* of their differences, but *because* of their differences. When, therefore, we seek equality in a relation of reciprocity what we require is some measure of value that can be applied to things that are different in kind. *Third,* the relationships within the society must be sufficiently fluid so that the same duty you owe me today, I may owe you tomorrow—in other words, the relationship of duty must in theory and in practice be reversible. Without this symmetry we are likely to be stumped by Rousseau's question, What is the reason that I, being myself, should act as if I were the other person, when I am virtually certain that I shall never be found in his situation?[16]

These, then, are the three conditions for an optimum realization of the notion of duty, the conditions that make a duty most

16. The passage from Rousseau occurs in *Emile,* Book IV, and is here quoted from Del Vecchio, *Justice* (1952), p. 96. Rousseau intends his question, of course, as a refutation of utilitarian theories of duty. Del Vecchio himself makes much of reciprocity in his analysis of justice. In distinguishing a mere demand from a claim of right, Del Vecchio points out that the latter presupposes a general principle, according to which if the positions of the parties were reversed, the same duty would be imposed in the opposite direction. This abstract reciprocity loses much of its appeal, however, if the reversal of positions cannot in fact occur. It is not much consolation to the slave, for example, to be told that if he had been born a master and his master, a slave, then it would have been his right to command what he must now render.

understandable and most palatable to the man who owes it. When we ask, "In what kind of society are these conditions most apt to be met?" the answer is a surprising one: in a society of economic traders. By definition the members of such a society enter direct and voluntary relationships of exchange. As for equality it is only with the aid of something like a free market that it is possible to develop anything like an exact measure for the value of disparate goods.[17] Without such a measure, the notion of equality loses substance and descends to the level of a kind of metaphor. Finally, economic traders frequently change roles, now selling, now buying. The duties that arise out of their exchanges are therefore reversible, not only in theory but in practice. The reversibility of role that thus characterizes a trading society exists nowhere else in the same degree, as becomes apparent when we consider the duties running between parent and child, husband and wife, citizen and government. Hayek sees the rule of law itself as dependent on a condition of society such that men may meet today to legislate their duties not knowing tomorrow whether they will owe these duties or be their beneficiaries. Understandably, Hayek identifies such a society with one organized on the market principle, and predicts a collapse of the rule of law for any society which abandons the market principle.[18]

This analysis suggests the somewhat startling conclusion that it is only under capitalism that the notion of the moral and legal duty can reach its full development. This was in fact the conclusion reached by a once famous Soviet writer, Eugene Pashukanis, perhaps the only Soviet thinker who can be said to have made a distinctive contribution to social philosophy.[19]

17. It should be recalled, however, that there are proposals (which have been put into at least partial operation within the Soviet bloc) for managing a socialist economy by market principles. See, for example, Oskar Lange, *On the Economic Theory of Socialism* (1936–37), reprinted in a volume with the same title, edited by Benjamin E. Lippincott (1938), pp. 55–129.

18. Chapter VI, "Planning and the Rule of Law," *The Road to Serfdom* (1944), pp. 72–87.

19. See Vol. V, 20th Century Legal Philosophy Series, *Soviet Legal Philosophy*, trans. Babb (1951), "The General Theory of Law and Marx-

Pashukanis' theory became known as the Commodity Exchange Theory of Law, though it might better have been called the Commodity Exchange Theory of Legal and Moral Duty. The theory was built on two pillars of Marxist thought: *first,* in the organization of society the economic factor is paramount; legal and moral principles and institutions therefore constitute a kind of "superstructure" reflecting the economic organization of society; *second,* in the finally achieved state of communism, law and the state will wither away.

In its main outlines Pashukanis' argument was quite simple. The economic organization of capitalist society is determined by exchange. It follows therefore that the legal and political institutions of such a society will be permeated with notions derived from exchange. So in bourgeois criminal law we find a table of crimes with a schedule of appropriate punishments or expiations —a kind of price list for misbehavior. In private law the dominant figure is that of the legal subject who owes duties, possesses rights, and is granted the legal power to settle his disputes with others by agreement. The legal subject is thus the legal counterpart of the economic trader. With communism economic exchange will be abolished, as will all the legal and political conceptions that derive from it. In particular communism will know nothing of legal rights and duties.

The same analysis was extended to the field of morals. With achieved communism, morality as it is usually understood (that is, as the morality of duty) will cease to perform any function. How far Pashukanis carried his theory may be seen in his attitude toward Kant. Kant's view that we should treat our fellow man as an end, and not merely as a means, is usually regarded as one of the noblest expressions of his philosophy. For Pashukanis it was merely the reflection of a market economy, for it is only by entering relationships of exchange that we are able to make others

---

ism," pp. 111–225. I have attempted a summary of Pashukanis' theory in "Pashukanis and Vyshinsky: A Study in the Development of Marxist Legal Theory," 47 *Michigan Law Review* 1157–66 (1949).

serve our ends at the same time we serve theirs. Indeed, any kind of reciprocity, however circuitously it may operate through social forms, casts men in a dual role, as ends in themselves and as means to the ends of others. Since there is no clear stop or breaking point between implicit reciprocity and explicit exchange, Pashukanis ends with the conclusion that when communism is finally achieved all moral duties will disappear.

These views proved too strong (or at least too inconvenient) for Pashukanis' contemporaries in Stalinist Russia, and he was liquidated in 1937. In justice to his memory it should be said that his theories have strong roots in the teachings of the communist forefathers. They obviously derive support from the twin doctrines of the superstructure and of the future withering away of state and law. They also have a remarkable emotional affinity with the whole tenor of Marx's thought, especially as revealed in the youthful "alienation theme." Marx seemed to have had a strong distaste for any principle or arrangement that could make one man serve the ends of another, though this compulsion is not only implicit in exchange but in any kind of formal social organization. This distaste reveals itself implicitly in his lifelong antipathy to the very notion of a formal division of labor, an antipathy all the more curious since it must have been plain to Marx that the economic production sought by communism would be impossible without the gains resulting from a specialization of function. This fundamental aversion to interdependence comes to most articulate expression in an early passage in which Marx describes life in bourgeois society—that is, in a trading society—as one in which man "treats others as means, reduces himself to the role of a means, and becomes the plaything of alien forces."[20]

With the bitter mood of this passage from Marx we may contrast the description of economic exchange given by Philip Wicksteed, a Unitarian minister turned economist:

> over the whole range of exchangeable things we can usually act more potently by the indirect method of pursuing or

20. Quoted from Tucker, *Philosophy and Myth in Karl Marx* (1961), p. 105. This book is highly recommended to anyone who wants to acquire a sense of what may be called the "moral feel" of Marx's thought.

furthering the immediate purposes of others than by the direct method of pursuing our own . . . We enter into business relations with others, not because our purposes are selfish, but because those with whom we deal are relatively indifferent to them, but are (like us) keenly interested in purposes of their own, to which we in our turn are relatively indifferent . . . There is surely nothing degrading or revolting to our higher sense in this fact of our mutually furthering each other's purposes because we are interested in our own . . . The economic nexus [that is, the nexus of exchange] indefinitely expands our freedom of combination and movement; for it enables us to form one set of groups linked by cohesion of [diverse] faculties and resources, and another set of groups linked by community of purpose, without having to find the "double coincidence" which would otherwise be necessary.[21]

If by some reversal of the flow of time Marx could have had this passage before him, and could have absorbed its thought and mood, the world might today bear a very different aspect for all of us.

Locating the Pointer on the Moral Scale

It is time now to return to a more general comparison between the concepts of economics and those of morality. In speaking of the relation of the two moralities, I suggested the figure of an ascending scale, starting at the bottom with the conditions obviously essential to social life and ending at the top with the loftiest strivings toward human excellence. The lower rungs of this scale represent the morality of duty; its higher reaches, the morality of aspiration. Separating the two is a fluctuating line of division, difficult to locate precisely, yet vitally important.

This line of division serves as an essential bulwark between the two moralities. If the morality of duty reaches upward beyond

21. *The Common Sense of Political Economy,* ed. Robbins (1933), pp. 156, 179–80.

its proper sphere the iron hand of imposed obligation may stifle experiment, inspiration, and spontaneity. If the morality of aspiration invades the province of duty, men may begin to weigh and qualify their obligations by standards of their own and we may end with the poet tossing his wife into the river in the belief—perhaps quite justified—that he will be able to write better poetry in her absence.

A similar relation holds between the economics of exchange and of marginal utility. Before the principle of marginal utility nothing is sacred; all existing arrangements are subject to being reordered in the interest of increased economic return. The economics of exchange is, in contrast, based on two fixed points: property and contract. While it permits interested calculation to reign everywhere else, such calculation is excluded when the question is fidelity to contract or respect for property. Without a self-sacrificing deference toward these institutions, a regime of exchange would lose its anchorage and no one would occupy a sufficiently stable position to know what he had to offer or what he could count on receiving from another. On the other hand, the rigidities of property and contract must be held within their proper boundaries. If they reach beyond those boundaries, society's effort to direct its resources toward their most effective use is frustrated by a system of vested personal and institutional interests, a "reserved market," for example, being a kind of property right reaching beyond its proper domain. Here we encounter again what is essentially the problem of locating the imaginary pointer at the right place. Once again the economist enjoys an advantage over the moralist. If he too has difficulty in drawing the line, he can at least shield his fumblings behind an impressive vocabulary, which in this case goes much beyond the innocent transparency of the word "ultility" and offers terms like monopoly, monopsony, parallel action, and sticky prices.

It may be suggested that a certain quality of stickiness is inherent in all duties, whether they be moral or legal and whether they arise out of an exchange or from some other relation. At the same time it is in the nature of all human aspirations toward perfection, including that which seeks maximum economic efficiency, to be pliable and responsive to changing conditions. A pervasive problem of social design is therefore that of maintaining a balance between supporting structure and adaptive fluidity. This problem is shared by morals, law, economics, aesthetics, and—as Michael Polanyi has shown—also by science.[22] The nature of this problem is not adequately perceived when we think of it in trite terms as an opposition between security and freedom, for we are concerned not merely with the question whether individuals are or feel free or secure, but with attaining a harmony and balance among the processes—often anonymous—of society as a whole.[23]

In a somewhat paradoxical sense even the essential social rigidities must maintain themselves, not simply by being there, but by pressing actively for recognition. Holmes once observed that every legal right tends to become absolute.[24] One may suggest that it is just this tendency toward the absolute that constitutes the essential meaning of "a right," whether it be legal or moral. In like manner one may say of the notion of duty that its meaning lies in a resistance to qualification. In contrast to mere desiderata, counsels of prudence, appeals to vague ideals and the like, rights and duties (whether they be moral or legal) represent sticking points in human resolution. In proper cases they may be qualified, but they may be counted on to resist qualification.

The view just expressed is closely akin to H. L. A. Hart's

22. *The Logic of Liberty* (1951); *Personal Knowledge* (1958).

23. It may be suggested that the question of the function of status, or of institutional role, is a part of this larger problem. Much of the analysis of this problem that has been made by Chester Barnard could, I think, be restated in the terms employed in the text. See Chapter IX in his *Organization and Management* (1948).

24. "All rights tend to declare themselves absolute to their logical extreme. Yet all in fact are limited by the neighborhood of principles of policy which are other than those on which the particular right is founded, and which become strong enough to hold their own when a certain point is reached." *Hudson County Water Company v. McCarter*, 209 U.S. 349, at p. 355 (1908).

notion of "defeasible concepts."[25] To say that a man has entered a contract is not just to tip the scales of justice indeterminately toward the conclusion that he may possibly have incurred an obligation. It is to say that he *is* obligated *unless* some specific ground of excuse, such as incapacity or duress, can be established. One may suggest that what is manifested here is an impulse of the morality of duty, expressing itself within the law, to maintain the integrity of its domain and to protect that domain from the erosions threatened by a view that attempts to solve too many simultaneous equations at once.

Rewards and Penalties

There remains for brief mention one final manifestation of the distinction between the morality of duty and that of aspiration. I refer to the way in which that distinction finds tacit recognition in our social practices concerning penalties and rewards.

In the morality of duty it is understandable that penalties should take precedence over rewards. We do not praise a man, or confer honors on him, because he has conformed to the minimum conditions of social living. Instead we leave him unmolested and concentrate our attention on the man who has failed in that conformity, visiting on him our disapproval, if not some more tangible unpleasantness. Considerations of symmetry would suggest that in the morality of aspiration, which strives toward the superlative, reward and praise should play the role that punishment and disapproval do in the morality of duty. To some extent this mirror image maintains itself in practice. But perfect symmetry is marred by the fact that the closer a man comes to the highest reaches of human achievement, the less competent are others to appraise his performance.

The business of distributing awards and penalties is a pervasive one in our society, extending beyond law into education,

25. "The Ascription of Responsibility and Rights," in A. G. N. Flew, ed., *Essays on Logic and Language* (1952), pp. 145–66.

industry, agriculture, and sports. Wherever distinctions are granted or deprivations imposed it is natural to select some umpire or committee to make the decision, and, no matter whether the issue be that of penalty or award, the deciding agency is expected to act with intelligence and impartiality. Nevertheless there is a great difference in the procedures generally established for meting out penalties as contrasted with those which grant awards. Where penalties or deprivations are involved we surround the decision with procedural guaranties of due process, often elaborate ones, and we are likely to impose an obligation of public accountability. Where awards and honors are granted we are content with more informal, less scrutinized methods of decision.

The reason for this difference is plain. Where penalties and deprivations are involved we are operating at the lower levels of human achievement where a defective performance can be recognized, if care is taken, with comparative certainty and formal standards for judging it can be established. At the level where honors and prizes become appropriate we see that there would be little sense, and a good deal of hypocrisy, in surrounding a decision that is essentially subjective and intuitive with the procedures appropriate to the trial of a law suit.

Many illustrations, in many corners of society, could be given of this difference. I shall mention only two. In union-management relations discharges are normally the first managerial function subjected to arbitrational review. Promotions may, under a particular contract, never be subjected to this review; if they are, they remain much less satisfactory material for the arbitrational process than do discharges. In baseball errors are formally judged by experts and publicly announced, while brilliant fielding plays —the Willie Mays catch, for example—depend for recognition on the informal opinion of fans and newspaper reporters. This practice may, of course, distort the pitcher's earned run average, but we accept this distortion as a small price to pay for escaping the obligation to measure with precision what cannot be so measured.

Generally we are content with informal methods of decision—often screened from the public—when selections are made for honorary degrees, military decorations, hero medals, literary and scientific prizes, foundation awards, and testimonial dinners. One outstanding exception to this laxness may seem to be presented by the elaborately formal procedure of beatification in the Roman Catholic Church. But this procedure does not in fact constitute an exception. Its object is not to honor a saint, but to authorize a cult. In the language of administrative law, it is a certification procedure. The required performance—including as it does the working of miracles—of necessity runs off the top of the scale of human achievement. Presumably, however, it falls within the lower rungs of the supernatural.

In the social practices I have just described there is a standing refutation for the notion, so common in moral argument, that we must know the perfectly good before we can recognize the bad or the barely adequate. If this were true, it would seem to be much easier to assess a five per cent deviation from perfection than to judge a ninety per cent departure. But when it actually comes to cases, our common sense tells us that we can apply more objective standards to departures from satisfactory performance than we can to performances reaching toward perfection. And it is on this common sense view that we build our institutions and practices.

THE MORALITY
THAT MAKES LAW POSSIBLE

[A] law which a man cannot obey, nor act according to it, is void and no law: and it is impossible to obey contradictions, or act according to them.
—Vaughan, C. J. in *Thomas v. Sorrell,* 1677

It is desired that our learned lawyers would answer these ensuing queries . . . whether ever the Commonwealth, when they chose the Parliament, gave them a lawless unlimited power, and at their pleasure to walk contrary to their own laws and ordinances before they have repealed them?
—Lilburne, *England's Birth-Right Justified,* 1645

This chapter will begin with a fairly lengthy allegory. It concerns the unhappy reign of a monarch who bore the convenient, but not very imaginative and not even very regal sounding name of Rex.

Eight Ways to Fail to Make Law

Rex came to the throne filled with the zeal of a reformer. He considered that the greatest failure of his predecessors had been in the field of law. For generations the legal system had known nothing like a basic reform. Procedures of trial were cumbersome, the rules of law spoke in the archaic tongue of another age, justice was expensive, the judges were slovenly and sometimes corrupt. Rex was resolved to remedy all this and to make his name in history as a great lawgiver. It was his unhappy fate to fail in this ambition. Indeed, he failed spectacularly, since not only did he not succeed in introducing the needed reforms, but he never even succeeded in creating any law at all, good or bad.

His first official act was, however, dramatic and propitious. Since he needed a clean slate on which to write, he announced to his subjects the immediate repeal of all existing law, of whatever kind. He then set about drafting a new code. Unfortunately, trained as a lonely prince, his education had been very defective. In particular he found himself incapable of making even the simplest generalizations. Though not lacking in confidence when it came to deciding specific controversies, the effort to give articulate reasons for any conclusion strained his capacities to the breaking point.

Becoming aware of his limitations, Rex gave up the project of a code and announced to his subjects that henceforth he would act as a judge in any disputes that might arise among them. In this way under the stimulus of a variety of cases he hoped that his latent powers of generalization might develop and, proceeding case by case, he would gradually work out a system of rules that could be incorporated in a code. Unfortunately the defects in his education were more deep-seated than he had supposed. The venture failed completely. After he had handed down literally hundreds of decisions neither he nor his subjects could detect in those decisions any pattern whatsoever. Such tentatives toward generalization as were to be found in his opinions only compounded the confusion, for they gave false leads to his subjects and threw his own meager powers of judgment off balance in the decision of later cases.

After this fiasco Rex realized it was necessary to take a fresh start. His first move was to subscribe to a course of lessons in generalization. With his intellectual powers thus fortified, he resumed the project of a code and, after many hours of solitary labor, succeeded in preparing a fairly lengthy document. He was still not confident, however, that he had fully overcome his previous defects. Accordingly, he announced to his subjects that he had written out a code and would henceforth be governed by it in deciding cases, but that for an indefinite future the contents of the code would remain an official state secret, known only to him and his scrivener. To Rex's surprise this sensible plan was deeply resented by his subjects. They declared it was very unpleasant to have one's case decided by rules when there was no way of knowing what those rules were.

Stunned by this rejection Rex undertook an earnest inventory of his personal strengths and weaknesses. He decided that life had taught him one clear lesson, namely, that it is easier to decide things with the aid of hindsight than it is to attempt to foresee and control the future. Not only did hindsight make it easier to decide cases, but—and this was of supreme importance to Rex—it made it easier to give reasons. Deciding to capitalize on this insight, Rex hit on the following plan. At the beginning of each calendar year he would decide all the controversies that had arisen among his subjects during the preceding year. He would accompany his decisions with a full statement of reasons. Naturally, the reasons thus given would be understood as not controlling decisions in future years, for that would be to defeat the whole purpose of the new arrangement, which was to gain the advantages of hindsight. Rex confidently announced the new plan to his subjects, observing that he was going to publish the full text of his judgments with the rules applied by him, thus meeting the chief objection to the old plan. Rex's subjects received this announcement in silence, then quietly explained through their leaders that when they said they needed to know the rules, they meant they needed to know them *in advance* so they could act on them. Rex muttered something to the effect that they might have made that point a little clearer, but said he would see what could be done.

Rex now realized that there was no escape from a published code declaring the rules to be applied in future disputes. Continuing his lessons in generalization, Rex worked diligently on a revised code, and finally announced that it would shortly be published. This announcement was received with universal gratification. The dismay of Rex's subjects was all the more intense, therefore, when his code became available and it was discovered that it was truly a masterpiece of obscurity. Legal experts who studied it declared that there was not a single sentence in it that could be understood either by an ordinary citizen or by a trained lawyer. Indignation became general and soon a picket appeared before the royal palace carrying a sign that read, "How can anybody follow a rule that nobody can understand?"

The code was quickly withdrawn. Recognizing for the first time that he needed assistance, Rex put a staff of experts to work on a revision. He instructed them to leave the substance untouched, but to clarify the expression throughout. The resulting code was a model of clarity, but as it was studied it became apparent that its new clarity had merely brought to light that it was honeycombed with contradictions. It was reliably reported that there was not a single provision in the code that was not nullified by another provision inconsistent with it. A picket again appeared before the royal residence carrying a sign that read, "This time the king made himself clear—in both directions."

Once again the code was withdrawn for revision. By now, however, Rex had lost his patience with his subjects and the negative attitude they seemed to adopt toward everything he tried to do for them. He decided to teach them a lesson and put an end to their carping. He instructed his experts to purge the code of contradictions, but at the same time to stiffen drastically every requirement contained in it and to add a long list of new crimes. Thus, where before the citizen summoned to the throne was given ten days in which to report, in the revision the time was cut to ten seconds. It was made a crime, punishable by ten years' imprisonment, to cough, sneeze, hiccough, faint or fall down in the presence of the king. It was made treason not to understand, believe in, and correctly profess the doctrine of evolutionary, democratic redemption.

When the new code was published a near revolution resulted.

Leading citizens declared their intention to flout its provisions. Someone discovered in an ancient author a passage that seemed apt: "To command what cannot be done is not to make law; it is to unmake law, for a command that cannot be obeyed serves no end but confusion, fear and chaos." Soon this passage was being quoted in a hundred petitions to the king.

The code was again withdrawn and a staff of experts charged with the task of revision. Rex's instructions to the experts were that whenever they encountered a rule requiring an impossibility, it should be revised to make compliance possible. It turned out that to accomplish this result every provision in the code had to be substantially rewritten. The final result was, however, a triumph of draftsmanship. It was clear, consistent with itself, and demanded nothing of the subject that did not lie easily within his powers. It was printed and distributed free of charge on every street corner.

However, before the effective date for the new code had arrived, it was discovered that so much time had been spent in successive revisions of Rex's original draft, that the substance of the code had been seriously overtaken by events. Ever since Rex assumed the throne there had been a suspension of ordinary legal processes and this had brought about important economic and institutional changes within the country. Accommodation to these altered conditions required many changes of substance in the law. Accordingly as soon as the new code became legally effective, it was subjected to a daily stream of amendments. Again popular discontent mounted; an anonymous pamphlet appeared on the streets carrying scurrilous cartoons of the king and a leading article with the title: "A law that changes every day is worse than no law at all."

Within a short time this source of discontent began to cure itself as the pace of amendment gradually slackened. Before this had occurred to any noticeable degree, however, Rex announced an important decision. Reflecting on the misadventures of his reign, he concluded that much of the trouble lay in bad advice he had received from experts. He accordingly declared he was reassuming the judicial power in his own person. In this way he could directly control the application of the new code and insure his country against another crisis. He began to spend practically all of his time hearing and deciding cases arising under the new code.

As the king proceeded with this task, it seemed to bring to a belated blossoming his long dormant powers of generalization. His opinions began, indeed, to reveal a confident and almost exuberant virtuosity as he deftly distinguished his own previous decisions, exposed the principles on which he acted, and laid down guide lines for the disposition of future controversies. For Rex's subjects a new day seemed about to dawn when they could finally conform their conduct to a coherent body of rules.

This hope was, however, soon shattered. As the bound volumes of Rex's judgments became available and were subjected to closer study, his subjects were appalled to discover that there existed no discernible relation between those judgments and the code they purported to apply. Insofar as it found expression in the actual disposition of controversies, the new code might just as well not have existed at all. Yet in virtually every one of his decisions Rex declared and redeclared the code to be the basic law of his kingdom.

Leading citizens began to hold private meetings to discuss what measures, short of open revolt, could be taken to get the king away from the bench and back on the throne. While these discussions were going on Rex suddenly died, old before his time and deeply disillusioned with his subjects.

The first act of his successor, Rex II, was to announce that he was taking the powers of government away from the lawyers and placing them in the hands of psychiatrists and experts in public relations. This way, he explained, people could be made happy without rules.

The Consequences of Failure

Rex's bungling career as legislator and judge illustrates that the attempt to create and maintain a system of legal rules may miscarry in at least eight ways; there are in this enterprise, if you will, eight distinct routes to disaster. The first and most obvious lies in a failure to achieve rules at all, so that every issue must be decided on an ad hoc basis. The other routes are: (2) a failure to publicize, or at least to make available to the affected party, the rules he is expected to observe; (3) the abuse of retroactive legislation, which not only cannot itself guide action, but undercuts the integrity of rules prospective in effect, since it puts them under the threat of retrospective change; (4) a failure to make rules understandable; (5) the enactment of contradictory rules or (6) rules that require conduct beyond the powers of the affected party; (7) introducing such frequent changes in the rules that the subject cannot orient his action by them; and, finally, (8) a failure of congruence between the rules as announced and their actual administration.

A total failure in any one of these eight directions does not simply result in a bad system of law; it results in something that is not properly called a legal system at all, except perhaps in the Pickwickian sense in which a void contract can still be said to be one kind of contract. Certainly there can be no rational ground for asserting that a man can have a moral obligation to obey a legal rule that does not exist, or is kept secret from him, or that came into existence only after he had acted, or was unintelligible, or was contradicted by another rule of the same system, or commanded the impossible, or changed every minute. It may not be impossible for a man to obey a rule that is disregarded by those charged with its administration, but at some point obedience becomes futile—as futile, in fact, as casting a vote that will never be counted. As the sociologist Simmel has observed, there is a kind of reciprocity between government and the citizen with respect to the observance of rules.[1] Government says to the citizen in

---

1. *The Sociology of Georg Simmel* (1950), trans. Wolff, §4, "Interaction in the Idea of 'Law,' " pp. 186–89; see also Chapter 4, "Subordination under a Principle," pp. 250–67. Simmel's discussion is worthy of study by those concerned with defining the conditions under which the ideal of "the rule of law" can be realized.

effect, "These are the rules we expect you to follow. If you follow them, you have our assurance that they are the rules that will be applied to your conduct." When this bond of reciprocity is finally and completely ruptured by government, nothing is left on which to ground the citizen's duty to observe the rules.

The citizen's predicament becomes more difficult when, though there is no total failure in any direction, there is a general and drastic deterioration in legality, such as occurred in Germany under Hitler.[2] A situation begins to develop, for example, in which though some laws are published, others, including the most important, are not. Though most laws are prospective in effect, so free a use is made of retrospective legislation that no law is immune to change ex post facto if it suits the convenience of those in power. For the trial of criminal cases concerned with loyalty to the regime, special military tribunals are established and these tribunals disregard, whenever it suits their convenience, the rules that are supposed to control their decisions. Increasingly the principal object of government seems to be, not that of giving the citizen rules by which to shape his conduct, but to frighten him into impotence. As such a situation develops, the problem faced by the citizen is not so simple as that of a voter who knows with certainty that his ballot will not be counted. It is more like

2. I have discussed some of the features of this deterioration in my article, "Positivism and Fidelity to Law," 71 *Harvard Law Review* 630, 648–57 (1958). This article makes no attempt at a comprehensive survey of all the postwar judicial decisions in Germany concerned with events occurring during the Hitler regime. Some of the later decisions rested the nullity of judgments rendered by the courts under Hitler not on the ground that the statutes applied were void, but on the ground that the Nazi judges misinterpreted the statutes of their own government. See Pappe, "On the Validity of Judicial Decisions in the Nazi Era," 23 *Modern Law Review* 260–74 (1960). Dr. Pappe makes more of this distinction than seems to me appropriate. After all, the meaning of a statute depends in part on accepted modes of interpretation. Can it be said that the postwar German courts gave full effect to Nazi laws when they interpreted them by their own standards instead of the quite different standards current during the Nazi regime? Moreover, with statutes of the kind involved, filled as they were with vague phrases and unrestricted delegations of power, it seems a little out of place to strain over questions of their proper interpretation.

that of the voter who knows that the odds are against his ballot being counted at all, and that if it is counted, there is a good chance that it will be counted for the side against which he actually voted. A citizen in this predicament has to decide for himself whether to stay with the system and cast his ballot as a kind of symbolic act expressing the hope of a better day. So it was with the German citizen under Hitler faced with deciding whether he had an obligation to obey such portions of the laws as the Nazi terror had left intact.

In situations like these there can be no simple principle by which to test the citizen's obligation of fidelity to law, any more than there can be such a principle for testing his right to engage in a general revolution. One thing is, however, clear. A mere respect for constituted authority must not be confused with fidelity to law. Rex's subjects, for example, remained faithful to him as king throughout his long and inept reign. They were not faithful to his law, for he never made any.

The Aspiration toward Perfection in Legality

So far we have been concerned to trace out eight routes to failure in the enterprise of creating law. Corresponding to these are eight kinds of legal excellence toward which a system of rules may strive. What appear at the lowest level as indispensable conditions for the existence of law at all, become, as we ascend the scale of achievement, increasingly demanding challenges to human capacity. At the height of the ascent we are tempted to imagine a utopia of legality in which all rules are perfectly clear, consistent with one another, known to every citizen, and never retroactive. In this utopia the rules remain constant through time, demand only what is possible, and are scrupulously observed by courts, police, and everyone else charged with their administration. For reasons that I shall advance shortly, this utopia, in which all eight of the principles of legality are realized to perfection, is not actually a useful target for guiding the impulse toward legality; the goal of perfection is much more complex.

Nevertheless it does suggest eight distinct standards by which excellence in legality may be tested.

In expounding in my first chapter the distinction between the morality of duty and that of aspiration, I spoke of an imaginary scale that starts at the bottom with the most obvious and essential moral duties and ascends upward to the highest achievements open to man. I also spoke of an invisible pointer as marking the dividing line where the pressure of duty leaves off and the challenge of excellence begins. The inner morality of law, it should now be clear, presents all of these aspects. It too embraces a morality of duty and a morality of aspiration. It too confronts us with the problem of knowing where to draw the boundary below which men will be condemned for failure, but can expect no praise for success, and above which they will be admired for success and at worst pitied for the lack of it.

In applying the analysis of the first chapter to our present subject, it becomes essential to consider certain distinctive qualities of the inner morality of law. In what may be called the basic morality of social life, duties that run toward other persons generally (as contrasted with those running toward specific individuals) normally require only forbearances, or as we say, are negative in nature: Do not kill, do not injure, do not deceive, do not defame, and the like. Such duties lend themselves with a minimum of difficulty to formalized definition. That is to say, whether we are concerned with legal or moral duties, we are able to develop standards which designate with some precision—though it is never complete—the kind of conduct that is to be avoided.

The demands of the inner morality of the law, however, though they concern a relationship with persons generally, demand more than forbearances; they are, as we loosely say, affirmative in nature: make the law known, make it coherent and clear, see that your decisions as an official are guided by it, etc. To meet these demands human energies must be directed toward specific kinds of achievement and not merely warned away from harmful acts.

Because of the affirmative and creative quality of its demands, the inner morality of law lends itself badly to realization through duties, whether they be moral or legal. No matter how desirable a direction of human effort may appear to be, if we assert there is a duty to pursue it, we shall confront the responsibility of defining at what point that duty has been violated. It is easy to assert that the legislator has a moral duty to make his laws clear and understandable. But this remains at best an exhortation unless we are prepared to define the degree of clarity he must attain in order to discharge his duty. The notion of subjecting clarity to quantitative measure presents obvious difficulties. We may content ourselves, of course, by saying that the legislator has at least a moral duty to try to be clear. But this only postpones the difficulty, for in some situations nothing can be more baffling than to attempt to measure how vigorously a man intended to do that which he has failed to do. In the morality of law, in any event, good intentions are of little avail, as King Rex amply demonstrated. All of this adds up to the conclusion that the inner morality of law is condemned to remain largely a morality of aspiration and not of duty. Its primary appeal must be to a sense of trusteeship and to the pride of the craftsman.

To these observations there is one important exception. This relates to the desideratum of making the laws known, or at least making them available to those affected by them. Here we have a demand that lends itself with unusual readiness to formalization. A written constitution may prescribe that no statute shall become law until it has been given a specified form of publication. If the courts have power to effectuate this provision, we may speak of a legal requirement for the making of law. But a moral duty with respect to publication is also readily imaginable. A custom, for example, might define what kind of promulgation of laws is expected, at the same time leaving unclear what consequences attend a departure from the accepted mode of publication. A formalization of the desideratum of publicity has obvious advantages over uncanalized efforts, even when they are intelligently and conscientiously pursued. A formalized standard of promulgation not only tells the lawmaker where to publish his laws; it also lets the subject—or a lawyer representing his interests—know where to go to learn what the law is.

One might suppose that the principle condemning retroactive laws could also be very readily formalized in a simple rule that no such law should ever be passed, or should be valid if enacted. Such a rule would, however, disserve the cause of legality. Curiously, one of the most obvious seeming demands of legality —that a rule passed today should govern what happens tomorrow, not what happened yesterday—turns out to present some of the most difficult problems of the whole internal morality of law.

With respect to the demands of legality other than promulgation, then, the most we can expect of constitutions and courts is that they save us from the abyss; they cannot be expected to lay out very many compulsory steps toward truly significant accomplishment.

Legality and Economic Calculation

In my first chapter I attempted to demonstrate how, as we leave the morality of duty and ascend toward the highest levels of a morality of aspiration, the principle of marginal utility plays an increasing role in our decisions. On the level of duty, anything like economic calculation is out of place. In a morality of aspiration, it is not only in place, but becomes an integral part of the moral decision itself—increasingly so as we reach toward the highest levels of achievement.

It is not difficult to show that something like an economic calculation may become necessary when a conflict arises between the internal and external moralities of law. From the standpoint of the internal morality of law, for example, it is desirable that laws remain stable through time. But it is obvious that changes in circumstances, or changes in men's consciences, may demand changes in the substantive aims of law, and sometimes disturbingly frequent changes. Here we are often condemned to steer a wavering middle course between too frequent change and no change at all, sustained by the conviction, not that the course chosen is the only right one, but that we must in all events keep clear of the shoals of disaster that lie on either side.

It is much less obvious, I suspect, that antinomies may arise within the internal morality of law itself. Yet it is easy to demonstrate that the various desiderata which go to make up that morality may at times come into opposition with one another. Thus, it is simultaneously desirable that laws should remain stable through time and that they should be such as impose no insurmountable barriers to obedience. Yet rapid changes in circumstances, such as those attending an inflation, may render obedience to a particular law, which was once quite easy, increasingly difficult, to the point of approaching impossibility. Here again it may become necessary to pursue a middle course which involves some impairment of both desiderata.

During a visit to Poland in May of 1961 I had a conversation with a former Minister of Justice that is relevant here. She told how in the early days of the communist regime an earnest and sustained effort was made to draft the laws so clearly that they would be intelligible to the worker and peasant. It was soon discovered, however, that this kind of clarity could be attained only at the cost of those systematic elements in a legal system that shape its rules into a coherent whole and render them capable of consistent application by the courts. It was discovered, in other words, that making the laws readily understandable to the citizen carried a hidden cost in that it rendered their application by the courts more capricious and less predictable. Some retreat to a more balanced view therefore became unavoidable.

These examples and illustrations could be multiplied. Enough has been said, I believe, to show that the utopia of legality cannot be viewed as a situation in which each desideratum of the law's special morality is realized to perfection. This is no special quality—and certainly no peculiar defect—of the internal morality of law. In every human pursuit we shall always encounter the problem of balance at some point as we traverse the long road that leads from the abyss of total failure to the heights of human excellence.

It is now time to pass in an extended review each of the eight demands of the law's inner morality. This review will deal with certain difficulties hitherto passed over, particularly those touching the relation between the internal and external moralities of law. It will also include some remarks on the ways in which problems of the law's inner morality have actually arisen in history.

The Generality of Law

The first desideratum of a system for subjecting human conduct to the governance of rules is an obvious one: there must be rules. This may be stated as the requirement of generality.

In recent history perhaps the most notable failure to achieve general rules has been that of certain of our regulatory agencies, particularly those charged with allocative functions. Like King Rex they were embarked on their careers in the belief that by proceeding at first case by case they would gradually gain an insight which would enable them to develop general standards of decision. In some cases this hope has been almost completely disappointed; this is notably so in the case of the Civil Aeronautics Board and the Federal Communications Commission. The reason for this failure lies, I believe, in the nature of the tasks assigned to these agencies; they are trying to do through adjudicative forms something that does not lend itself to accomplishment through those forms.[3] But whatever the reason, considered as attempts to create coherent legal systems these agencies have been notably unsuccessful.

3. I have attempted to analyze the limitations of the adjudicative process in two articles: "Adjudication and the Rule of Law," *Proceedings of the American Society of International Law* (1960), pp. 1–8; "Collective Bargaining and the Arbitrator," *Wisconsin Law Review* 3–46 (1963). I plan later to publish a more general analysis to be called *The Forms and Limits of Adjudication*. See also pp. 170–77, infra.

The complaint registered against these agencies is not so much that their rules are unfair, but that they have failed to develop any significant rules at all. This distinction is important because the desideratum of generality is sometimes interpreted to mean that the law must act impersonally, that its rules must apply to general classes and should contain no proper names. Constitutional provisions invalidating "private laws" and "special legislation" express this principle.[4] But the principle protected by these provisions is a principle of fairness, which, in terms of the analysis presented here, belongs to the external morality of the law.

This principle is different from the demand of the law's internal morality that, at the very minimum, there must be rules of some kind, however fair or unfair they may be. One can imagine a system of law directed toward a single named individual, regulating his conduct with other named individuals. Something like this can exist between employer and employee. If the employer wants to avoid the necessity of standing over the employee and directing his every action, he may find it essential to articulate and convey to the employee certain general principles of conduct. In this venture there are open to the employer all the routes to failure traversed by King Rex. He may not succeed in articu-

---

4. See the entry, "Special, Local or Private Laws," in *Index Digest of State Constitutions* (2d ed. 1959), published by the Legislative Drafting Research Fund of Columbia University. Provisions of this sort have produced much difficulty for courts and legislatures. Sometimes their requirements are met by such apparently disingenuous devices as a provision that a particular statute shall apply "to all cities in the state which according to the last census had a population of more than 165,000 and less than 166,000." Before condemning this apparent evasion we should recall that the one-member class or set is a familiar and essential concept of logic and set theory. Sometimes the prohibition of special laws is directed against rather obvious misuses of legislative power. The California Constitution, for example, prohibits special laws "for the punishment of crimes . . . regulating the practice of courts of justice . . . granting divorces . . . declaring any person of age." (Article VI §25, as amended to Nov. 4, 1952.) The same Article, however, contains a general prohibition of special or local laws "in all cases where a general law can be made applicable." This has produced a veritable donnybrook of litigation.

lating general rules; if he does, he may not succeed in conveying them to the employee, etc. If the employer succeeds in bringing into existence a functioning system of rules, he will discover that this success has been bought at a certain cost to himself. He must not only invest some effort and intelligence in the enterprise, but its very success limits his own freedom of action. If in distributing praise and censure, he habitually disregards his own rules, he may find his system of law disintegrating, and without any open revolt, it may cease to produce for him what he sought to obtain through it.

In actual systems for controlling and directing human conduct a total failure to achieve anything like a general rule is rare. Some generalization is implicit in the act of communicating even a single wish. The command to a dog, "Shake hands," demands some power of generalization in both master and dog. Before he can execute the command the dog has to understand what range of slightly different acts will be accepted as shaking hands. Furthermore, a well-trained dog will come in time to perceive in what kinds of situations he is likely to be asked to shake hands and will often extend his paw in anticipation of a command not yet given. Obviously something like this can and does happen in human affairs, even when those possessing the power to command have no desire to lay down general rules. But if a total failure of generalization requires the special talent for ineptitude of a King Rex, the fact is that many legal systems, large and small, suffer grievously from a lack of general principle.[5]

The problem of generality receives a very inadequate treatment in the literature of jurisprudence. Austin correctly perceived that a legal system is something more than a series of patternless exercises of political power. Yet his attempt to distinguish between general and particular commands was so arbitrary and so unrelated to his system as a whole that the Anglo-American

5. Herbert Wechsler's complaint that some of the recent decisions of the Supreme Court on constitutional issues lack the degree of reasoned generality that will assure the Court's "neutrality" is the latest expression of a plaint that goes back to the beginnings of law itself. See Wechsler, *Principles, Politics, and Fundamental Law* (1961).

literature since his time has scarcely recovered from this original misdirection.[6]

Perhaps the basic defect of Austin's analysis lay in his failure to distinguish two questions: (1) what is essential for the efficacy of a system of legal rules, and (2) what shall we call "a law"? In the analysis presented in these lectures the requirement of generality rests on the truism that to subject human conduct to the control of rules, there must be rules. This in no way asserts that every governmental act possessing "the force of law"—such as a judicial decree directed against a particular defendant—must itself take the form of laying down a general rule. Nor is there any attempt here to rule on such issues of linguistic convenience as deciding whether we should call a statute which establishes a tax collection office in Centerville a law.

Promulgation

Turning now to the promulgation of laws, this is an ancient and recurring problem, going back at least as far as the Secession of the Plebs in Rome.[7] Obvious and urgent as this demand seems, it must be recognized that it is subject to the marginal utility principle. It would in fact be foolish to try to educate every citizen into the full meaning of every law that might conceivably be applied to him, though Bentham was willing to go a long way in that direction.[8]

6. See Austin, *Lectures on Jurisprudence* (1879), Lecture I, pp. 94–98; Gray, *The Nature and Sources of the Law* (2d ed. 1921), pp. 161–62; Brown, *The Austinian Theory of Law* (1906), note on pp. 17–20; cf. Kelsen, *General Theory of Law and State* (1945), pp. 37–39; Somló, *Juristische Grundlehre* (2d ed. 1927), §20, pp. 64–65. The best treatment in English that I have encountered is in Patterson, *Jurisprudence—Men and Ideas of the Law* (1953), ch. 5.

7. Relevant discussions will be found in Austin, *Lectures on Jurisprudence* (1879), pp. 542–44; Gray, *Nature and Sources of the Law* (2d ed., 1921), pp. 162–70. Austin accepts without cavil a view traditional in England according to which an act of Parliament is considered to be effective without publication.

8. See, for example, the educative efforts recommended in *Rationale of Judicial Evidence*, Ch. IV, "Of Preappointed Evidence," *Works*, Bowring's ed., *4*, 508–85.

The need for this education will, of course, depend upon how far the requirements of law depart from generally shared views of right and wrong. Over much of its history the common law has been largely engaged in working out the implications of conceptions that were generally held in the society of the time. This large measure of coincidence between moral and legal demands reduced greatly the force of the objection that the rules of the common law were, in contrast with those of a code, difficult of access.

The problem of promulgation is complicated by the question, "Just what counts as law for purposes of this requirement?" Deciding agencies, especially administrative tribunals, often take the view that, though the rules they apply to controversies ought to be published, a like requirement does not attach to the rules and practices governing their internal procedures. Yet every experienced attorney knows that to predict the outcome of cases it is often essential to know, not only the formal rules governing them, but the internal procedures of deliberation and consultation by which these rules are in fact applied. Perhaps it is in recognition of this that the otherwise bizarre seeming requirement has developed in Switzerland and Mexico that certain courts must hold their deliberations in public.

The man whom Thurman Arnold sometimes calls the "mere realist" (when he is not reserving that role for himself)[9] might be tempted to say something like this of the requirement of promulgation: "After all, we have thousands of laws, only the smallest fraction of which are known, directly or indirectly, to the ordi-

9. Sometimes Judge Arnold seems to be able to combine the roles. In Professor Hart's "Theology," 73 *Harvard Law Review* 1298, at p. 1311 (1960), he rises eloquently above the "mere realist" by declaring, "Without a constant and sincere pursuit of the shining but never completely attainable ideal of the rule of law above men, of 'reason' above 'personal preference,' we would not have a civilized government." But in the same article he castigates Professor Henry M. Hart for suggesting that the Supreme Court ought to spend more time in "the maturing of collective thought." Arnold declares, "There is no such process as this, and there never has been; men of positive views are only hardened in those views by . . . conference" (p. 1312).

nary citizen. Why all this fuss about publishing them? Without reading the criminal code, the citizen knows he shouldn't murder and steal. As for the more esoteric laws, the full text of them might be distributed on every street corner and not one man in a hundred would ever read it." To this a number of responses must be made. Even if only one man in a hundred takes the pains to inform himself concerning, say, the laws applicable to the practice of his calling, this is enough to justify the trouble taken to make the laws generally available. This citizen at least is entitled to know, and he cannot be identified in advance. Furthermore, in many activities men observe the law, not because they know it directly, but because they follow the pattern set by others whom they know to be better informed than themselves. In this way knowledge of the law by a few often influences indirectly the actions of many. The laws should also be given adequate publication so that they may be subject to public criticism, including the criticism that they are the kind of laws that ought not to be enacted unless their content can be effectively conveyed to those subject to them. It is also plain that if the laws are not made readily available, there is no check against a disregard of them by those charged with their application and enforcement. Finally, the great bulk of modern laws relate to specific forms of activity, such as carrying on particular professions or businesses; it is therefore quite immaterial that they are not known to the average citizen. The requirement that laws be published does not rest on any such absurdity as an expectation that the dutiful citizen will sit down and read them all.

Retroactive Laws

In this country the problem of retroactive laws is explicitly dealt with in certain provisions of the United States Constitution[10]

10. The third paragraph of Article I, Section IX, provides, "No bill of attainder or ex post facto law shall be passed" by the Congress. Despite the breadth of its language, the provision concerning ex post facto laws has been construed to apply only to criminal statutes. (See the articles cited in

and in scattered measures in certain state constitutions.[11] Outside the areas covered by these provisions, the validity of retroactive legislation is largely regarded as a problem of due process. I shall not concern myself with the intricacies and uncertainties of this body of constitutional law.[12] Instead I shall deal with certain basic problems concerning the relation between retroactivity and the other elements of legality.[13]

---

note 12, infra.) By bills of attainder the Constitution meant primarily punitive legislative acts directed against individuals. The prohibition of such bills was supported not only by the belief that laws ought to be prospective in effect, but also, and perhaps primarily, by a conviction that punitive measures ought to be imposed by rules of general application.

The prohibition of bills of attainder and ex post facto laws is extended to the states by Article I, Section X. This Section adds a provision that no "state shall . . . pass . . . any law impairing the obligation of contract." This last provision is generally regarded as invalidating a particular kind of "retroactive" law. However, as I shall indicate later in the text, there are real difficulties in developing a precise definition of a "retroactive law." These become particularly acute in connection with the "impairment clause."

11. See the entries "Ex Post Facto Laws and Retrospective Laws" in the *Index Digest of State Constitutions* (2d ed. 1959). The spirit of these statutes finds vigorous expression in Part I, Section 23, of the New Hampshire Constitution of 1784: "Retrospective laws are highly injurious, oppressive, and unjust. No such laws, therefore, should be made, either for the decision of civil causes, or the punishment of offenses."

12. See Hale, "The Supreme Court and the Contract Clause," 57 *Harvard Law Review* 512–57, 612–74, 852–92 (1944); Hochman, "The Supreme Court and the Constitutionality of Retroactive Legislation," 73 *Harvard Law Review* 692–727 (1960); "Prospective Overruling and Retroactive Application in the Federal Courts," 71 *Yale Law Journal* 907–51 (1962), (unsigned note).

13. The literature of jurisprudence pays but scant attention to retroactive laws. Gray discusses at considerable length the ex post facto effect of judicial decisions (*The Nature and Sources of the Law* [2d ed. 1921], pp. 89–101, 218–33) but has only this to say of statutes: "The legislature . . . can, in the absence of any Constitutional prohibition, even make the new statute retroactive." (Ibid., p. 187.) Kelsen seems slightly bothered by retroactive laws, but observes that since it is generally recognized that ignorance of law does not excuse, and hence a law may properly be applied to one who did not know of it, the retroactive statute only carries this a bit further by applying a law to one who could not possibly have known of it. *General Theory of Law and State* (1945), pp. 43–44, 73, 146, 149. For

Taken by itself, and in abstraction from its possible function in a system of laws that are largely prospective, a retroactive law is truly a monstrosity. Law has to do with the governance of human conduct by rules. To speak of governing or directing conduct today by rules that will be enacted tomorrow is to talk in blank prose. To ask how we should appraise an imaginary legal system consisting exclusively of laws that are retroactive, and retroactive only, is like asking how much air pressure there is in a perfect vacuum.

If, therefore, we are to appraise retroactive laws intelligently, we must place them in the context of a system of rules that are generally prospective. Curiously, in this context situations can arise in which granting retroactive effect to legal rules not only becomes tolerable, but may actually be essential to advance the cause of legality.

Like every other human undertaking, the effort to meet the often complex demands of the internal morality of law may suffer various kinds of shipwreck. It is when things go wrong that the retroactive statute often becomes indispensable as a curative measure; though the proper movement of law is forward in time, we sometimes have to stop and turn about to pick up the pieces. Suppose a statute declares that after its effective date no marriage shall be valid unless a special stamp, provided by the state, is affixed to the marriage certificate by the person performing the ceremony. A breakdown of the state printing office results in the stamps' not being available when the statute goes into effect.

Somló the question is one of fairness; there is no intrinsic reason in the nature of law itself why laws cannot be retrospective. *Juristische Grundlehre* (2d ed. 1927), 302–03. Only Austin seems to consider retroactive laws as presenting a serious problem for legal analysis. Regarding law as a command to which a sanction is attached, he observes that "injury or wrong supposes unlawful *intention,* or one of those modes of unlawful *inadvertence* which are styled negligence, heedlessness, and rashness. For unless the party knew that he was violating his duty, or unless he *might* have known that he was violating his duty, the sanction could not operate, at the moment of the wrong, to the end of impelling him" to obey the command. *Lectures on Jurisprudence* (4th ed. 1879), p. 485.

Though the statute is duly promulgated, it is little publicized, and the method by which it would ordinarily become known, by word of mouth among those who perform marriages, fails because the stamps are not distributed. Many marriages take place between persons who know nothing of the law, and often before a minister who also knows nothing of it. This occurs after the legislature has adjourned. When it is called back into session, the legislature enacts a statute conferring validity on marriages which by the terms of the previous statute were declared void. Though taken by itself, the retrospective effect of the second statute impairs the principle of legality, it alleviates the effect of a previous failure to realize two other desiderata of legality: that the laws should be made known to those affected by them and that they should be capable of being obeyed.[14]

One might be tempted to derive from this illustration the lesson that retrospective laws are always justified, or at least are innocent, when their intent is to cure irregularities of form. Before hastening to this conclusion it would be well to recall the Roehm Purge of 1934. Hitler had decided that certain elements in the Nazi party gathered about Roehm were an encumbrance to his regime. The normal procedure for a dictatorship in such a case would be to order sham trials to be followed by conviction and execution. However, time was pressing, so Hitler and his associates took a hurried trip south during which they shot down nearly a hundred persons. Returning to Berlin Hitler promptly arranged to have passed a retroactive statute converting these murders into lawful executions. Afterward Hitler declared that during the affair "the Supreme Court of the German people consisted of myself," thus indicating that to his mind the shoot-

14. Because their draftsmen commonly overlook the occasional need for "curative" laws, flat constitutional prohibitions of retroactive laws have sometimes had to be substantially rewritten by the courts. Thus Article I, §20, of the Tennessee Constitution of 1870 provides that "no retrospective law, or law impairing the obligation of contract, shall be made." This was at an early time interpreted as if it read "no retrospective law, or other law, impairing the obligation of contract, shall be made." The early cases are discussed in *Wynne's Lessee v. Wynne*, 32 Tenn. 405 (1852).

ings were attended by a mere irregularity of form which consisted in the fact that he held in his hand a pistol rather than the staff of justice.[15] And, on this view of the matter, he might even have quoted the language of our Supreme Court in upholding an enactment which it called "a curative statute aptly designed to remedy . . . defects in the administration of government."[16]

A second aspect of retrospective lawmaking relates not so much to any positive contribution it may on occasion make to the internal morality of the law, but rather to the circumstance that it unavoidably attaches in some measure to the office of judge. It is important to note that a system for governing human conduct by formally enacted rules does not of necessity require courts or any other institutional procedure for deciding disputes about the meaning of rules. In a small and friendly society, governed by relatively simple rules, such disputes may not arise. If they do, they may be settled by a voluntary accommodation of interests. Even if they are not so resolved, a certain number of continuing controversies on the periphery may not seriously impair the efficacy of the system as a whole.

I emphasize this point because it is so often taken for granted that courts are simply a reflection of the fundamental purpose of law, which is assumed to be that of settling disputes. The need for rules—so it seems to be thought—arises wholly out of man's selfish, quarrelsome, and disputatious nature. In a society of angels there would be no need for law.

But this depends on the angels. If angels can live together and accomplish their good works without any rules at all, then, of course, they need no law. Nor would they need law if the rules on which they acted were tacit, informal, and intuitively perceived. But if, in order to discharge their celestial functions effectively, angels need "made" rules, rules brought into existence

15. Relevant references will be found in my article in 71 *Harvard Law Review* 650 (1958).
16. *Graham v. Goodcell*, 282 U.S. 409, 429 (1930).

by some explicit decision, then they need law as law is viewed in these essays. A King Rex called in to govern them and to establish rules for their conduct would lose no opportunity to bungle his job simply because his subjects were angels. One might object that at least the problem of maintaining congruence between official action and enacted rule would not arise; but this is not true, for Rex might easily fall into the pit of addressing particular requests to his angelic subjects that conflicted with the general rules he had laid down for their conduct. This practice might produce a state of confusion in which the general rules would lose their directive force.

In a complex and numerous political society courts perform an essential function. No system of law—whether it be judge-made or legislatively enacted—can be so perfectly drafted as to leave no room for dispute. When a dispute arises concerning the meaning of a particular rule, some provision for a resolution of the dispute is necessary. The most apt way to achieve this resolution lies in some form of judicial proceeding.

Suppose, then, a dispute arises between *A* and *B* concerning the meaning of a statutory rule by which their respective rights are determined. Their dispute is submitted to a court. After weighing all the arguments carefully the judge may consider that they are about evenly balanced between the position taken by *A* and that taken by *B*. In that sense the statute really gives him no clear standard for deciding the case. Yet the principles relevant to its decision lie in this statute, the requirements of which would in nine cases out of ten raise no problem at all. If the judge fails to render a decision, he fails in his duty to settle disputes arising out of an existing body of law. If he decides the case, he inevitably engages in an act of retrospective legislation.

Obviously the judge must decide the case. If every time doubt arose as to the meaning of a rule, the judge were to declare the existence of a legal vacuum, the efficacy of the whole system of prospective rules would be seriously impaired. To act on rules confidently, men must not only have a chance to learn what the rules are, but must also be assured that in case of a dispute about their meaning there is available some method for resolving the dispute.

In the case just supposed the argument for a retrospective decision is very strong. Suppose, however, that the court acts not to clarify a doubt about the law, but to overrule one of its own precedents. Following the case of *A v. B*, for example, the same dispute arises between *C* and *D*. *C* refuses to settle the dispute on the basis of the decision rendered in *A v. B*, and instead takes the case to court. *C* convinces the court that its decision in *A v. B* was mistaken and should be overruled. If this overruling is made retrospective, then *D* loses out though he relied on a legal decision that was clearly in his favor. On the other hand, if the decision in *A v. B* was wrong and ought to have been overruled, then *C* has performed a public service in refusing to accept it and in taking it to court to be reexamined. It is surely ironic if the only reward *C* receives for this service is to have a now admittedly mistaken rule applied against him. If the court were to overrule the precedent prospectively, so that the new rule would apply only to cases arising after the overruling decision, it is difficult to see how a private litigant would ever have any incentive to secure the repeal of a decision that was mistaken or that had lost its justification through a change in circumstances. (It has been pointed out that this argument loses its force in the case of what may be called "the institutional litigant," say, a labor union or a trade association which has a continuing interest in the development of the law that extends beyond specific controversies.)[17]

The situations just discussed concerned civil disputes. Quite different considerations apply to criminal cases. This has come to be recognized in cases involving the overruling of precedents, as for example where a court has construed a criminal statute not to apply to a certain form of activity, then in a later case changes its mind and overrules its previous interpretation.[18] If this over-

17. See the note in the *Yale Law Journal* cited in n. 12, supra.
18. See reference of last note.

ruling decision were projected retrospectively, then men would be branded as criminals who acted in reliance on a judicial interpretation of the law.

It has been supposed that different considerations apply to cases where the court settles previously unresolved uncertainties in the application of a criminal statute and that such cases are to be treated just like the civil case of *A v. B* discussed above. This view is, I believe, mistaken. It is true that there are certain safeguards here that mitigate what appears to be the gross injustice of retrospectively making criminal what was previously not clearly so. If the criminal statute as a whole is uncertain of application it may be declared unconstitutionally vague. Furthermore, it is an accepted principle of interpretation that a criminal statute should be construed strictly, so that acts falling outside its normal meaning are not to be considered criminal simply because they present the same kind of danger as those described by the language of the statute. Yet it is possible that a criminal statute may be so drawn that, though its meaning is reasonably plain in nine cases out of ten, in the tenth case, where some special situation of fact arises, it may be so unclear as to give the particular defendant no real warning that what he was doing was criminal. This is especially likely to be the case where economic regulations are involved. The courts have generally assumed that in this kind of case they have no choice but to resolve the doubt, thus creating retrospective criminal law. The problem is treated, in other words, as if it were just like a civil suit. Yet in a criminal case like that supposed an acquittal leaves no dispute unresolved; it simply means that the defendant goes free.

I suggest that a principle ought to be recognized according to which a defendant should not be held guilty of crime where the statute, as applied to his particular situation, was so unclear that, had it been equally unclear in all applications, it would have been held void for uncertainty. This principle would eliminate the false analogy to civil suits, and would bring the treatment of what may be called specific uncertainty into harmony with the law concerning criminal statutes that are uncertain as a whole.

There remains for examination the most difficult problem of all, that of knowing when an enactment should properly be regarded as retrospective. The easiest case is that of the statute which purports to make criminal an act that was perfectly legal when it was committed. Constitutional provisions prohibiting ex post facto laws are chiefly directed against such statutes. The principle *nulla poena sine lege* is one generally respected by civilized nations. The reason the retrospective criminal statute is so universally condemned does not arise merely from the fact that in criminal litigation the stakes are high. It arises also—and chiefly—because of all branches of law, the criminal law is most obviously and directly concerned with shaping and controlling human conduct. It is the retroactive criminal statute that calls most directly to mind the brutal absurdity of commanding a man today to do something yesterday.

Contrast with the ex post facto criminal statute a tax law first enacted, let us say, in 1963 imposing a tax on financial gains realized in 1960 at a time when such gains were not yet subject to tax. Such a statute may be grossly unjust, but it cannot be said that it is, strictly speaking, retroactive. To be sure, it bases the amount of the tax on something that happened in the past. But the only act it requires of its addressee is a very simple one, namely, that he pay the tax demanded. This requirement operates prospectively. We do not, in other words, enact tax laws today that order a man to have paid taxes yesterday, though we may pass today a tax law that determines the levy to be imposed on the basis of events occurring in the past.

To the ordinary citizen the argument just advanced would probably appear as the merest quibble. He would be likely to say that just as a man may do an act because he knows it to be legal under the existing criminal law, so he may enter a transaction because he knows that under the existing law the gain it yields is not subject to tax. If the ex post facto criminal law is heinous because it attaches a penalty to an act that carried no punishment when it was done, there is an equal injustice in a law that levies a tax on a man because of an activity that was tax-free when he engaged in it.

The answer to this argument would call attention to the consequences that would follow if its implications were fully accepted. Laws of all kinds, and not merely tax laws, enter into men's calculations and decisions. A man may decide to study for a particular profession, to get married, to limit or increase the size of his family, to make a final disposition of his estate— all with reference to an existing body of law, which includes not only tax laws, but the laws of property and contract, and perhaps, even, election laws which bring about a particular distribution of political power. If every time a man relied on existing law in arranging his affairs, he were made secure against any change in legal rules, the whole body of our law would be ossified forever.

To this argument a reply could be made along the following lines: Tax laws are not just like other laws. For one thing, they enter more directly into the planning of one's affairs. Moreover— and much more importantly—their principal object is often not merely to raise revenue, but to shape human conduct in ways thought desirable by the legislator. In this respect they are close cousins to the criminal law. The laws of property and contract neither prescribe nor recommend any particular course of action; their object is merely to protect acquisitions resulting from unspecified activities. Tax laws, on the other hand, coax men into, or dissuade them from, certain kinds of behavior and this is often precisely their objective. When they thus become a kind of surrogate for the criminal law, they lose, as it were, their primitive innocence. In the case with which this discussion began (where the law originally imposed no tax on certain kinds of gains) the purpose of the law may have been to induce men to enter transactions of the kind that would yield these very gains. When a tax is later imposed on gains arising from these transactions, men are in effect penalized for doing what the law itself originally induced them to do.

At this point a replication may be entered to the following effect. Laws of every kind may induce men toward, or deter them from, particular forms of behavior. The whole law of contracts, for example, might be said to have the purpose of inducing men to organize their affairs through "private enterprise." If business operations are planned in part by taking into account the existing law of contracts, is that law to be forever immune from change? Suppose a man unable to read or write becomes a real estate broker at a time when oral brokerage contracts are enforceable. Is he to be protected against a later law that might require such contracts to be evidenced by a signed writing? As for the argument that tax laws often have the explicit purpose of attracting men into, or deterring them from, certain activities, who can say what the precise function of a tax is, except that it raises revenue? One legislator may have favored a tax for one reason, another for a quite different reason. What shall we say of the tax on alcoholic beverages? Was its purpose to discourage drinking or was it to raise revenue by imposing a special levy on those whose habits of life indicate that they are especially able to help defray the costs of government? There can be no clear answer to questions like these.

At this point we must cut short this dialogue and leave its issues unresolved. The purpose of presenting it has been merely to indicate some of the difficulties surrounding the concept of the retroactive law, difficulties that are by no means confined to the law of taxation. In meeting these difficulties the courts have often resorted to the notion of a contract between the government and the citizen. Thus, if a tax exemption is granted in favor of certain activities and then later repealed, the test often applied is to ask whether the state can fairly be considered to have entered a contract to maintain the exemption. It should be observed that this notion of a contract between state and citizen is capable of indefinite extension. As Georg Simmel has shown, the state's position of superior power rests ultimately on a tacit reciprocity.[19] This reciprocity, once made explicit, can be extended to all eight of the principles of legality. If King Rex, instead of being an hereditary monarch, had been elected to office for life on a promise to reform the legal system, his subjects might well have

19. See note 1, supra.

felt they had a right to depose him. The notion that a revolution may be justified by a breach of contract by the government is, of course, an ancient one. It is a concept that is generally thought to lie completely beyond the usual premises of legal reasoning. Yet a milder cousin of it appears within the legal system itself when the validity of retrospective legislation is made to depend upon the state's fidelity to a contract between itself and the citizen.

In this discussion of retrospective laws much stress has been placed on difficulties of analysis. For that reason I should not like to leave the subject without a reminder that not every aspect of it is shrouded with obscurity. As with the other desiderata that make up the internal morality of the law, difficulties and nuances should not blind us to the fact that, while perfection is an elusive goal, it is not hard to recognize blatant indecencies. Nor in seeking examples of obvious abuses do we need to confine our search to Hitlerite Germany or Stalinist Russia. We, too, have legislators who, in their own more modest way, give evidence of believing that the end justifies the means. Take, for example, a federal statute enacted in 1938. This statute made it "unlawful for any person who has been convicted of a crime of violence . . . to receive any firearm or ammunition which has been shipped or transported in interstate or foreign commerce." The draftsmen of the statute quite justifiably considered that persons falling within its language do not as a whole constitute our most trustworthy citizens. They also quite understandably harbored a wish that they might make their statute retroactive. Realizing, however, that this was impossible they sought to do the next best thing. They wrote into the statute a rule that if any firearm was received in interstate commerce by a person meeting the description of the act, then it should be presumed that the receipt took place after the effective date of the act. This piece of legislative overcleverness was stricken down by the Supreme Court in *Tot v. United States*.[20]

20. *Tot v. United States*, 319 U.S. 463 (1942). The Court also struck down another presumption contained in the Act. This provided that pos-

The Clarity of Laws

The desideratum of clarity represents one of the most essential ingredients of legality.[21] Though this proposition is scarcely subject to challenge, I am not certain it is always understood what responsibilities are involved in meeting this demand.

Today there is a strong tendency to identify law, not with rules of conduct, but with a hierarchy of power or command. This view—which confuses fidelity to law with deference for established authority—leads easily to the conclusion that while judges, policemen, and prosecuting attorneys can infringe legality, legislatures cannot, except as they may trespass against explicit constitutional restrictions on their power. Yet it is obvious that obscure and incoherent legislation can make legality unattainable by anyone, or at least unattainable without an unauthorized revision which itself impairs legality. Water from a tainted spring

session of a firearm or ammunition by a person falling within the description contained in the Act should give rise to a presumption that it had been received after being shipped in interstate or foreign commerce.

21. There is little discussion of this desideratum in the literature of jurisprudence. The short treatment in Bentham's posthumous work, *The Limits of Jurisprudence Defined,* Everett, ed. (1945), p. 195, is entirely devoted to a labored attempt to develop a nomenclature capable of distinguishing various kinds of unclarity. One might have expected Austin to list among "laws improperly so-called" (*Lectures,* pp. 100–01) the wholly unintelligible statute. But it does not appear in his discussion. The neglect of this subject by positivistic writers is, however, quite understandable. A recognition that laws may vary in clarity would entail a further recognition that laws can have varying degrees of efficacy, that the unclear statute is, in a real sense, less a law than the clear one. But this would be to accept a proposition that runs counter to the basic assumptions of positivism.

In this country it has been urged that, quite without reference to any standards impliedly imposed by constitutions, the courts should refuse to make any attempt to apply statutes drastically lacking in clarity. Aigler, "Legislation in Vague or General Terms," 21 *Michigan Law Review* 831–51 (1922). As the law has developed, however, the requirement of clarity has been incorporated in a doctrine of unconstitutional vagueness, the application of this doctrine being almost entirely confined to criminal cases. See the extensive note, "The Void-for-Vagueness Doctrine in the Supreme Court," 109 *University of Pennsylvania Law Review* 67–116 (1960).

can sometimes be purified, but only at the cost of making it something other than it was. Being at the top of the chain of command does not exempt the legislature from its responsibility to respect the demands of the internal morality of law; indeed, it intensifies that responsibility.

To put a high value on legislative clarity is not to condemn out of hand rules that make legal consequences depend on standards such as "good faith" and "due care." Sometimes the best way to achieve clarity is to take advantage of, and to incorporate into the law, common sense standards of judgment that have grown up in the ordinary life lived outside legislative halls. After all, this is something we inevitably do in using ordinary language itself as a vehicle for conveying legislative intent. Nor can we ever, as Aristotle long ago observed, be more exact than the nature of the subject matter with which we are dealing admits. A specious clarity can be more damaging than an honest open-ended vagueness.

On the other hand, it is a serious mistake—and a mistake made constantly—to assume that, though the busy legislative draftsman can find no way of converting his objective into clearly stated rules, he can always safely delegate this task to the courts or to special administrative tribunals. In fact, however, this depends on the nature of the problem with which the delegation is concerned. In commercial law, for example, requirements of "fairness" can take on definiteness of meaning from a body of commercial practice and from the principles of conduct shared by a community of economic traders. But it would be a mistake to conclude from this that all human conflicts can be neatly contained by rules derived, case by case, from the standard of fairness.

There is need, then, to discriminate when we encounter Hayek's sweeping condemnation of legal provisions requiring what is "fair" or "reasonable":

> One could write a history of the decline of the Rule of Law . . . in terms of the progressive introduction of these

vague formulas into legislation and jurisdiction,[22] and of the increasing arbitrariness and uncertainty of, and the consequent disrespect for, the law and the judicature.[23]

A much needed chapter of jurisprudence remains at present largely unwritten. This chapter would devote itself to an analysis of the circumstances under which problems of governmental regulation may safely be assigned to adjudicative decision with a reasonable prospect that fairly clear standards of decision will emerge from a case-by-case treatment of controversies as they arise. In dealing with problems of this fundamental character, a policy of "wait and see" or of "social experimentation" has little to recommend it.

Contradictions in the Laws

It is rather obvious that avoiding inadvertent contradictions in the law may demand a good deal of painstaking care on the part of the legislator. What is not so obvious is that there can be difficulty in knowing when a contradiction exists, or how in abstract terms one should define a contradiction.

It is generally assumed that the problem is simply one of logic. A contradiction is something that violates the law of identity by which A cannot be not-A. This formal principle, however, if it has any value at all, has none whatever in dealing with contradictory laws.[24]

Let us take a situation in which a contradiction "in the logical sense" seems most evident. In a single statute, we may suppose, are to be found two provisions: one requires the automobile

22. "Adjudication" is no doubt meant, not "jurisdiction."
23. *The Road to Serfdom* (1944), p. 78.
24. Kelsen's highly formal analysis of the problem of contradictory norms does not, I submit, offer any aid at all to the legislator seeking to avoid contradictions or to the judge seeking to resolve them. *General Theory of Law and State* (1945), pp. 374–75 et passim; see index entry "Non-contradiction, principle of." Nor is much to be gained from Bentham's discussion of "repugnancies." Everett, *Bentham's Limits of Jurisprudence Defined* (1945), pp. 195–98.

owner to install new license plates on January first; the other makes it a crime to perform any labor on that date. Here there seems to be a violation of the law of identity; an act cannot be both forbidden and commanded at the same time. But is there any violation of logic in making a man do something and then punishing him for it? We may certainly say of this procedure that it makes no sense, but in passing this judgment we are tacitly assuming the objective of giving a meaningful direction to human effort. A man who is habitually punished for doing what he was ordered to do can hardly be expected to respond appropriately to orders given him in the future. If our treatment of him is part of an attempt to build up a system of rules for the governance of his conduct, then we shall fail in that attempt. On the other hand if our object is to cause him to have a nervous breakdown, we may succeed. But in neither event will we have trespassed against logic.

One of the accepted principles for dealing with apparent contradictions in the law is to see whether there is any way of reconciling the seemingly inconsistent provisions. Pursuant to this principle a court might hit upon the idea of finding the man who installed his plates on New Year's Day guilty of a crime and of then remitting his punishment because he worked under the compulsion of a statute. This seems a rather labored solution, but stranger procedures have been adopted in the history of the law. At one time in canonical law there was a principle according to which any promise made under oath was binding and another principle according to which certain kinds of promises, such as those extorted or usurious, imposed no obligation. What should the courts do then in the case of a usurious promise under oath? The solution was to order the promisor to render performance to the promisee and then immediately to compel the promisee to return what he had just received.[25] There may even have been a certain symbolic value in this curious procedure. By first enforcing the contract the court would dramatize the rule that men

25. Rudolph von Jhering, *Geist des römischen Rechts*, II² (6th and 7th ed. 1923), §45, p. 491.

are bound by promises under oath, and then by undoing its decree, the court would remind the promisee of what his overreaching had cost him.

Assuming that the court confronted with the New Year's Day statute would see no value in convicting the defendant and then remitting his fine, it might adopt one of two interpretations of the statute: (1) that the section making work on New Year's Day a crime overrides the provision concerning license plates, so that the automobile owner may lawfully postpone installing his plates until January second; or (2) that the provision concerning license plates overrides the work prohibition, so that the owner must install his plates on the first, but commits no crime in doing so. A less obvious, but much better solution would be to combine these interpretations, so that the owner who installs his plates on the first violates no law, while the owner who postpones providing his car with new plates until the second is equally within the law. This solution would recognize that the basic problem presented by the statute is that it gives a confused direction to the citizen so that he ought to be allowed to resolve that confusion in either way without injuring himself.

It will be well to consider another "self-contradictory" statute —this time as presented in an actual decision. In *United States v. Cardiff* the president of a company manufacturing food had been convicted of the crime of refusing to permit a federal inspector to enter his factory to determine whether it was complying with the Federal Food, Drug, and Cosmetic Act.[26] Section 704 of that Act defines the conditions under which an inspector may enter a factory; one of these conditions is that he first obtain the permission of the owner. Section 331 makes it a crime for the owner of the factory to refuse "to permit entry or inspection as authorized by section 704." The Act seems, then, to say that the inspector has a right to enter the factory but that the owner has a right to keep him out by refusing permission. There is, however, a very simple way of removing this apparent contra-

26. 344 U.S. 174 (1952).

diction. This would be to interpret the Act to mean that the owner violates the Act if *after* granting his consent that the inspector should enter, he *then* refuses entry. That this would make his liability depend on his own voluntary act is no anomaly; a man doesn't have to make a promise, but if he does, he may fasten a liability on himself by doing so.

The Supreme Court considered this interpretation but refused to accept it. The trouble with it is not that it is lacking in logic, but that it does not correspond to any sensible legislative purpose. It is understandable that Congress might wish to insure that the inspector be able to enter the factory over the owner's protest. It is not understandable that it should limit the inspector's right to enter to the improbable case of an eccentric factory owner who might first grant permission and then shut the door. Sense could be made of the statute by construing the requirement that the inspector first secure permission as relating to the normal courtesies affecting a convenient time and date, though the language counts against this interpretation. The Supreme Court held that the clash of the two provisions produced a result too ambiguous to give adequate warning of the nature of the crime; the Court therefore set the conviction aside.

So far this discussion has related to contradictions as they arise within the frame of a single enactment. More difficult problems can be presented when a statute enacted, say, in 1963 is found to conflict with the provisions of a quite distinct statute passed in 1953. Here the solution sanctioned by usage is to regard as impliedly repealed any provisions in the earlier statute inconsistent with the later enactment, the consecrated maxim being *lex posterior derogat priori*.[27] But in some cases an apter way of dealing with the problem might be to follow the principle now

27. In an early treatise on interpretation Lord Ellesmere laid down the rule that where repugnancies arise within a single statute the first provision —that is, the provision that comes first in the reading order of the text— should control. Thorne, *A Discourse upon the Statutes* (1942), pp. 132–33. One wonders what the basis for this curious view could have been. Was it perhaps an assumption that legislative draftsmen characteristically become weary and less attentive as they near the end of their task?

applied where contradictions arise within the frame of a single statute, that is, by effecting a reciprocal adjustment between the two statutes, interpreting each in the light of the other. This solution would, however, involve its own difficulties. One would be to know where to stop, for the courts might easily find themselves embarked on the perilous adventure of attempting to remake the entire body of our statutory law into a more coherent whole. The reinterpretation of old statutes in the light of new would also present embarrassing problems of retrospective legislation. I shall not attempt to pursue these issues. Enough has been intimated, however, to convey one clear lesson: legislative carelessness about the jibe of statutes with one another can be very hurtful to legality and there is no simple rule by which to undo the damage.

It has been suggested that instead of speaking of "contradictions" in legal and moral argument we ought to speak of "incompatibilities,"[28]—of things that do not go together or do not go together well. Another term, a great favorite in the history of the common law, is useful here. This is the word "repugnant." It is especially apt because what we call contradictory laws are laws that fight each other, though without necessarily killing one another off as contradictory statements are assumed to do in logic. Another good term that has fallen into disuse is the word "inconvenient" in its original sense. The inconvenient law was one that did not fit or jibe with other laws. (Cf. modern French, *convenir,* to agree or come together.)

It should be apparent from the analysis presented here that to determine when two rules of human conduct are incompatible we must often take into account a host of considerations extrinsic to the language of the rules themselves. At one time in history the command, "Cross this river, but don't get wet," contained a repugnancy. Since the invention of bridges and boats this is no longer true. If today I tell a man to jump in the air, but to keep his feet in contact with the ground, my order seems self-contra-

28. Perelman and Olbrechts-Tyteca, *La Nouvelle Rhétorique—Traité de l'Argumentation* (1958), pp. 262–76.

dictory simply because we assume there is no way open to him to take the ground along with him in his leap. The context that must be taken into account in determining the issue of incompatibility is, of course, not merely or even chiefly technological, for it includes the whole institutional setting of the problem—legal, moral, political, economic, and sociological. To test this assertion one may suppose that the New Year's Day statute required the installation of license plates on that day, but in another section levied an excise tax of one dollar on any person performing work on that day. It would be instructive to reflect how one would go about demonstrating that these provisions are "repugnant" and that their inclusion in a single statute must have been the result of legislative oversight.

Laws Requiring the Impossible

On the face of it a law commanding the impossible seems such an absurdity that one is tempted to suppose no sane lawmaker, not even the most evil dictator, would have any reason to enact such a law.[29] Unfortunately the facts of life run counter to this assumption. Such a law can serve what Lilburne called "a law-

29. The question may be raised at this point whether most of the other desiderata that make up the internal morality of the law are not also ultimately concerned with the possibility of obedience. There is no question that the matter may be viewed in this light. Just as it is impossible to obey a law that requires one to become ten feet tall, so it is also impossible to obey a law that cannot be known, that is unintelligible, that has not yet been enacted, etc. But in justification for the separation effected in the text it should be observed that my concern is not to engage in an exercise in logical entailment, but to develop principles for the guidance of purposive human effort. The logician may, if he wishes, view a law that contradicts itself as a special case of the impossibility of observance, though in adopting this view he may, as I have indicated, find it difficult to define what he means by a "contradiction." From the standpoint of the lawmaker, in any event, there is an essential difference between the precautions he must take to keep his enactments consistent with one another and those he must take to be sure that the requirements of the law lie within the powers of those subject to them. Essential differences of this sort would be obscured by any attempt to telescope everything under the head of "impossibility of obedience."

70

less unlimited power" by its very absurdity; its brutal pointless-
ness may let the subject know that there is nothing that may not
be demanded of him and that he should keep himself ready to
jump in any direction.

The technique of demanding the impossible is subject to more
subtle and sometimes even to beneficent exploitation. The good
teacher often demands of his pupils more than he thinks they
are capable of giving. He does this with the quite laudable motive
of stretching their capacities. Unfortunately in many human contexts the line can become blurred between vigorous exhortation
and imposed duty. The legislator is thus easily misled into believing his role is like that of the teacher. He forgets that the
teacher whose pupils fail to achieve what he asked of them can,
without insincerity or self-contradiction, congratulate them on
what they did in fact accomplish. In a similar situation the
government official faces the alternative of doing serious injustice
or of diluting respect for law by himself winking at a departure
from its demands.

The principle that the law should not demand the impossible
of the subject may be pressed toward a quixotic extreme in which
it ends by demanding the impossible of the legislator. It is sometimes assumed that no form of legal liability can be justified unless it rests either on (1) an intent to do a harmful act, or (2) some
fault or neglect. If a man is held accountable for a condition of
affairs for which he was not to blame—either because he inten-
tionally brought it about or because it occurred through some
neglect on his part—then he has ascribed to him responsibility
for an occurrence that lay beyond his powers. When the law is
interpreted to reach such a result it in effect holds a man for
violating a command, "This must not happen," which it was
impossible for him to obey.

The air of reasonableness that surrounds this conclusion obscures the true extent of what it actually demands. With respect
to the proof of fault, for example, the law faces an insoluble
dilemma. If we apply to a particular defendant an objective standard—traditionally that of "the reasonable man"—we obviously

71

run the risk of imposing on him requirements he is incapable of meeting, for his education and native capacities may not bring this standard within his reach. If we take the opposite course and attempt to ask whether the man before us, with all his individual limitations and quirks, fell short of what he ought to have achieved, we enter upon a hazardous inquiry in which all capacity for objective judgment may be lost. This inquiry requires a sympathetic identification with the life of another. Obviously differences of class, race, religion, age, and culture may obstruct or distort that identification. The result is that though an aloof justice is bound at times to be harsh, an intimate justice, seeking to explore and grasp the boundaries of a private world, cannot in the nature of things be evenhanded. The law knows no magic that will enable it to transcend this antinomy. It is, therefore, condemned to tread an uncertain middle course, tempering the standard of the reasonable man in favor of certain obvious deficiencies, but formalizing even its definitions of these.

The difficulties just described, it may be said, arise because a determination of fault involves what is essentially a moral judgment. In contrast, determining the intention with which an act was done seems to require only an inquiry of fact. But, again the reality is more complex. If intention is a fact, it is a private fact inferred from outward manifestations. There are times when the inference is relatively easy. Holmes once remarked that even a dog knows the difference between being stumbled over and being kicked. But at times the intention required by the law is a highly specific one, as where criminal penalties are made dependent upon proof that the defendant knowingly violated the law. This sort of provision is sometimes found in complex economic regulations, its purpose being to avoid the injustice of punishing a man for doing an act which may on its face have seemed quite innocent. From my own observation it is often a question whether in this case the cure is not worse than the disease. The required intent is so little susceptible of definite proof or disproof that the trier of fact is almost inevitably driven to asking, "Does he look like the kind who would stick by the rules or one who would cheat on them when he saw a chance?" This question, unfortunately, leads easily into another, "Does he look like my kind?"[30]

These, then, are the difficulties encountered when, in order to keep the law within the citizen's capacity for obedience, his liability is limited to cases where fault or wrongful intent can be demonstrated. There are, however, numerous instances in our law of legal liability that is explicitly made independent of any proof of fault or intent.

One rather pervasive form of a liability of this sort presents no serious problem for the law's inner morality. A lunatic, let us suppose, steals my purse. His mental condition may be such that it is impossible for him to understand or to obey the laws of private property. This circumstance furnishes a good reason for not sending him to jail, but it offers no reason at all for letting him keep my purse. I am entitled under the law to get my purse back, and he is, in this sense, under a legal liability to return it, even though in taking it he acted without fault and without any intention of doing wrong. Another case illustrating the same principle arises when in a settlement of accounts a debtor over-pays his creditor, both acting innocently and sharing the same mistaken belief as to what is due. Here the creditor is compelled to return the overpayment, though his receipt of it was in no sense a wrongful act.

A considerable body of law has to do with preventing or rectifying the unjust enrichment that may come about when men act inadvertently, or under mistake, or without the ordinary ca-

30. In this connection attention should be called to an article, "The Modern Conception of Animus," 19 *Green Bag* 12–33 (1906), by Brooks Adams, brother of Henry and grandson of John Quincy. In this article Adams presents an ingenious and curiously Marxist argument that the ruling classes have always manipulated in their own interest the definition of intent (animus) required for particular crimes or torts. Adams also seeks to demonstrate that a similar manipulation has been worked on the rules of evidence that determine what suffices to prove or disprove the required intent. Though its main thesis is at times more ingenious than convincing, the article is worth reading for its demonstration of the difficulties of proof involved where liability is made to depend on intent.

pacity to comprehend the nature of their acts. Some of this law is explicitly assigned to quasi contracts; the rest of it makes its presence felt as an influence—often a silent influence—in the law of contracts and torts. Analysis has been confused, both in the common law and in the Roman law, by the fact that actions formally classified as "delictual" or as "sounding in tort" have been used to rectify the unjust enrichment of one party at the expense of another in situations where any wrongdoing by the defendant is quite immaterial.

The existence of a body of law having to do with the rectification of inadvertencies may seem to suggest an objection to the analysis presented in these essays. Law has here been considered as "the enterprise of subjecting human conduct to the governance of rules." Yet when men act under mistake or through inadvertence they obviously do not and cannot pattern their actions after the law; no one studies the law of quasi contracts to learn what he should do in moments when he does not quite know what he is doing. The solution of this difficulty is fairly obvious. To preserve the integrity of a system of legal relations set by advertence there is need for a supplementary system of rules for healing the effects of inadvertence. There is here a close parallel to the problem of retrospective laws. A system of law composed exclusively of retrospective rules could exist only as a grotesque conceit worthy of Lewis Carroll or Franz Kafka. Yet a retrospective "curative" statute can perform a useful function in dealing with mishaps that may occur within a system of rules that are generally prospective.[31] So it is with the rules that cure the effects of inadvertence. If everything happened through inadvertence, there would be no way even of conceiving of the problem of correcting inadvertence. Rules designed for that purpose derive not only their justification, but their very meaning from their function as an adjunct to a larger system of rules intended to be taken as a guide for conduct.

The principle of rectifying the unjust enrichment that results from inadvertence cannot, however, explain all the instances

31. See pp. 53–54, supra.

where legal liability arises without fault or intent. There exists, in fact, a very considerable body of law concerned with imposing a strict or absolute liability for harms resulting from certain forms of activity. Thus, blasting operations may be attended by an accountability for all harm that may result to others even though no intent to harm or any neglect of proper precautions can be demonstrated.[32] In cases like this the law decrees, in the consecrated phrase, that "men act at their peril."

Strict liability of this sort is most readily justified by the economic principle that the foreseeable social costs of an enterprise ought to be reflected in the private costs of conducting that enterprise. Thus, the dangers inherent in a blasting operation are such that no amount of care or foresight can prevent occasional unintended injury to persons or property. If the highway contractor who blasts a cut through a hillside is held accountable only for demonstrated fault, his incentive to accomplish his excavations by a safer means is reduced. His economic calculations, in other words, are falsified and the price of this falsification is borne by the public. To rectify this situation we impose on his blasting operations a kind of tax in the form of a rule that he must respond for any damage that results from these operations, whether or not they can be attributed to any negligence on his part.

The analogy of a tax is useful in clarifying the relation between a strict liability of this sort and the internal morality of law. We do not view a general sales tax as ordering men not to sell goods; we consider that it merely imposes a kind of surcharge on the act of selling. So we should not view the special rule about blasting operations as commanding the man using explosives never to cause any damage, however innocently. Rather we should regard the rule as attaching a special liability to entry upon a certain line of conduct. What the internal morality of law demands of a rule of strict liability is not that it cease commanding the impossible, but that it define as clearly as possible the kind of activity that carries a special surcharge of legal responsibility.

The principle that enterprises creating special risks ought to

32. American Law Institute, *Restatement of Torts* (1938), §519, "Miscarriage of Ultrahazardous Activities Carefully Carried On."

bear the cost of the injuries resulting from their operation is capable of a very considerable expansion. In some countries, for example, the principle has been extended to the operation of automobiles, including those used for pleasure or private convenience. It is a kind of cliché that there exists today "a general trend" toward strict liability. It seems, indeed, often to be assumed that this trend is carrying us remorselessly toward a future in which the concepts of fault and intent will cease to play any part in the law.

I think we can be reasonably sure that no such future lies ahead of us. If strict liability were to attend, not certain specified forms of activity, but *all* activities, the conception of a causal connection between the act and the resulting injury would be lost. A poet writes a sad poem. A rejected lover reads it and is so depressed that he commits suicide. Who "caused" the loss of his life? Was it the poet, or the lady who jilted the deceased, or perhaps the teacher who aroused his interest in poetry? A man in a drunken rage shoots his wife. Who among those concerned with this event share the responsibility for its occurrence —the killer himself, the man who lent the gun to him, the liquor dealer who provided the gin, or was it perhaps the friend who dissuaded him from securing a divorce that would have ended an unhappy alliance?

Some inkling of the nature of this sort of problem we can get from the difficulties encountered in administering those forms of strict liability we already have. One such liability is that imposed by the Workmen's Compensation Laws. Obviously some causal connection must be established between the employee's job and the illness or injury to be compensated. The phrase used in the statutes is that the injury or illness must "arise out of and in the course of the employment." The interpretation of this clause has given rise to a most unsatisfactory and often bizarre body of law. To see what a universal application of strict liability would involve we need only ask how we would apply a rule that required only that the plaintiff's loss or injury should "arise out of" the defendant's conduct.

The account just given of the problem of strict civil liability is by no means exhaustive. Some forms of such liability exist that are not readily explained on the grounds examined here. There are also numerous instances of uncertain or mixed legislative motives, one common supplementary justification for rules of strict accountability being, for example, that they tend to insure due care more effectively than rules making liability turn explicitly on proof that due care was lacking. Some instances of strict liability are probably to be regarded as anomalies, resulting either from analytical confusion or historical accident. Then, too, the line between strict liability and liability founded on fault is often obscured by presumptions of fault, some of those being quite stiff in the sense that they impose a heavy burden on those who seek to rebut them. Finally, it should be recalled that contractual liability is generally "strict"; though certain catastrophic and unexpected interferences with performance may excuse, it is generally not a defense for the defaulting contractor to plead that he did his best. It scarcely requires demonstration that this last form of strict liability presents no problem for the internal morality of law; the law ought not itself to impose an impossible burden on a man, but it is not bound to protect him from contractually assuming responsibility for an occurrence that lies beyond his powers.

We come now to the most serious infringement of the principle that the law should not command the impossible. This lies in laws creating a strict criminal liability—laws under which a man may be found guilty of a crime though he acted with due care and with an innocent intent. In modern times the most generous use of such laws has been in the field of economic, health, and safety regulations, though it is not uncommon also to impose a strict criminal liability in areas having to do with the possession of narcotics, gambling apparatus, and prohibited liquors.

Strict criminal liability has never achieved respectability in our law. Wherever laws imposing such a liability have been enacted they have called forth protests and a defense that seldom goes beyond apologizing for an assumed necessity. There is, however, no mystery about the reason for their continued and perhaps expanding appearance in modern legislation: they serve mightily the convenience of the prosecutor. Their apparent injustice, he is likely to assure us, is removed by "selective enforcement." Though theoretically such laws are a trap for the innocent, it is only the real villains who are pursued in practice. As for them, their being brought to justice is greatly facilitated because the government in making out its case is relieved from having to prove intent or fault, a particularly difficult task when complicated regulatory measures are involved. When absolute liability is coupled with drastic penalties—as it often is—the position of the prosecutor is further improved. Usually he will not have to take the case to trial at all; the threat of imprisonment or a heavy fine is enough to induce a plea of guilty, or—where this is authorized—a settlement out of court. Drastic penalties also enhance the public relations of the agencies of enforcement. The innocent stumbler who knows that he could have been found guilty is deeply grateful when he is let off and therefore saved from being branded as a criminal. He promises in all sincerity to be more intelligently cooperative in the future.

The conveniences of what has been called "jawbone enforcement"—it might less charitably be called "enforcement by blackmail"—became widely known during the hectic days of World War II, when overworked administrators of complex economic regulations had to find some way of simplifying their task. The continued use of this device should be a source of concern to everyone who likes to think of fidelity to law as respect for duly enacted rules, rather than as a readiness to settle quietly any claim that may be made by the agencies of law enforcement. Fortunately, influential and persuasive voices have recently been raised against this evil and the other abuses that go with strict criminal liability.[33]

33. Hall, *General Principles of Criminal Law* (2d ed. 1960), Chapter X, pp. 325–59; Hart, "The Aims of Criminal Law," 23 *Law & Contemporary Problems* 401–41 (1958); The American Law Institute, *Model Penal Code, Proposed Official Draft* (1962), Sections 1.04(5), 2.01–2.13.

Before leaving the subject of laws commanding the impossible, two further observations need to be made. One is simply and obviously to the effect that no hard and fast line can be drawn between extreme difficulty and impossibility. A rule that asks somewhat too much can be harsh and unfair, but it need not contradict the basic purpose of a legal order, as does a rule that demands what is patently impossible. Between the two is an indeterminate area in which the internal and external moralities of law meet.

My final observation is that our notions of what is in fact impossible may be determined by presuppositions about the nature of man and the universe, presuppositions that are subject to historical change. Today opposition to laws purporting to compel religious or political beliefs is rested on the ground that such laws constitute an unwarranted interference with individual liberty. Thomas Jefferson took a different view. In the original draft of the Preamble to the Virginia Statute of Religious Freedom he condemned such laws as attempting to compel the impossible:

> Well aware that the opinions and beliefs of men depend not upon their own will, but follow involuntarily the evidence proposed to their minds . . .[34]

One may raise the question whether there is not in this conception a profounder respect both for truth and for human powers than there is in our own.

Constancy of the Law through Time

Of the principles that make up the internal morality of the law, that which demands that laws should not be changed too frequently seems least suited to formalization in a constitutional restriction. It is difficult to imagine, for example, a constitutional convention unwise enough to resolve that no law should be

34. Boyd, *The Papers of Thomas Jefferson,* II, 545.

changed more often than, say, once a year. Restrictions on retroactive legislation, on the other hand, have been a favorite among
constitution makers.[35] Yet there is a close affinity between the
harms done by retrospective legislation and those resulting from
too frequent changes in the law. Both follow from what may be
called legislative inconstancy. It is interesting to note that Madison, when he sought to defend the provisions in the Constitution
prohibiting ex post facto laws and laws impairing the obligation
of contract, used language more apt for describing the evil of
frequent change than that resulting from retroactive laws:

> The sober people of America are weary of the fluctuating
> policy which has directed the public councils. They have
> seen with regret and indignation that sudden changes and
> legislative interferences . . . become . . . snares to the more-
> industrious and less-informed part of the community. They
> have seen, too, that one legislative interference is but the
> first link of a long chain of repetitions.[36]

The affinity between the problems raised by too frequent or
sudden changes in the law and those raised by retrospective legislation receives recognition in the decisions of the Supreme Court.
The evil of the retrospective law arises because men may have
acted upon the previous state of the law and the actions thus
taken may be frustrated or made unexpectedly burdensome by a
backward looking alteration in their legal effect. But sometimes
an action taken in reliance on the previous law can be undone,
provided some warning is given of the impending change and
the change itself does not become effective so swiftly that an in-
sufficient time is left for adjustment to the new state of the law.
Thus the Court has said:

> it is well settled that [statutes of limitations] may be modified
> by shortening the time prescribed, but only if this is done
> while the time is still running, and so that a reasonable time

35. See notes 10 and 11, supra pp. 51–52.
36. *The Federalist,* No. 44.

still remains for the commencement of an action before the bar takes effect.[37]

Congruence between Official Action and Declared Rule

We arrive finally at the most complex of all the desiderata that make up the internal morality of the law: congruence between official action and the law. This congruence may be destroyed or impaired in a great variety of ways: mistaken interpretation, inaccessibility of the law, lack of insight into what is required to maintain the integrity of a legal system, bribery, prejudice, indifference, stupidity, and the drive toward personal power.

Just as the threats toward this congruence are manifold, so the procedural devices designed to maintain it take, of necessity, a variety of forms. We may count here most of the elements of "procedural due process," such as the right to representation by counsel and the right of cross-examining adverse witnesses. We may also include as being in part directed toward the same objective habeas corpus and the right to appeal an adverse decision to a higher tribunal. Even the question of "standing" to raise constitutional issues is relevant in this connection; haphazard and fluctuating principles concerning this matter can produce a broken and arbitrary pattern of correspondence between the Constitution and its realization in practice.

In this country it is chiefly to the judiciary that is entrusted the task of preventing a discrepancy between the law as declared and as actually administered. This allocation of function has the advantage of placing the responsibility in practiced hands, subjecting its discharge to public scrutiny, and dramatizing the integrity of the law. There are, however, serious disadvantages in any system that looks solely to the courts as a bulwark against the lawless administration of the law. It makes the correction of abuses dependent upon the willingness and financial ability of the affected party to take his case to litigation. It has proved

37. *Ochoa v. Hernandez y Morales,* 230 U.S. 139, at pp. 161–62 (1913).

relatively ineffective in controlling lawless conduct by the police, this evil being in fact compounded by the tendency of lower courts to identify their mission with that of maintaining the morale of the police force. For an effective control of police lawlessness much can be said for some overseeing agency, like the Scandinavian ombudsman, capable of acting promptly and flexibly on informal complaints.

In those areas where the law is judge-made it may be said that, though the essential congruence between law and official action can be impaired by lower courts, it cannot be impaired by the supreme court since it makes the law. The supreme court of a jurisdiction, it may seem, cannot be out of step since it calls the tune. But the tune called may be quite undanceable by anyone, including the tune-caller. All of the influences that can produce a lack of congruence between judicial action and statutory law can, when the court itself makes the law, produce equally damaging departures from other principles of legality: a failure to articulate reasonably clear general rules and an inconstancy in decision manifesting itself in contradictory rulings, frequent changes of direction, and retrospective changes in the law.

The most subtle element in the task of maintaining congruence between law and official action lies, of course, in the problem of interpretation. Legality requires that judges and other officials apply statutory law, not according to their fancy or with crabbed literalness, but in accordance with principles of interpretation that are appropriate to their position in the whole legal order. What are those principles? The best short answer I know dates back to 1584 when the Barons of the Exchequer met to consider a difficult problem of interpretation in Heydon's Case:

> And it was resolved by them, that for the sure and true interpretation of all statutes in general (be they penal or beneficial, restrictive or enlarging of the common law,) four things are to be discerned and considered:—
>
> *1st.* What was the common law before the making of the Act.

2nd. What was the mischief and defect for which the common law did not provide.

3rd. What remedy the Parliament hath resolved and appointed to cure the disease of the commonwealth.

And, *4th.* The true reason of the remedy; and then the office of all the Judges is always to make such construction as shall suppress the mischief, and advance the remedy.[38]

If any criticism can be made of this analysis, it is that it should have included a fifth point to be "discerned and considered," which might read somewhat as follows: "How would those who must guide themselves by its words reasonably understand the intent of the Act, for the law must not become a snare for those who cannot know the reasons of it as fully as do the Judges."

Keeping before us the central truth of the Resolution in Heydon's Case, namely, that to understand a law you must understand "the disease of the commonwealth" it was appointed to cure, will enable us to clear the problem of interpretation of the confusions that have typically beclouded it. Some of these have a specious air of common sense about them that has conferred on them an undeserved longevity. This is particularly true of the thought contained in the following passage from Gray:

> Interpretation is generally spoken of as if its chief function was to discover what the meaning of the Legislature really was. But when a Legislature has had a real intention, one way or another, on a point, it is not once in a hundred times that any doubt arises as to what its intention was . . . The fact is that the difficulties of so-called interpretation

38. 3 Co. Rep. 7a. It is apparent that in the passage quoted the word "mischief" is used in a sense no longer current. As used in Heydon's Case it was in fact a close cousin to two other words that were then great favorites: "repugnancy" and "inconvenience." All of these terms described a situation where things did not fit together, chunks of chaos not yet reduced through human effort to reasoned order.

It should perhaps also be suggested that since the report of the Resolution is by Coke, it is possible that he reports what the Barons ought to have resolved rather than what they did in fact think and say.

arise when the Legislature has had no meaning at all; when the question which is raised on the statute never occurred to it . . . [In such cases] when the judges are professing to declare what the Legislature meant, they are in truth, themselves legislating to fill up *casus omissi*.[39]

Now it is, of course, true that occasionally in the drafting of a statute some likely situation is entirely forgotten, so that one may imagine the draftsman saying something like "Oops!" when this oversight is called to his attention. But cases of this sort are far from typical of the problems of interpretation. More commonly the statute turns out to be blunt and incomplete rather than so directed as to miss an obvious target.

Underlying Gray's view is an atomistic conception of intention, coupled with what may be called a pointer theory of meaning. This view conceives the mind to be directed toward individual things, rather than toward general ideas, toward distinct situations of fact rather than toward some significance in human affairs that these situations may share. If this view were taken seriously, then we would have to regard the intention of the draftsman of a statute directed against "dangerous weapons" as being directed toward an endless series of individual objects: revolvers, automatic pistols, daggers, Bowie knives, etc. If a court applies the statute to a weapon its draftsman had not thought of, then it would be "legislating," not "interpreting," as even more obviously it would be if it were to apply the statute to a weapon not yet invented when the statute was passed.[40]

This atomistic view of intention exercises, directly and indirectly, so much influence on theories of interpretation that it becomes essential to set explicitly off against it a truer view of the problem. To that end let me suggest an analogy. An inventor

39. *The Nature and Sources of the Law* (2d ed. 1921), pp. 172–73.
40. The "atomistic" view of intention described in the text is related to, and may be regarded as an expression of, philosophic nominalism. I have dealt with the influence of this view on the movement known as legal realism in my article, "American Legal Realism," 82 *University of Pennsylvania Law Review* 429, 443–47 (1934).

of useful household devices dies leaving the pencil sketch of an invention on which he was working at the time of his death. On his deathbed he requests his son to continue work on the invention, though he dies without having had a chance to tell the son what purpose the invention was to serve or anything about his own plans for completing it. In carrying out his father's wish the son's first step would be to decide what the purpose of the projected invention was, what defect or insufficiency of existing devices it was intended to remedy. He would then try to grasp the underlying principle of the projected invention, the "true reason of the remedy" in the language of Heydon's Case. With these problems solved he would then proceed to work out what was essential to complete the design for the projected device.

Let us now ask of the son's action questions of the sort commonly asked concerning the interpretation of statutes. Was the son faithful to his father's intention? If we mean, "Did he carry out an intention the father had actually formed concerning the manner of completing the design?" why, of course, the question is quite unanswerable for we do not know whether the father had any such intention, and if so, what it was. If we mean, "Did he remain within the framework set by the father, accepting the father's conception of a need for the projected device and his father's general approach to the problem of supplying that need?" then the answer, on the facts supposed, is yes. If the son were able to call on his father's spirit for help, the chances are that this help would take the form of collaborating with the son in the solution of a problem the father had left unsolved. So it is usually with difficult problems of interpretation. If the draftsman of a statute were called into direct consultation, he would normally have to proceed in the same manner as the judge by asking such questions as the following: Does this case fall within the mischief which the statute sought to remedy? Does it fall within the "true reason of the remedy" appointed by the statute, that is, is the prescribed remedy apt for dealing with this particular manifestation of the general mischief at which the statute was aimed?

85

The analogy of the incomplete invention may also be helpful in clarifying an obscurity that runs through the vocabulary of interpretation. We tend to think of intention as a phenomenon of individual psychology, though what we are interpreting is a corporate act. Thus we ask after the intention of "the legislator," though we know there is no such being. At other times we speak of the intention of "the legislature," though we know that those who voted for a statute often do so with a variety of views as to its meaning and often with no real understanding of its terms. Moving closer to individual psychology we may speak of the intention of "the draftsman." But again we are in trouble. There may be a number of draftsmen, acting at different times and without any common understanding as to the exact purpose sought. Furthermore, any private and uncommunicated intention of the draftsman of a statute is properly regarded as legally irrelevant to its proper interpretation.[41] Let us turn to the analogy of the incomplete invention to see if it offers any aid in this impasse. It is clear that the son may in working out his problem find it helpful to put himself, as it were, in the frame of his father's thinking, recalling his modes of thought and his characteristic ways of solving problems. Yet it is also plain that this procedure may neither be essential nor helpful. Indeed, if the incomplete design came from the hand of some quite unknown inventor the son's task might not be essentially changed. He would look to the diagram itself to see what purpose was to be served by the invention and what general principle or principles underlay the projected design. We could speak in such a case of "the intention of the design." This might involve a metaphor but it is at least a useful one that does not misdescribe the nature of

41. Speaking of the Statute of Frauds, Lord Nottingham said in *Ash v. Abdy*, 3 Swanston 664 (1678), "I had some reason to know the meaning of this law; for it had its first rise from me." Cf. "If Lord Nottingham drew it, he was the less qualified to construe it, the author of an act considering more what he privately intended than the meaning he has expressed." Campbell's *Lives of the Lord Chancellors of England, 3* (3d ed. 1848), 423 n.

the son's task. So in speaking of legislative intention I think it would be better if we spoke of "the intention of the statute," just as Mansfield in dealing with contractual intention once spoke of "the intent of the transaction."[42]

Fidelity to enacted law is often identified with a passive and purely receptive attitude on the part of the judge. If he acts "creatively," it must be that he is going beyond his assignment as an interpreter. Those who prefer judge-made law to statutes are apt to welcome this departure and rejoice to see the judge apparently make so much from so little. On the other hand, those who distrust judicial power are apt to discern in any creative role an abandonment of principle and a reaching for personal power. When issue is joined in these terms the whole problem is misconceived. In the case of the incomplete invention when the son assumed a creative role he did not, for that act alone, deserve either praise or blame. He was simply meeting the demands of his assignment by doing what he had to do to carry out his father's wish. The time for praise or blame would come when we could survey what he had accomplished in this inescapably creative role. So it is with judges.

It may be objected that the analogy that has been exploited here is misleading. A statute, it may be said, does not serve a purpose as simple and as easily defined as, for example, that of a vacuum cleaner. The social mischief it seeks to remedy is often subtle and complex, its very existence being perceptible only to those holding certain value judgments. Again, the remedy which a statute appoints for curing "a disease of the commonwealth" is not like a shaft connecting one mechanism with another. Often the legislature has to choose among a wide range of possible remedies, some providing a very oblique kind of cure for the defect sought to be corrected.

All this may be conceded and yet I suggest that it is precisely at this point of apparent default that the figure of the incomplete invention becomes most useful. Some obscurity concerning the

42. *Kingston v. Preston*, 2 Douglas 689 (1773).

mischief sought to be remedied by a statute can be tolerated. But if this obscurity exceeds a certain crucial point, then no virtuosity in draftsmanship nor skill in interpretation can make a meaningful thing of a statute afflicted with it. Again, some looseness of thought about the connection between the remedy and the defect it is appointed to cure does not inevitably vitiate a statute. But if this connection is fundamentally misconceived, then all possibility of coherent interpretation is lost. To suppose otherwise would be like assuming that an invention basically mistaken in conception could be rescued by being incorporated in a neat blueprint.

Let me give an historic example of a statutory provision that was vitiated by a fundamental defect in its design. I refer to Paragraph 5 of Section 4 of the Statute of Frauds, passed in 1677. Section 4 of the Statute was predicated on the assumption that certain kinds of contracts ought not to be legally enforceable unless proof of their existence was backed by a signed document. On the other hand, it was thought unwise to extend so stringent a requirement to all contracts, some of which ought to be legally valid though expressed orally. Accordingly, the draftsmen faced the necessity of deciding what kinds of contracts ought to be required to be in writing and what kinds could safely be left to oral expression. One such decision was incorporated in the following language: "no action shall be brought . . . (5) upon any agreement that is not to be performed within the space of one year from the making thereof; unless the agreement upon which such action shall be brought . . . shall be in writing, and signed by the party to be charged therewith."

It is probably safe to say that few statutory enactments have given rise to so many discordant and bizarre interpretations as the words just quoted. What went wrong? The statute is expressed in simple, straightforward English. The mischief aimed at seems fairly obvious. It is also fairly easy to see why the draftsmen should select, as especially needing the security of written evidence, contracts scheduled to run over a considerable period of time; in Holt's words, "the design of the statute was, not to trust to the memory of witnesses for a longer time than one year."[43]

Difficulty arose because the draftsmen had simply not thought through the relation between the mischief and the remedy they appointed to cure it. In the first place it is clear that there is no direct relation between the time when a witness will be called to testify and the time required to perform the contract; a contract might be scheduled for completion within one month and yet first come into proof in court two years later. Furthermore, the draftsmen failed to ask themselves what the courts should do with the very common case of contracts as to which it is impossible to say in advance how much time their performance will require, such as contracts to employ a man for life or to pay a monthly sum to him until he is cured of an illness. By imagining unexpected events that accelerate or postpone performance this class of contracts can be greatly expanded. In a case coming up for decision shortly after the Statute was passed it was suggested that the validity of the contract should depend on the actual course of events.[44] If it turned out that performance came due within a year, the oral contract was valid; if not, then the contract was unenforceable. But this solution was never accepted and could not be. Parties need to know from the outset, or at least as soon as trouble develops, whether or not they have a contract. To make the existence of a binding contract depend upon later events would invite all kinds of jockeying for position and produce the greatest imaginable confusion. In short, the courts were confronted with a statute which simply could not be applied in a way to carry out the loosely conceived intention of its draftsmen. The British finally found in 1954 the only cure for this situation: outright repeal of the section in question. We still reach for the solution to a puzzle that has no solution.

My second instance of fundamentally misconceived legislation is more modern by nearly three centuries. It concerns a statute which suffers from the defect that it is impossible to define

43. *Smith v. Westfall,* 1 Lord Raymond 317 (1697).
44. See the case cited in the last note.

in any clear terms just what mischief it was intended to cure. With the repeal of prohibition Americans highly resolved "to prevent the return of the old saloon." What did this mean? The old saloon was a complex thing, combining architectural, atmospheric, artistic, commercial, legal, and sociological aspects. It was highly improbable that it would, or even could, return in its old form after an absence of fifteen years during which fundamental social changes took place. Still, to make assurance doubly sure it was thought in many states "there ought to be a law."

How do you legislate against a thing like "the old saloon"? Well, the old saloon had swinging doors; let it therefore be made illegal to serve drinks behind anything that may fairly be called swinging doors. In the old saloon the patrons stood up to their drinks; let it therefore be decreed that they must now sit down— though surely as an original proposition there is much reason for assuming that the cause of temperance would be advanced by requiring the drinkers to stand during their imbibitions. You could not buy a meal in the old saloon, though you might be given one for nothing. Let us create something of the atmosphere of a family restaurant in the new saloon by imposing a legal requirement that it serve meals. But this must not be carried too far. It would be grossly unfair to require the thirsty customer to buy food before he could be served a drink. Let the legal requirement be, then, that the new saloon be prepared to serve food to any who may order it, however few they may be among its patrons.

The primary responsibility for administering this allopathic concoction of rules was of course vested, not with the prosecutor, but with the licensing authority. Can anyone imagine deriving any sense of useful social function from serving on such an authority? Is it any wonder that this area of regulation is notorious for inefficiency and corruption? Even if a conscientious bureaucrat could be found who would consider his life filled with mission if he were simply allowed to enforce rules, however senseless, the problem would still not be solved. There would remain insoluble problems of interpretation, in deciding, for example, what constitutes being adequately prepared to serve a meal to a diner who never comes.

At this point our discussion of the problem of interpretation must be broken off. It is too richly textured a subject to be exhausted by any one analogy or metaphor. Its demands depend so much on context that illustrative cases can serve only to disclose general principles, but cannot convey the nuances that attend the application of those principles to particular branches of the law. With all its subtleties, the problem of interpretation occupies a sensitive, central position in the internal morality of the law. It reveals, as no other problem can, the cooperative nature of the task of maintaining legality. If the interpreting agent is to preserve a sense of useful mission, the legislature must not impose on him senseless tasks. If the legislative draftsman is to discharge his responsibilities he, in turn, must be able to anticipate rational and relatively stable modes of interpretation. This reciprocal dependence permeates in less immediately obvious ways the whole legal order. No single concentration of intelligence, insight, and good will, however strategically located, can insure the success of the enterprise of subjecting human conduct to the governance of rules.

Legality as a Practical Art

To the lengthy analysis just concluded some final observations should be added concerning practical applications of the principles of legality.

First, a warning about the word "law" is in order. In 1941 there was added to the Annotated Laws of Massachusetts (Ch. 2, §9) a provision to the effect that the chickadee should be the Official Bird of the Commonwealth. Now it is apparent that the public weal would have suffered no serious setback if this law had been kept secret from the public and made retroactive to the landing of the Mayflower. Indeed, if we call by the name of law any official act of a legislative body, then there may be circumstances under which the full details of a law must be kept secret. Such a case might arise where a legislative appropriation was made to finance research into some new military weapon. It is always unfortunate when any act of government must be concealed from the public and thus shielded from public criticism. But there are times when we must bow to grim necessity. The Constitution itself in Article V provides that each "house shall keep a journal of its proceedings, and from time to time publish the same, excepting such parts as may in their judgment require secrecy." All of this has very little relevance, however, to the laws that are the subject under discussion.[45] I can conceive, for example, of no emergency that would justify withholding from the public knowledge of a law creating a new crime or changing the requirements for making a valid will.

Secondly, infringements of legal morality tend to become cumulative. A neglect of clarity, consistency, or publicity may beget the necessity for retroactive laws. Too frequent changes in the law may nullify the benefits of formal, but slow-moving procedures for making the law known. Carelessness about keeping the laws possible of obedience may engender the need for a discretionary enforcement which in turn impairs the congruence between official action and enacted rule.

Thirdly, to the extent that the law merely brings to explicit expression conceptions of right and wrong widely shared in the community, the need that enacted law be publicized and clearly stated diminishes in importance. So also with the problem of retroactivity; where law is largely a reflection of extralegal morality, what appears in form as retrospective legislation may in substance represent merely the confirmation of views already widely held, or in process of development toward the rule finally enacted. When toward the end of the sixteenth century the English courts finally gave legal sanction to the executory bilateral contract they only caught up with commercial practice by allowing

45. A discussion of some problems of publicity as they affect governmental action other than the passage of laws in the usual sense will be found in my article, "Governmental Secrecy and the Forms of Social Order," in 2 *Nomos* ("Community") 256–68 (1959).

parties to do directly what they had previously been compelled to achieve by indirection.

Fourthly, the stringency with which the eight desiderata as a whole should be applied, as well as their priority of ranking among themselves, will be affected by the branch of law in question, as well as by the kinds of legal rules that are under consideration. Thus, it is generally more important that a man have a clear warning of his legal duties than that he should know precisely what unpleasantness will attend a breach; a retroactive statute creating a new crime is thoroughly objectionable, a similar statute lengthening the term of imprisonment for an existing crime is less so. A familiar distinction between rules of law is that which distinguishes rules imposing duties from rules conferring legal capacities. Both sorts of rules are affected in some measure by all eight of the demands of legal morality. At the same time, rules granting and defining legal powers seldom have any counterpart in the practices of everyday life—shaking hands on a deal has never been accepted as an adequate legal formality. Hence as to rules defining legal powers the requirements of publicity and clarity are apt to be especially demanding. Contrariwise, conferring retroactive validity on what was under existing law a vain attempt to exercise a legal power will often be seen as advancing the cause of legality by preventing a confusion of legal rights.

Fifthly and finally, it should be recalled that in our detailed analysis of each of the demands of legal morality we have generally taken the viewpoint of a conscientious legislator, eager to understand the nature of his responsibility and willing to face its difficulties. This emphasis on nuances and difficult problems should not make us forget that not all cases are hard. Each of the demands of legality can be outraged in ways that leave no doubt. Caligula, for example, is said to have respected the tradition that the laws of Rome be posted in a public place, but saw to it that his own laws were in such fine print and hung so high that no one could read them.

The paradox that a subject can be at once so easy and so

difficult may be illumined by a figure from Aristotle. In his *Ethics* Aristotle raises the question whether it is easy to deal justly with others. He observes that it might seem that it would be, for there are certain established rules of just dealing that can be learned without difficulty. The application of a simple rule ought itself to be simple. But this is not so, Aristotle says, invoking at this point a favorite analogy, that of medicine: "It is an easy matter to know the effects of honey, wine, hellebore, cautery and cutting. But to know how, for whom, and when we should apply these as remedies is no less an undertaking than being a physician."[46]

So we in turn may say: It is easy to see that laws should be clearly expressed in general rules that are prospective in effect and made known to the citizen. But to know how, under what circumstances, and in what balance these things should be achieved is no less an undertaking than being a lawgiver.

46. *Nichomachean Ethics,* Book V, 1137a.

THE CONCEPT
OF LAW

III

As ideas of what law is for are so largely implicit in ideas of what law is, a brief survey of ideas of the nature of law . . . will be useful.—Roscoe Pound

Das Vergessen der Absichten ist die häufigste Dummheit, die gemacht wird.—Friedrich Nietzsche

The purpose of the present chapter is to put the analysis presented in my second chapter into its proper relation with prevailing theories of and about law. This task is taken up, not primarily to vindicate what I have said against the opposing views of others, but by way of a further clarification of what has so far been said here. While I agree that a book on legal theory ought not to be merely "a book from which one learns what other books contain,"[1] the fact remains that what one has learned from other books (sometimes indirectly and without having read them) acts as a prism through which any new analysis is viewed. Some setting off of one's own views against those deeply en-

1. Hart, *The Concept of Law* (1961), viii.

95

trenched in the vocabulary and thought of one's subject is an essential part of exposition.

Legal Morality and Natural Law

Proceeding with that exposition, then, the first task is to relate what I have called the internal morality of the law to the ages-old tradition of natural law. Do the principles expounded in my second chapter represent some variety of natural law? The answer is an emphatic, though qualified, yes.

What I have tried to do is to discern and articulate the natural laws of a particular kind of human undertaking, which I have described as "the enterprise of subjecting human conduct to the governance of rules." These natural laws have nothing to do with any "brooding omnipresence in the skies." Nor have they the slightest affinity with any such proposition as that the practice of contraception is a violation of God's law. They remain entirely terrestrial in origin and application. They are not "higher" laws; if any metaphor of elevation is appropriate they should be called "lower" laws. They are like the natural laws of carpentry, or at least those laws respected by a carpenter who wants the house he builds to remain standing and serve the purpose of those who live in it.

Though these natural laws touch one of the most vital of human activities they obviously do not exhaust the whole of man's moral life. They have nothing to say on such topics as polygamy, the study of Marx, the worship of God, the progressive income tax, or the subjugation of women. If the question be raised whether any of these subjects, or others like them, should be taken as objects of legislation, that question relates to what I have called the external morality of law.

As a convenient (though not wholly satisfactory) way of describing the distinction being taken we may speak of a procedural, as distinguished from a substantive natural law. What I have called the internal morality of law is in this sense a procedural version of natural law, though to avoid misunderstanding the word "procedural" should be assigned a special and expanded sense so that it would include, for example, a substantive accord between official action and enacted law. The term "procedural" is, however, broadly appropriate as indicating that we are concerned, not with the substantive aims of legal rules, but with the ways in which a system of rules for governing human conduct must be constructed and administered if it is to be efficacious and at the same time remain what it purports to be.

In the actual history of legal and political thinking what association do we find between the principles I have expounded in my second chapter and the doctrine of natural law? Do those principles form an integral part of the natural law tradition? Are they invariably rejected by the positivist thinkers who oppose that tradition? No simple answer to these questions is possible.

With the positivists certainly no clear pattern emerges. Austin defined law as the command of a political superior. Yet he insisted that "laws properly so-called" were general rules and that "occasional or particular commands" were not law.[2] Bentham, who exploited his colorful vocabulary in castigating the law of nature, was at all times concerned with certain aspects of what I have called the internal morality of law. Indeed, he seemed almost obsessed with the need to make the laws accessible to those subject to them. On the other hand, in more recent times Gray has treated the question whether law ought to take the form of general rules as a matter of "little importance practically," though admitting that specific and isolated exercises of legal power do not make a fit subject for jurisprudence.[3] For Somló retroactive laws might be condemned as unfair, but in no sense are to be regarded as violating any general premise underlying the concept of law itself.[4]

2. See note 6, Chapter 2, p. 49.
3. Ibid.
4. "Es kann somit bloss ein Rechtsinhaltsprinzip sein, das die rück-wirkende Kraft von Rechtsnormen ausschliesst, nicht ein Voraussetzungs-prinzip." *Juristische Grundlehre* (2d ed. 1927), p. 302. See also note 13, Chapter 2, supra p. 52.

With respect to thinkers associated with the natural law tradition it is safe to say that none of them would display the casualness of a Gray or Somló toward the demands of legal morality. On the other hand, their chief concern is with what I have called substantive natural law, with the proper ends to be sought through legal rules. When they treat of the demands of legal morality it is, I believe, usually in an incidental way, though occasionally one aspect of the subject will receive considerable elaboration. Aquinas is probably typical in this respect. Concerning the need for general rules (as contrasted with a case-by-case decision of controversies) he develops a surprisingly elaborate demonstration, including an argument that wise men being always in short supply it is a matter of economic prudence to spread their talents by putting them to work to draft general rules which lesser men can then apply.[5] On the other hand, in explaining why Isidore required laws to be "clearly expressed" he contents himself with saying that this is desirable to prevent "any harm ensuing from the law itself."[6]

With writers of all philosophic persuasions it is, I believe, true to say that when they deal with problems of legal morality it is generally in a casual and incidental way. The reason for this is not far to seek. Men do not generally see any need to explain or to justify the obvious. It is likely that nearly every legal philosopher of any consequence in the history of ideas has had occasion to declare that laws ought to be published so that those subject to them can know what they are. Few have felt called upon to expand the argument for this proposition or to bring it within the cover of any more inclusive theory.

From one point of view it is unfortunate that the demands of legal morality should generally seem so obvious. This appearance has obscured subtleties and has misled men into the belief that no painstaking analysis of the subject is necessary or even possible. When it is asserted, for example, that the law ought not to contradict itself, there seems nothing more to say.

5. *Summa Theologica*, Pt. I–II, ques. 95, Art 1.
6. Ibid., Art. 3.

Yet, as I have tried to show, in some situations the principle against contradiction can become one of the most difficult to apply of those which make up the internal morality of the law.[7]

To the generalization that in the history of political and legal thought the principles of legality have received a casual and incidental treatment—such as befits the self-evident—there is one significant exception. This lies in a literature that arose in England during the seventeenth century, a century of remonstrances, impeachments, plots and civil war, a period during which existing institutions underwent a fundamental reexamination.

It is to this period that scholars trace the "natural law foundations" of the American Constitution. Its literature—curiously embodied chiefly in the two extremes of anonymous pamphlets and judicial utterances—was intensely and almost entirely concerned with problems I have regarded as those of the internal morality of law. It spoke of repugnancies, of laws impossible to be obeyed, of parliaments walking contrary to their own laws before they have repealed them. Two representative samples of this literature appear at the head of my second chapter.[8] But the most famous pronouncement to come down from that great period is that of Coke in *Dr. Bonham's Case.*

Henry VIII had given to the Royal College of Physicians (in a grant later confirmed by Parliament) broad powers to license and regulate the practice of medicine in London. The College was granted the right to try offenses against its regulations and to impose fines and imprisonments. In the case of a fine, one half was to go to the King, the other half to the College itself. Thomas Bonham, a doctor of medicine of the University of Cambridge, undertook the practice of medicine in London without the certificate of the Royal College. He was tried by the College, fined and later imprisoned. He brought suit for false imprisonment.

7. Supra pp. 65–70.
8. Supra p. 33. A splendid account of this literature will be found in Gough, *Fundamental Law in English Constitutional History* (1954); (reprinted with minor changes, 1961).

In the course of Coke's judgment upholding Bonham's cause, this famous passage appears:

> The censors [of the Royal College] cannot be judges, ministers and parties; judges to give sentence or judgment; ministers to make summons; and parties to have the moiety of the forfeiture, *quia aliquis non debet esse Judes in propria causa, imo iniquum est aliquem suae rai esse judicem;* and one cannot be Judge and attorney for any of the parties. . . . And it appears in our books, that in many cases, the common law will controul Acts of Parliament, and sometimes adjudge them to be utterly void: for when an Act of Parliament is against common right and reason, or repugnant, or impossible to be performed, the common law will controul it, and adjudge such Act to be void.[9]

Today this pronouncement is often regarded as the quintessence of the natural law point of view. Yet notice how heavily it emphasizes procedures and institutional practices. Indeed, there is only one passage that can be said to relate to substantive rightness or justice, that speaking of parliamentary acts "against common right and reason." Yet by "common right" Coke may very well have had in mind rights acquired through the law and then taken away by law, the kind of problem, in other words, often presented by retrospective legislation. It may seem odd to speak of repugnant statutes in a context chiefly concerned with the impropriety of a man's acting as judge in his own cause. Yet for Coke there was here a close association of ideas. Just as legal rules can be repugnant to one another, so institutions can be repugnant. Coke and his associates on the bench strove to create an atmosphere of impartiality in the judiciary, in which it would be unthinkable that a judge, say, of Common Pleas should sit in

9. 8 Rep. 118a (1610). For an interesting analysis of the relevance this famous passage had for the actual decision of the lawsuit brought by Dr. Bonham, see Thorne, "Dr. Bonham's Case," 54 *Law Quarterly Review* 543–52 (1938).

judgment of his own case. Then came the King and Parliament sticking an ugly, incongruous finger into this effort, creating a "court" of physicians for judging infringements of their own monopoly and collecting half the fines for themselves. When Coke associated this legislative indecency with repugnancy he was not simply expressing his distaste for it; he meant that it contradicted essential purposive efforts moving in an opposite direction.

The view, common among modern scholars, that in the quoted passage Coke betrays a naïve faith in natural law, tells us little that will help us understand the intellectual climate of the seventeenth century. It tells us a great deal about our own age, an age that in some moods at least thinks itself capable of believing that no appeal to man's nature, or to the nature of things, can ever be more than a cover for subjective preference, and that under the rubric "subjective preference" must be listed indifferently propositions as far apart as that laws ought to be clearly expressed and that the only just tax is one that makes the citizen pay the exact equivalent of what he himself receives from government.

Those who actually created our republic and its Constitution were much closer in their thinking to the age of Coke than they are to ours. They, too, were concerned to avoid repugnancies in their institutions and to see to it that those institutions should suit the nature of man. Hamilton rejected the "political heresy" of the poet who wrote:

> For forms of government let fools contest—
> That which is best administered is best.[10]

In supporting the power of the judiciary to declare acts of Congress unconstitutional Hamilton pointed out that the judiciary can never be entirely passive toward legislation; even in the absence of a written constitution judges are compelled, for example, to develop some rule for dealing with contradictory enactments,

10. *The Federalist,* No. 68.

this rule being derived not "from any positive law, but from the nature and reason of the thing."[11]

A continuing debate in this country relates to the question whether in interpreting the Constitution the courts should be influenced by considerations drawn from "natural law."[12] I suggest that this debate might contribute more to a clarification of issues if a distinction were taken between a natural law of substantive ends and a natural law concerned with procedures and institutions. It should be confessed, however, that the term "natural law" has been so misused on all sides that it is difficult to recapture a dispassionate attitude toward it.

What is perfectly clear is that many of the provisions of the Constitution have the quality I have described as that of being blunt and incomplete.[13] This means that in one way or another their meaning must be filled out. Surely those whose fate in any degree hinges on the creative act of interpretation by which this meaning is supplied, as well as those who face the responsibility of the interpretation itself, must wish that it should proceed on the most secure footing that can be obtained, that it should be grounded insofar as possible in the necessities of democratic government and of human nature itself.

I suggest that this ideal lies most nearly within our reach in the area of constitutional law concerned with what I have called the internal morality of the law. Within this area, interpretation can often depart widely from the explicit words of the Constitution and yet rest secure in the conviction that it is faithful to an intention implicit in the whole structure of our government. There is, for example, no explicit prohibition in the Constitution of vague or obscure legislation. Yet I doubt if anyone could regard as a judicial usurpation the holding that a criminal statute violates "due process of law" if it fails to give a reasonably clear

11. Ibid., No. 78.
12. Within the Court itself the debate was initiated by an exchange between Justices Black and Frankfurter in *Adamson v. California,* 332 U.S. 46 (1947).
13. P. 84, supra.

description of the act it prohibits.[14] When one reflects on the problems of drafting a constitution the justification for this holding becomes obvious. If an express provision directed against vague laws were included in the Constitution, some standard, explicit or tacit, would have to determine what degree of obscurity should vitiate. This standard would have to run in quite general terms. Starting with the premise that law governs and judges men's actions by general rules, any criminal statute ought to be sufficiently clear to serve the double purpose of giving to the citizen an adequate warning of the nature of the act prohibited and of providing adequate guidelines for adjudication in accordance with law. If one wished to summarize all this in a phrase, it would be hard to find a better expression than "due process of law."

The Constitution invalidates any "law *impairing* the obligation of contracts." Yet the courts have held that a law unduly *enhancing* the obligation of existing contracts may be equally objectionable and therefore unconstitutional.[15] This seems a surprising result but it rests on a secure constitutional basis. The context of the impairment clause makes it clear that it was regarded as one of several manifestations of the general evil of retrospective legislation, the draftsmen having refrained (wisely in view of the difficulty of the task) from attempting any comprehensive measure covering the subject. When we judge the impairment clause against the background of its general purpose, it becomes plain that the same objection that applies to laws reducing the obligations of existing contracts may equally apply to laws enlarging those obligations. In assuming the risks inherent in a contractual engagement, a man may properly take into account what the existing law prescribes as his obligation in case of default. If that law is then radically changed to his disfavor, the legislature has broken faith with him.

In these last remarks I may seem to be assigning contradictory

14. See the references in note 21, Chapter 2, p. 63, supra.
15. The cases are discussed in Hale, "The Supreme Court and the Contracts Clause," 57 *Harvard Law Review* 512, 514–16 (1944).

qualities to the internal morality of the law. I have suggested that this morality lends itself awkwardly to formulation in a written constitution. I have at the same time asserted that in dealing with questions touching the internal morality of the law judicial interpretation can proceed with an unusual degree of confidence in its objectivity, and this despite the fragmentary and inadequate constitutional expressions on which it must build. How can a task so difficult for the draftsman that he must leave his job half-done be thought to provide relatively firm guidelines for judicial interpretation?

The answer to this question has, I think, already been given, though in somewhat unfamiliar terms. I have described the internal morality of law as being chiefly a morality of aspiration, rather than of duty.[16] Though this morality may be viewed as made up of separate demands or "desiderata"—I have discerned eight—these do not lend themselves to anything like separate and categorical statement.[17] All of them are means toward a single end, and under varying circumstances the optimum marshalling of these means may change. Thus an inadvertent departure from one desideratum may require a compensating departure from another; this is the case where a failure to give adequate publicity to a new requirement of form may demand for its cure a retrospective statute.[18] At other times, a neglect of one desideratum may throw an added burden on another; thus, where laws change frequently, the requirement of publicity becomes increasingly stringent. In other words, under varying circumstances the elements of legality must be combined and recombined in accordance with something like an economic calculation that will suit them to the instant case.

These considerations seem to me to lead to the conclusion that it is within the constitutional area I have designated as that of the law's internal morality that the institution of judicial review is both most needed and most effective. Wherever the choice is

16. See pp. 42–44, supra.
17. See pp. 42–46, supra, et passim in the second chapter.
18. See p. 92, supra.

reasonably open to it, the court ought to remain within this area. *Robinson v. California*[19] is, I submit, a case where the Supreme Court quite plainly took the wrong turn. As the majority viewed the issues in that case the question presented was whether a statute might constitutionally make the state or condition of being a drug addict a crime punishable by six months' imprisonment. It was assumed as a scientific fact that this condition might come about innocently. The Court held that the statute violated the Eighth Amendment by imposing a "cruel and unusual punishment."

Surely it is plain that being sent to jail for six months would not normally be regarded as "cruel and unusual punishment"— a phrase that calls to mind at once the whipping post and the ducking stool. In attempting to meet this objection the Court argued that in deciding whether a given punishment was cruel and unusual one had to take into account the nature of the offense for which it was imposed. Thus the Court needlessly took on its shoulders a general responsibility—surely oppressive, even if it has been described as sublime—for making the punishment fit the crime.

This excursion into substantive justice was, I submit, quite unnecessary. We have an express constitutional prohibition of ex post facto criminal laws, and a well-established rule of constitutional law that a statutory definition of crime must meet certain minimum standards of clarity. Both of these restraints on legislative freedom proceed on the assumption that the criminal law ought to be presented to the citizen in such a form that he can mold his conduct by it, that he can, in short, obey it. Being innocently in a state or condition of drug addiction cannot be construed as an act, and certainly not as an act of disobedience. Bringing the decision in *Robinson v. California* within the traditional confines of due process would certainly have presented no greater difficulty than would be presented by a case, say, where a criminal statute was kept secret by the legislature until

19. 370 U.S. 660 (1962).

an indictment was brought under it. (It should be recalled that our Constitution has no express requirement that laws be published.)

Legal Morality and the Concept of Positive Law

Our next task is to bring the view of law implicit in these chapters into its proper relation with current definitions of positive law. The only formula that might be called a definition of law offered in these writings is by now thoroughly familiar: law is the enterprise of subjecting human conduct to the governance of rules. Unlike most modern theories of law, this view treats law as an activity and regards a legal system as the product of a sustained purposive effort. Let us compare the implications of such a view with others that might be opposed to it.

The first such theory I shall consider is one that in mood and emphasis stands at the opposite pole from these chapters and yet, paradoxically, advances a thesis that is easily reconciled with my own. This is Holmes' famous predictive theory of law: "The prophecies of what the courts will do in fact, and nothing more pretentious, are what I mean by law."[20]

Now clearly the ability to prophesy presupposes order of some sort. The predictive theory of law must therefore assume some constancy in the influences that determine what "the courts will do in fact." Holmes chose to abstract from any study of these influences, concentrating his attention on the cutting edge of the law.

He himself explained that he made this abstraction in order to effect a sharp distinction between law and morality. But he could think he had succeeded in this objective only by refraining from any attempt to describe the actual process of prediction itself. If we are to predict intelligently what the courts will do in fact, we must ask what they are trying to do. We must indeed go further and participate vicariously in the whole purposive ef-

20. "The Path of the Law," 10 *Harvard Law Review* 457–78, at p. 461 (1897).

fort that goes into creating and maintaining a system for directing human conduct by rules. If we are to understand that effort, we must understand that many of its characteristic problems are moral in nature. Thus, we need to put ourselves in the place of the judge faced with a statute extremely vague in its operative terms yet disclosing clearly enough in its preamble an objective the judge considers plainly unwise. We need to share the anguish of the weary legislative draftsman who at 2:00 A.M. says to himself, "I know this has got to be right and if it isn't people may be hauled into court for things we don't mean to cover at all. But how long must I go on rewriting it?"

A concentration on the order imposed by law in abstraction from the purposive effort that goes into creating it is by no means a peculiarity of Holmes' predictive theory. Professor Friedmann, for example, in an attempt to offer a neutral concept of law that will not import into the notion of law itself any particular ideal of substantive justice, proposes the following definition:

> the rule of law simply means the "existence of public order." It means organized government, operating through the various instruments and channels of legal command. In this sense, all modern societies live under the rule of law, fascist as well as socialist and liberal states.[21]

Now it is plain that a semblance of "public order" can be created by lawless terror, which may serve to keep people off the streets and in their homes. Obviously, Friedmann does not have this sort of order in mind, for he speaks of "organized government, operating through the various instruments and channels of legal command." But beyond this vague intimation of the kind of order he has in mind he says nothing. He plainly indicates, however, a conviction that, considered just "as law," the law of Nazi Germany was as much law as that of any other nation. This proposition, I need not say, is completely at odds with the analysis presented here.

21. *Law and Social Change* (1951), p. 281.

Most theories of law either explicitly assert, or tacitly assume, that a distinguishing mark of law consists in the use of coercion or force. That distinguishing mark is not recognized in this volume. In this respect the concept of law I have defended contradicts the following definition, proposed by an anthropologist seeking to identify the distinctive "legal" element among the various forms of social order that make up a primitive society:

> for working purposes law may be defined in these terms: A social norm is legal if its neglect or infraction is regularly met, in threat or in fact, by the application of physical force by an individual or group possessing the socially recognized privilege of so acting.[22]

The notion that its authorization to use physical force can serve to identify law and to distinguish it from other social phenomena is a very common one in modern writings. In my opinion it has done great harm to clarity of thought about the functions performed by law. It will be well to ask how this identification came about.

In the first place, given the facts of human nature, it is perfectly obvious that a system of legal rules may lose its efficacy if it permits itself to be challenged by lawless violence. Sometimes violence can only be restrained by violence. Hence it is quite predictable that there must normally be in society some mechanism ready to apply force in support of law in case it is needed. But this in no sense justifies treating the use or potential use of force as the identifying characteristic of law. Modern science depends heavily upon the use of measuring and testing apparatus; without such apparatus it could not have achieved what it has. But no one would conclude on this account that science should be defined as the use of apparatus for measuring and testing. So it is with law. What law must foreseeably do to achieve its aims is something quite different from law itself.

There is another factor tending toward an identification of

22. Hoebel, *The Law of Primitive Man* (1954), p. 28.

law with force. It is precisely when the legal system itself takes up weapons of violence that we impose on it the most stringent requirements of due process. In civilized nations it is in criminal cases that we are most exigent in the demand for guarantees that the law remain faithful to itself. Thus, that branch of law most closely identified with force is also that which we associate most closely with formality, ritual, and solemn due process. This identification has a particular relevance to primitive society, where the first steps toward a legal order are likely to be directed toward preventing or healing outbreaks of private violence.

These considerations explain, but do not justify, the modern tendency to see physical force as the identifying mark of law. Let us test this identification with a hypothetical case. A nation admits foreign traders within its borders only on condition that they deposit a substantial sum of money in the national bank guaranteeing their observance of a body of law specially applicable to their activities. This body of law is administered with integrity and, in case of dispute, is interpreted and applied by special courts. If an infraction is established the state pursuant to court order levies a fine in the form of a deduction from the trader's deposit. No force, but a mere bookkeeping operation, is required to accomplish this deduction; no force is available to the trader that could prevent it. Surely it would be perverse to deny the term "law" to such a system merely because it had no occasion to use force or the threat of force to effectuate its requirements. We might, however, quite properly refuse to call it a system of law if it were determined that its published rules and robed judges were a mere façade for what was in fact a lawless act of confiscation.

The considerations implicit in this illustration relieve us, I think, from having to explore in any detail a further question: Just what is meant by force when it is taken as the identifying mark of law? If in a theocratic society the threat of hell-fire suffices to secure obedience to its laws, is this "a threat of force"? If so, then force begins to take on a new meaning and simply indicates that a legal system, to be properly called such, has to achieve some minimum efficacy in practical affairs, whatever the basis of that efficacy—a proposition both unobjectionable and quite unexciting.

In most theories of law the element of force is closely associated with the notion of a formal hierarchy of command or authority. In the passage quoted from Hoebel this association was absent because, as an anthropologist, Hoebel was concerned with primitive law, where any clearly defined hierarchic ordering of authority is generally lacking. Since the emergence of the national state, however, a long line of legal philosophers running from Hobbes through Austin to Kelsen and Somló have seen the essence of law in a pyramidal structure of state power. This view abstracts from the purposive activity necessary to create and maintain a system of legal rules, contenting itself with a description of the institutional framework within which this activity is assumed to take place.

Legal philosophy has paid a heavy price for this abstraction. Within the school accepting it many disputes are left without any intelligible principle for resolving them. Take, for example, the argument whether "law" includes only rules of some generality, or should be regarded as embracing also "particular or occasional commands." Some say that law implies generality of some sort, others deny this. Those who agree on the necessity for generality disagree on the proper way of defining it; does it require a class of acts, a class of persons, or both?[23] The whole argument, resting merely on affirmation and counteraffirmation, ends in a blind alley. I suggest that this debate is without intelligible content unless one starts with the obvious truth that the citizen cannot orient his conduct by law if what is called law confronts him merely with a series of sporadic and patternless exercises of state power.

If we ask what purpose is served by the conception of law as a hierarchy of command, the answer may be that this conception represents the legal expression of the political national state. A

23. See note 6, Chapter 2, p. 49.

110

less vague and, I believe, juster answer would be to say that it expresses a concern with the problem of resolving conflicts within the legal system. Indeed, one may say that it converts one principle of the internal morality of law—that condemning contradictory laws—into an absolute to the neglect of all others. With Kelsen and Somló this concentration on internal coherence becomes explicit as a fundamental element of their theories.[24] Certainly it is desirable that unresolved contradictions within a legal system should be avoided or should be subject to resolution when they arise. But viewing the matter without precommitment, what reason can there be for any preference between a legal system that is full of contradictions and one in which the rules are so vague it is impossible to know whether they contradict one another or not?

It may be answered that common sense and a concern to make his measures effective will ordinarily lead the legislator to make his laws reasonably clear, whereas contradictions among the rules applied by the various agencies of government constitute a perennial problem. Before accepting this answer we should certainly reflect on the very real temptations a government may have to make its laws vague. But more fundamentally the whole issue is misconceived when, instead of clarifying our problems and seeking apt solutions, we attempt to foreclose our difficulties by definitional fiat. It is all very well to define law in such a way that it cannot be self-contradictory because in theory there is always a higher instance that can resolve disputes on a lower level. But this leaves the practical problems of contradiction untouched, particularly that of clarifying what in close cases shall be regarded as being a contradiction. Though Kelsen and Somló make much of the problem of resolving contradictions, so far as I can determine neither ever discusses a single problem of the sort likely to cause difficulties in actual practice. Instead the whole discussion deals with such abstractions as that "it is logically

24. See Kelsen, *General Theory of Law and State* (1945), pp. 401–04 and index entry "Non-contradiction, principle of"; Somló, *Juristische Grundlehre* (2d ed. 1927), index entry "Widersprüche des Rechts."

impossible to assert both 'A ought to be' and 'A ought not to be' "[25]—a proposition certainly not likely to help a judge struggling with a statute that in one section seems to say Mr. A ought to pay a tax and in another that he is exempt from it. Nor would a judge faced with such a statute derive much assistance from Somló's principle that where there is a "real," as contrasted with an "apparent," contradiction the opposing rules should be regarded as canceling one another.[26]

Even if we could solve all the problems of contradiction by a definition, it is by no means clear that a neatly defined hierarchy of authority is always the best way of resolving conflicts within a legal system. In discussing what the law is when the lower courts disagree, Gray presupposes a judicial hierarchy and gives the obvious answer that in such a case what the supreme court says is the law.[27] But one can easily conceive of a system of courts of equal standing, in which the judges would come together from time to time to iron out any conflicts among them by a process of discussion and reciprocal accommodation. Something like this no doubt occurred when appellate judges used to preside over trials and bring doubtful cases for discussion before the whole court.

In unionized industries in this country we have an institution that has been called "industrial jurisprudence." The rules regulating relations within an industrial plant are set, not through enactment by some legislative body, but by contract between management and a labor union. The judiciary of this legal system is constituted by arbitrators, again chosen by agreement. In such a system there are, of course, opportunities for failure. The fundamental charter of the parties' rights, the collective bargaining agreement, may not come into existence because of a failure of agreement between management and the union. When a dispute arises under a successfully negotiated agreement, the parties may fail to agree in nominating an arbitrator. Usually some

25. Kelsen, p. 374.
26. Somló, p. 383.
27. *The Nature and Sources of the Law* (2d ed. 1921), p. 117.

formal provision is made in anticipation of this possibility; when the parties cannot agree on an arbitrator the American Arbitration Association may, for example, be authorized to nominate him. But such a provision is neither indispensable to success, nor a guarantee against failure. All legal systems can break down, including those with the most neatly ordered chains of command.

In his discussion of theories that identify law with a hierarchic ordering of authority, Pashukanis shrewdly observes[28] that if a neat chain of command were the most significant quality of law then we should regard the military as the archetypal expression of juristic order. Yet any such view would violate the most elementary common sense. The source of this tension between theory and everyday wisdom lies, quite obviously, in a concentration by theory on formal structure to the neglect of the purposive activity this structure is assumed to organize. There is no need here to attempt any elaborate analysis of the differences between the kind of hierarchic ordering required for military purposes and that which may be thought essential to a legal system. One need only recall the common and quite troublesome problem faced by a legal order in knowing what to do when a lay citizen relies on an erroneous interpretation of the law rendered by an agency occupying a lower rung of the legal ladder. Plainly no similar question could arise within a military order except in times of martial law, when the military takes over the function of governing lay conduct.

Our discussion of theories of law would be incomplete if we made no mention of the principle of parliamentary sovereignty, the doctrine according to which, in the United Kingdom for example, the Parliament is regarded as possessing an unlimited competence in lawmaking. This doctrine deserves examination here because of its intimate association with theories that accept a hierarchic ordering of authority as the essential mark of a legal system.

28. Pashukanis, *The General Theory of Law and Marxism* (1927), trans. Babb in *Soviet Legal Philosophy,* 20th Century Legal Philosophy Series, *5* (1951), 111–225, at p. 154.

Parliamentary sovereignty can, of course, be supported entirely by an argument of political prudence to the effect that it is always desirable to have a reserve of lawmaking power ready to meet unforeseen circumstances. Explicit limitations on the power of the legislature that seem wise and beneficial when adopted may later serve to block measures necessary to deal with drastically changed conditions. If the pressure of circumstance mounts too high, the restraint may be circumvented by dodges and fictions that themselves carry a high cost in the distortions they introduce into the moral atmosphere of government and even into its institutional structure. These points can be illustrated hypothetically by a reference to the most stringent restraint contained in our own Constitution. This is the provision that no state shall, without its consent, "be deprived of its equal suffrage in the Senate."[29] This is the only constitutional restraint now operative that is removed even from the effect of change by amendment of the Constitution itself.

Now it is possible that there might occur—perhaps as the result of some natural disaster—a radical reduction in the population of certain of the states, so that, let us say, one third of the states would contain a population of only about one thousand persons each. In such a situation equal representation in the Senate might become a political absurdity. If the right to equal representation is respected, the whole political life of the nation might be mortally crippled. In such a situation the possibility of some legal maneuver comes naturally to mind. Could we perhaps use the amending power to reduce the role of the Senate to something like that of the House of Lords? Or abolish the Senate in favor of a unicameral assembly? Or is public opinion sufficiently behind us to make it enough simply to rename the Senate "The Council of Elders" and then reallocate representation in it?

In comparing the obvious rigidities of a written constitution with the principle of parliamentary supremacy we must not be misled by the appearance of rugged simplicity which the latter

29. Art. V.

principle presents. Parliamentary sovereignty means, in effect, that the parliament stands above the law in the sense that it can change any law that is not to its liking. But, paradoxically, it gains this position of being above the law only by subjecting itself to law—the law of its own internal procedure. For a corporate body to pass laws it must conform to laws that will determine when a law has been passed. This body of laws is itself subject to all the kinds of shipwreck that can visit any other legal system —it can be too vague or contradictory to give sure guidance, and, above all, its standards can be so disregarded in practice as to default in time of need. The kind of crisis that can cause a breakdown in rigid constitutional restrictions on legislative power can also, and perhaps as easily, cause a breakdown in the lawful processes of legislation. Even in England, where men tend to stick by the rules and to keep things straight, it is said that the courts once applied as law—on the basis of an entry in the Parliamentary Roll—a measure that had never actually been passed by Parliament.[30] The structure of authority, so often glibly thought of as organizing law, is itself a product of law.

In the country where the doctrine of parliamentary sovereignty is most vigorously cultivated discussions of it run, not in terms of its wisdom, but turn rather on points of law. Those who support the doctrine have generally regarded it as a principle of law to be sustained or refuted entirely by legal arguments; critics of the doctrine have generally accepted this joinder of issue. It is when the argument takes this form that an opening is presented for the entry of theories about the nature of law. The theories that have actually shaped the doctrine are those which display what I have described as a fatal abstraction from the enterprise of creating and administering a system of rules for the control of human conduct.

The effects of this abstraction become apparent in a crucial passage in Dicey's classic defense of the rule of parliamentary sovereignty. In the concluding paragraph of his main argument

30. Dicey, *The Law of the Constitution* (10th ed., 1960), Intro., xl.

he asserts that certain laws passed by Parliament constitute "the highest exertion and crowning proof of sovereign power."[31]

What are the enactments that possess these extraordinary qualities? In Dicey's own words they are "Acts such as those which declare valid marriages which, owing to some mistake of form or otherwise, have not been properly celebrated," and statutes "the object of which is to make legal transactions which when they took place were illegal, or to free individuals to whom the statute applies from liability for having broken the law."[32] It was of such enactments that Dicey wrote, "being as it were the legalisation of illegality" they constitute "the highest exertion and crowning proof of sovereign power."

It is only a theory that disregards completely the realities of creating and administering a legal system that could pass such a sweeping—though fortunately highly metaphorical—judgment on retrospective laws. It should be recalled that other adherents of the same general school of thought as that to which Dicey belonged have viewed retroactive laws as a routine exercise of legislative power, presenting no special problems for legal theory.[33] These diametrically opposed views, arising within the framework of the same general theory, are, I submit, symptomatic of a lack of any real concern with the problems of law-making.

A similar lack of concern is revealed in the conclusions Dicey is willing to draw from the rule of parliamentary supremacy. The most famous such conclusion is expressed in the following words: "Parliament could extinguish itself by legally dissolving itself and leaving no means whereby a subsequent Parliament could be legally summoned."[34] This is about like saying that the life force manifests itself even in the act of suicide—a statement that may have a certain existential poetry about it, but is about as remote from the ordinary affairs and concerns of men as is Dicey's legal authorization of the suicide of a legal order.

31. Ibid., p. 50.
32. Ibid., pp. 49–50.
33. See esp. Somló, supra n. 4, p. 97.
34. Ibid., pp. 68–70 n.

The tradition in discussing Parliament's legal omnipotence is to test statements that are extreme to the point of absurdity by illustrations that are equally absurd. This tradition is fully respected in my next illustration. Let us put together two of Dicey's assertions, that Parliament may legally end itself, and "that Parliament . . . has under the English constitution, the right to make or unmake any law whatever."[35] Now let us suppose that in some psychotic future the Parliament were to enact the following measures: (1) that all the persons then members of the Parliament should henceforth be free from the restraint of any laws whatever, and should be authorized to rob, kill and rape without legal penalty; (2) that any interference with the actions of such persons should be a crime, subject to capital punishment; (3) that all other laws of whatever kind were repealed; and (4) that the Parliament be permanently dissolved. Surely it is difficult to imagine any solicitor advising his client, after consulting Dicey, that "as a matter of strict law" the rampaging and ravishing M.P.s were within their legal rights and that the client would have to face for himself the moral issue whether to violate the law by lifting his hand against them. At some point we take leave of the gravitational field within which the distinction between law and not-law makes sense. I suggest that that point is reached far short of the situation I have described, and is indeed reached when we begin to ask whether parliamentary suicide is possible, or whether Parliament can formally assign all its powers to a dictator, or whether Parliament can decide that all future laws enacted by it shall be kept secret from those subject to them. The first two questions are easy grist for Dicey's mill; the third, of course, he does not consider, though in terms of the experience of history it is the least fanciful of the three.

This concludes my criticism of certain theories of law that may be opposed to the analysis presented in these chapters. In summary of the view I have advanced I may repeat that I have tried to see law as a purposive activity, typically attended by certain difficulties that it must surmount if it is to succeed in attain-

35. Ibid., pp. 39–40.

117

ing its ends. In contrast, the theories I have rejected seem to me to play about the fringe of that activity without ever concerning themselves directly with its problems. Thus, law is defined as "the existence of public order" without asking what kind of order is meant or how it is brought about. Again, the distinguishing mark of law is said to lie in a means, namely "force," that is typically employed to effectuate its aims. There is no recognition that, except as it makes the stakes higher, the use or nonuse of force leaves unchanged the essential problems of those who make and administer the laws. Finally, there are theories that concentrate on the hierarchic structure that is commonly thought to organize and direct the activity I have called law, though again without recognizing that this structure is itself a product of the activity it is thought to put in order.

At this point I am sure there will be those who, though agreeing generally with my negations and rejections, will nevertheless feel a certain discomfort about the view of law I have presented as my own. To them the concept of law that underlies these writings will seem too loose, too accommodating, too readily applied over too wide a range of instances, to serve significantly as a distinctive way of looking at law. These are criticisms that I shall deal with shortly. But first I should like to explore an analogy that may serve to support the conception advanced here.

The Concept of Science

The analogy I have in mind is that of science, by which I mean primarily what are called the physical and biological sciences.

Science, too, may be regarded as a particular direction of human effort, encountering its special problems and often failing in certain typical ways to solve them. Just as there are philosophies of law, so there are philosophies of science. Some philosophers of science, notably Michael Polanyi, are primarily concerned with the activity of the scientist, seeking to discern its proper aims and the practices and institutions conducive to attaining them. Others seem to embroider their theories, in various ingenious ways, about the periphery of the scientist's work. Such browsing in the literature as I have done would indicate that the parallels between legal and scientific philosophies are indeed striking. Holmes' definition of law in terms of its cutting edge is certainly not lacking in affinity for Bridgman's "operational theory of concepts."[36] One advocate of "scientific empiricism" has expressly asserted that his philosophy has nothing to say about the act of scientific discovery itself, for, he says, this "escapes logical analysis."[37] One is reminded at once of Kelsen's relegation of all the important problems involved in the making and interpreting of laws to the realm of the "meta-juristic."

I shall not attempt here, however, any further excursion into the actual literature of scientific philosophy. Instead I shall construct three hypothetical definitions of science after the models presented by legal theory.

In defining science it is quite possible, and indeed quite customary, to concentrate on its results, rather than on the activity that produces those results. Thus, corresponding to the view that law is simply "the existence of public order," we may assert that "science exists when men have the ability to predict and control the phenomena of nature." As a parallel to the view that law is characterized by the use of force, we may, as I have already suggested, suppose a theory of science defining it as the use of certain kinds of instruments. Seeking an analogue for hierarchic theories of law we encounter the difficulty that, except in a totalitarian context, we cannot very well think of science as a hierarchic ordering of scientific authority. But we may recall that with Kelsen the legal pyramid presents, not a hierarchy of human agencies, but a hierarchy of norms. Building on this conception we may then define science as consisting of "an arrangement of propositions about natural phenomena in an ascending order of generality."

36. *The Logic of Modern Physics* (1949), pp. 3–9 et passim.
37. Reichenbach, *The Rise of Scientific Philosophy* (1951), p. 231.

Now it cannot be said that any of these views is false. It is simply that none of them would start the lay citizen on his way toward any real understanding of science and its problems. Nor would they serve the scientist usefully who wanted to clarify for himself the aims of science and the institutional arrangements that would promote those aims.

Recently there has been a movement of reform in scientific education, particularly in the teaching of general courses in science intended for those who do not expect to become scientists. The older courses of this sort generally offered a kind of panoramic view of the achievements of science, supplemented by a fairly abstract discussion of some of the problems of scientific method, notably induction and verification. Newer courses have sought to give the student an insight into the manner in which the scientist reaches for new truths. In the course pioneered by Conant this is done through a study of case histories. The object is to give the student a vicarious experience in the act of scientific discovery. In this way it is hoped that he will come to have some understanding of the "tactics and strategy of science."[38]

Michael Polanyi's greatest achievement has probably been in his theories of what may be called broadly the epistemology of scientific discovery. But as touching the theme of these essays, his most distinctive contribution lies in his conception of the scientific enterprise.[39] With him this enterprise is a collaborative one, seeking the institutional forms and practices appropriate to its peculiar aims and problems. Though men of genius may introduce revolutionary turns of theory, they are able to do so only by building on the thought, the findings, and the mistakes of their predecessors and contemporaries. Within the scientific community the freedom of the individual scientist is not simply an opportunity for self-assertion, but an indispensable means for organizing effectively the common search for scientific truth.

The calling of the scientist has its distinctive ethos, its internal morality. Like the morality of law, it must, by the very nature of

38. *Science and Common Sense* (1951).
39. *The Logic of Liberty* (1951); *Personal Knowledge* (1958).

120

the demands it has to meet, be a morality of aspiration, not of duty. A single example will suffice, I think, to make clear why this must be so.

A scientist believes that he has made a fundamental discovery of the sort that may touch upon and advance the researches of others. When should he publish? It is clear that if he has in fact made an important discovery, he must make it known to the scientific community even though, for example, he can foresee that a rival scientist, building on it, may perhaps be enabled to make a further discovery overshadowing his own. On the other hand, he must be sure that he has in fact made the discovery he believes he has, for by rushing into print he may waste the time of others by giving a false lead to their researches.

It is questions of this sort that Polanyi has in mind when, borrowing a legal term, he speaks of a "fiduciary" concept of science. There is, indeed, a close correspondence between the moralities of science and of law. Outrageous departures are in both cases easily recognized. Within both fields an adherence to traditional ways, or a coincidence between self-interest and the ethics of the profession, may prevent any moral issue from arising. Yet both moralities may at times present difficult and subtle problems no simple formula of duty can possibly resolve. As to both moralities the general level of perceptiveness and of behavior may vary appreciably from one nation to another, or within a single nation, from one social context to another.

Without some understanding of the tactics and strategy of the scientific enterprise, and of its distinctive ethos, the lay citizen cannot, I submit, have an intelligently informed opinion on questions like the following: What should be the policy of government toward science? How can scientific research be most effectively introduced and cultivated in newly emerging nations? What precisely is the cost society pays directly and indirectly, when the responsibilities of scientific morality are ignored or loosely observed? I think I need not labor to prove that all these questions have close cousins in the law. Nor is there any need to demonstrate that the legal questions corresponding to these of science

121

must remain unanswered in any philosophy of law that abstracts from the nature of the activity we call law.

Objections to the View of Law Taken Here

I now turn to certain objections that may be raised against any analysis that treats law as "the enterprise of subjecting human conduct to the governance of rules."

The *first* such objection would run in terms something like these: To speak of a legal system as an "enterprise" implies that it may be carried on with varying degrees of success. This would mean that the existence of a legal system is a matter of degree. Any such view would contradict the most elementary assumptions of legal thinking. Neither a rule of law nor a legal system can "half exist."

To this my answer is that, of course, both rules of law and legal systems can and do half exist. This condition results when the purposive effort necessary to bring them into full being has been, as it were, only half successful. The truth that there are degrees of success in this effort is obscured by the conventions of ordinary legal language. These conventions arise from a laudable desire not to build into our ways of speech a pervasive encouragement to anarchy. It is probably well that our legal vocabulary treats a judge as a judge, though of some particular holder of the judicial office I may quite truthfully say to a fellow lawyer, "He's no judge." The tacit restraints that exclude from our ordinary ways of talking about law a recognition of imperfections and shades of gray have their place and function. They have no place or function in any attempt to analyze the fundamental problems that must be solved in creating and administering a system of legal rules.

Of no other complex human undertaking would it ever be assumed that it could meet with anything other than varying degrees of success. If I ask whether education "exists" in a particular country, the expected response, after the addressee of my question had recovered from some puzzlement as to its form, would be something like this: "Why, yes, their achievements in this field are very fine," or "Well, yes, but only in a very rudimentary way." So it would be with science, literature, chess, obstetrics, conversation, and the mortuary art. Disputes might arise, to be sure, about the proper standards for judging achievement, and of course, any attempt at quantitative appraisal (such as "half"-success) would have to be considered as metaphorical. Nevertheless the normal expectation would be of some performance falling between zero and a theoretical perfection.

Only with law is it different. It is truly astounding to what an extent there runs through modern thinking in legal philosophy the assumption that law is like a piece of inert matter—it is there or not there. It is only such an assumption that could lead legal scholars to assume, for example, that the "laws" enacted by the Nazis in their closing years, considered as laws and in abstraction from their evil aims, were just as much laws as those of England and Switzerland. An even more grotesque outcropping of this assumption is the notion that the moral obligation of the decent German citizen to obey these laws was in no way affected by the fact that they were in part kept from his knowledge, that some of them retroactively "cured" wholesale murder, that they contained wide delegations of administrative discretion to redefine the crimes they proscribed, and that, in any event, their actual terms were largely disregarded when it suited the convenience of the military courts appointed to apply them.[40]

A possible *second* objection to the view taken here is that it permits the existence of more than one legal system governing the same population. The answer is, of course, that such multiple systems do exist and have in history been more common than unitary systems.

In our country today the citizen in any given state is subject to two distinct systems of law, that of the federal government and that of the state. Even in the absence of a federal system, there may be one body of law governing marriage and divorce,

40. See the discussion and references supra, p. 40.

another regulating commercial relations and still a third governing what is left over, all three systems being separately administered by special courts.

Multiple systems may give rise to difficulties both for theory and for practice. Difficulties of the first sort can arise only if theory has committed itself to the view that the concept of law requires a neatly defined hierarchy of authority with a supreme legislative power at the top that is itself free from legal restraints. One way of accommodating this theory to the facts of political life is to say that although there may appear to be three systems, *A, B* and *C,* actually *B* and *C* exist only by the legal tolerance of *A.* Carrying this a step further it may be asserted that what the supreme legal power permits it impliedly commands, so that what appears as three systems is actually one—"in contemplation of law."

Practical difficulties can arise when there is a real rub between systems because their boundaries of competence have not been and perhaps cannot be clearly defined. One solution of this problem as it affects the division of competence between nation and state in a federal system is to subject disputes to judicial decision under the terms of a written constitution. This device is useful, but not in all cases indispensable. Historically dual and triple systems have functioned without serious friction, and when conflict has arisen it has often been solved by some kind of voluntary accommodation. This happened in England when the common law courts began to absorb into their own system many of the rules developed by the courts of the law merchant, though the end of this development was that the merchants' courts were finally supplanted by those of the common law.

A possible *third* criticism points to the same basic objection as the second, but sees it this time magnified many times over. If law is considered as "the enterprise of subjecting human conduct to the governance of rules," then this enterprise is being conducted, not on two or three fronts, but on thousands. Engaged in this enterprise are those who draft and administer rules governing the internal affairs of clubs, churches, schools, labor unions, trade associations, agricultural fairs, and a hundred and one other forms of human association. If, therefore, we are prepared to apply with consistency the conception of law advanced in these chapters, it must follow that there are in this country alone "systems of law" numbering in the hundreds of thousands. Since this conclusion seems absurd, it may be said that any theory that can give rise to it must be equally absurd.

Before attempting any general answer to this critcism, let us consider a hypothetical instance of the workings of one such legal system in miniature. A college enacts and administers a set of parietal rules governing the conduct of students in its dormitories. A student or faculty council is entrusted with the task of passing on infractions and when it is established that a violation has occurred, the council is understood to have the power to impose disciplinary measures, which in serious cases may include the organizational equivalent of capital punishment, that is, expulsion.

If we extract from the word "law" any connotation of the power or authority of the state, there is not the slightest difficulty in calling this a system of law. Furthermore, a sociologist or philosopher interested primarily in the law of the state, might study the rules, institutions, and problems of this body of parietal law for the insight he might thus obtain into the processes of law generally. However, so inveterate has become the association of the word "law" with the law of the political state that to call a system of parietal rules in all seriousness a "system of law" suggests an offense against the rules of linguistic propriety. If this were our only problem we might at once make peace with our critics by entering a stipulation that they may regard any such usage as metaphorical and that they may qualify it as much as they like with that ancient question-beggar: "quasi."

The difficulty runs deeper, however. Suppose that under the system of parietal rules a student is tried by the council, and being found guilty of a serious infraction, is expelled from the school. He files suit and asks the court to order his reinstatement.

125

There is abundant authority that the courts may and should take jurisdiction of such a case, and this without reference to the question whether the school involved is private or public.[41]

How will the court decide such a case? If the expelled student contends that, although his expulsion was in accord with the published rules, the rules themselves are grossly unfair, the court may, though normally with reluctance, pass judgment on that contention. Assuming no such objection is raised, the court will address itself to a question that may be expressed in these terms: Did the school in creating and administering its parietal rules respect the internal morality of law? Were these rules promulgated?—a question in this case expressed by asking whether the student was given proper notice of them. Were they reasonably clear in meaning, so as to let the student know what actions on his part would constitute an infraction? Was the finding of the council in accordance with the rules? Were the procedures of inquiry so conducted as to insure that the result would be grounded in the published rules and based on an accurate knowledge of the relevant facts?

Whether the court reinstates the student or upholds his expulsion, it takes its standard of decision from the college's own rules. If to acquire the force of law these rules need the imprimatur of the state, they have now received it insofar as they affect the issue decided by the court. Once we accept the parietal rules as establishing the law of the case, binding both on the college authorities and the courts, the situation is not essentially different from that in which an appellate court reviews the decision of a trial judge.

Why, then, do we hesitate to describe the parietal rules simply as law? The easy answer is to say that such an extension of the word would violate ordinary linguistic usage. This begs the question why linguistic usage has taken the turn it has. I think the answer lies in considerations something like the following: We

41. For the best general treatment see "Private Government on the Campus—Judicial Review of University Expulsions," 72 *Yale Law Journal* 1362–1410 (1963).

intuitively realize that in cases like that I have been discussing we are confronted with delicate issues of maintaining a proper balance of institutional function within our society. That such issues are at stake becomes apparent if the case brought for judicial determination involves a student expelled from a school run by a religious order because of heresy or from a private military academy because "he is constitutionally incapable of accepting military discipline in the proper spirit." When issues as delicate as those here suggested are under consideration we hesitate to throw into the balance a word as heavily loaded with implications of sheer power and established authority as is the word "law."

One may approve the motives that prompt this restraint. I suggest, however, that the real source of difficulty lies in philosophies that have invested the word "law" with connotations which unfit it for use precisely where it is most needed. For in the case at hand it is badly needed. Without it, we face this dilemma: On the one hand, we are forbidden to call law the rules by which a college determines expulsions. On the other hand, these rules are plainly given the force of law in judicial decisions. That the courts may strike down rules that are grossly unfair does not differentiate them from Acts of Congress which may also be declared void when they violate constitutional restrictions on the legislative power. Being denied the term "law" we are compelled to look about for some other conceptual shelter under which we can house these rules. This is generally found in a notion of private law: contract. The parietal rules, it is said, constitute a contract between the school and the student by which their respective rights are determined.[42]

This "thoroughly artificial nexus of contract"[43] has given a great deal of trouble. In considering its inconveniences and short-

42. I am leaving out of account here the limited use courts have made of property concepts and the law of defamation in dealing with some expulsion cases, particularly those involving social clubs.

43. Lloyd, "Disqualifications Imposed by Trade Associations—Jurisdiction of Court and Natural Justice," 21 *Modern Law Review* 661, at p. 668 (1958).

comings we should recall that the school expulsion cases constitute only a small sampling drawn from a vast body of precedent dealing with similar problems as they arise in labor unions,
churches, social clubs, and a whole host of other institutional
forms. As a device for dealing with this wide range of problems
the concept of contract defaults in several important respects.
For one thing, it points to remedies that are inappropriate to the
context. For another, it suggests that if the institution or association sees fit to do so, it may contractually stipulate for an unrestricted privilege of canceling membership. Most fundamentally, the contract theory is inconsistent with the responsibility actually assumed by the courts in these cases. It is easy to say,
for example, that the parietal rules constitute a contract between
the college and the student, but how are we to explain the deference accorded by the courts to the interpretation put on those
rules by the college authorities in the process of applying them
to an alleged infraction? When parties quarrel about what a contract means we do not ordinarily defer to the interpretation made
by either of them but judge between the two impartially. These
difficulties, and others I have left unmentioned, can be cured by
the device of assuming that the contract in question is a very
special one, in which all the necessary deviations from ordinary
contract law are to be understood as tacitly intended by the
parties. But when this is done the "contract" becomes an empty
fiction, offering a convenient rack on which to hang any result
deemed appropriate to the situation.

The objection to the contract theory is that, like any legal fiction, it tends to obscure the real issues involved and postpones a
direct confrontation with them. I submit that the body of law I
have been discussing is essentially a branch of constitutional law,
largely and properly developing outside the framework of our
written constitutions. It is constitutional law in that it involves
the allocation among the various institutions of our society of
legal power, that is, the authority to enact rules and to reach
decisions that will be regarded as properly binding on those affected by them. That this body of constitutional law should have

grown up outside our written constitutions should not be a source of concern. It would have been impossible for the draftsmen of our first written constitutions to have anticipated the rich institutional growth that has occurred since their time. Furthermore, the intellectual climate of the late eighteenth century was such as to obscure a recognition of the centers of authority created when men form voluntary associations.[44] In the light of these considerations we should be no more disturbed to find that we have a body of unwritten constitutional law than the British have been to discover that since the Statute of Westminster of 1931 they have acquired the rudiments of a written constitution living comfortably in the midst of their unwritten constitution.

A view that seeks to understand law in terms of the activity that sustains it, instead of considering only the formal sources of its authority, may sometimes suggest a use of words that violates the normal expectations of language. This inconvenience may, I suggest, be offset by the capacity of such a view to make us perceive essential similarities. It may help us to see that the imperfectly achieved systems of law within a labor union or a university may often cut more deeply into the life of a man than any court judgment ever likely to be rendered against him. On the other hand, it may also help us to realize that all systems of law, big and little, are subject to the same infirmities. In no case can the legal achievement outrun the perception of the human beings who guide it. The judicial review of institutional disciplinary measures performs its most obvious service when it corrects outrageous injustice; in the long run it can be most useful if it helps to create an atmosphere within institutions and associations that will render it unnecessary.[45]

---

44. Wyzanski, "The Open Window and the Open Door," 35 *California Law Review* 336–51, at pp. 341–45 (1947).

45. For a general survey of the law, amounting to a short treatise, see the note, "Developments in the Law—Judicial Control of Actions of Private Associations," 76 *Harvard Law Review* 983–1100 (1963). The best general introduction is still Chafee's very readable article, "The Internal Affairs of Associations Not for Profit," 43 *Harvard Law Review* 993 (1930).

I come now to the *fourth*—and so far as my own account can go—final criticism that may be made of the view of law taken here. This is that it does not sufficiently distinguish between law and morality. Morality, too, is concerned with controlling human conduct by rules. It, too, is concerned that these rules should be clear, consistent with one another and understood by those who ought to obey them. A view that seems to recognize as the characteristic mark of law a set of concerns shared with morality invites the criticism that it obscures an essential distinction.

This criticism conceals, I think, several distinct issues. One is presented when we ask how, when we are confronted with a system of rules, we decide whether the system as a whole shall be called a system of law or one of morality. The only answer to that question ventured here is that contained in the word "enterprise" when I have asserted that law, viewed as a direction of purposive human effort, consists in "the enterprise of subjecting human conduct to the governance of rules."

One can imagine a small group—transplanted, say, to some tropical island—living successfully together with only the guidance of certain shared standards of conduct, these standards having been shaped in various indirect and informal ways by experience and education. What may be called the legal experience might first come to such a society when it selected a committee to draw up an authoritative statement of the accepted standards of conduct. Such a committee would find itself *ex necessitate rei* embarked on the enterprise of law. Contradictions in standards, previously latent and unnoticed, would have to be resolved. Realizing that clarification could not be accomplished without some change of meaning the committee would have to concern itself with the possible harshness of a retrospective application of the standards set forth in its statement. As the society gradually acquired the other familiar instruments of a legal system —such as judges and a legislative assembly—it would find itself more deeply involved in the enterprise of law. Or, again, instead of starting with an attempt to draft an authoritative statement of the rules, the society in question might start by appointing some one to serve as judge. Nothing, it seems to me, hinges upon the particular manner in which the members of the society, or some of them, are plunged into what I have called the "enterprise" of law.

Though it can be said that law and morality share certain concerns—for example, that the rules should be clear—it is as these concerns become increasingly the objects of an explicit responsibility that a legal system is created. Generality, for example, is taken for granted in morality and can hardly be called a problem. It becomes a problem, and a pressing one, however, when a judge sentences a man to jail and can find no way of expressing any general principle by which his decision can be explained or justified.

These observations admittedly leave uncertain the precise point at which a legal system can be said to have come into being. I see no reason to pretend to see black and white where reality presents itself in shades of gray. Certainly there is little point in imposing on the situation some definitional fiat, by saying, for example, that we shall consider law to exist only where there are courts.

The question just dismissed, though much discussed in the literature of jurisprudence, is not one of great interest in practice. Here the difficult problem is rather that of defining the proper relationship between what is unquestionably an established and functioning system of law, on the one hand, and general standards of morality, on the other. In dealing with this problem I do not think it can be said that the view of law taken in these essays in any sense obscures or distorts the essential issues.

On the contrary I submit that the distinction between the external and internal moralities of the law may offer a helpful clarification. Take, for example, the problems that may confront a judge in interpreting a statute. So far as the external aims of the statute are concerned, it is a part of the ethos of his office that the judge should remain, insofar as human capacity admits, neutral among the moral positions that may have been taken in the statute with regard to such questions as divorce, contraception, gambling, or the requisition of private property for public use.

But the very same considerations that require an attitude of neutrality with regard to the external aims of the law demand a commitment by the judge to the law's internal morality. It would, for example, be an abdication of the responsibilities of his office if the judge were to take a neutral stand between an interpretation of a statute that would bring obedience to it within the capacity of the ordinary citizen and an interpretation that would make it impossible for him to comply with its terms.

The distinction between the external and internal moralities of law is, of course, a tool of analysis and should not be regarded as a substitute for the exercise of judgment. I have been at pains to show that along the spectrum occupied by these two moralities there may appear, in certain applications, a middle area where they overlap.[46] The two moralities, in any event, interact with one another in ways that I shall analyze in my final chapter.[47] Suffice it for the present to point out that a judge faced with two equally plausible interpretations of a statute might properly prefer that which would bring its terms into harmony with generally accepted principles of right and wrong. Though this result may be rested on a presumed legislative intent, it can also be justified on the ground that such an interpretation would be less likely to make of the statute a trap for the innocent, thus bringing the problem within the considerations relevant to the law's internal morality.

A perennial debate relates to the problem of "legislating morals." Recently there has been a lively discussion of the proper relation of the law to sexual behavior and more particularly to homosexual practices.[48] I must confess that I find this argument

46. See especially the discussion of the problems of generality (supra, pp. 46–48 and infra, pp. 157–59), contradictions (supra, pp. 69–70), and the possibility of obedience (supra, p. 79).

47. See infra, pp. 155–67.

48. P. A. Devlin, *The Enforcement of Morals* (1959), *Law and Morals* (1961); H. L. A. Hart, *Law, Liberty and Morality* (1963).

quite inconclusive on both sides, resting as it does on initial assumptions that are not made explicit in the argument itself. I would, however, have no difficulty in asserting that the law ought not to make it a crime for consenting adults to engage privately in homosexual acts. The reason for this conclusion would be that any such law simply cannot be enforced and its existence on the books would constitute an open invitation to blackmail, so that there would be a gaping discrepancy between the law as written and its enforcement in practice. I suggest that many related issues can be resolved in similar terms without our having to reach agreement on the substantive moral issues involved.

Hart's The Concept of Law

So far I have passed over the important recent book from which I have borrowed the title for this chapter. *The Concept of Law*[49] by H. L. A. Hart is certainly a contribution to the literature of jurisprudence such as we have not had in a long time. It is not a collection of essays disguised as a book. It is not a textbook in the usual sense. Instead, it represents an attempt to present in short compass the author's own solutions for the major problems of jurisprudence.

Many things about the book are excellent. It is beautifully written and filled with brilliant aperçus. I have learned many things from it. With its fundamental analysis of the concept of law, however, I am in virtually complete disagreement.

In my final chapter I shall have some critical comments on the treatment Hart accords to what I have called the internal morality of law. In summary the criticism I shall there advance is that Hart's whole analysis proceeds in terms that systematically exclude any consideration of the problems I attempted to analyze in my second chapter.

In the present context my quarrel is with "the rule of recognition," a concept Hart seems to regard as the central theme of his

49. Oxford University Press, 1961.

book and its chief contribution. In developing this concept Hart begins with a distinction between rules imposing duties and rules conferring legal powers. So far there can be no complaint. The distinction is a familiar one, especially in this country where it has served as the keystone of the Hohfeldian analysis.[50] Plainly there is an important difference between a rule that says, "Thou shalt not kill," and one that says, "If you want to make a valid will, put it in writing and sign it before three witnesses."

It should be observed that this distinction, usefully clarifying as it is in some cases, may be misapplied in such a way as to obfuscate the simplest issues almost beyond redemption. Of this there is abundant evidence in some of the writings based on the Hohfeldian analysis.

Let me develop briefly the ambiguities implicit in the distinction with the aid of two illustrations. In the first we shall pose for ourselves the problem of classifying a rule that reads, "Where a trustee has paid out of his own pocket expenses properly chargeable to the trust estate, he has a right to reimburse himself out of trust funds in his possession." The use of the word "right" suggests a corresponding duty on the part of the beneficiary, yet the trustee has no need to enforce this duty; by a species of lawful self-help he simply effects a legally valid transfer from the trust funds to his own account. Accordingly we may conclude that we are here dealing with a power-conferring rule, rather than a duty-imposing rule. But suppose that the instrument creating the trust gives the beneficiary, in turn, a power on coming of age to effect a transfer of the trust estate directly to himself. Suppose, further, that the beneficiary exercises this power before the trustee has had a chance to reimburse himself out of the trust funds. Plainly

50. See Hohfeld, *Fundamental Legal Conceptions* (1923). The best introduction to the Hohfeldian system is Corbin, "Legal Analysis and Terminology," 29 *Yale Law Journal* 163–73 (1919). The Hohfeldian analysis discerns four basic legal relations: right–duty, no-right–privilege, power–liability, and disability–immunity. Of these, however, the second and fourth are simply the negations of the first and third. Accordingly the basic distinction on which the whole system is built is that between right–duty and power–liability; this distinction coincides exactly with that taken by Hart.

the beneficiary now has a legal duty to reimburse the trustee. The fundamental principle is, however, the same in both cases, namely, that the trustee is entitled to reimbursement at the expense of the beneficiary; whether he is given a power to help himself, as it were, or a right against the beneficiary (with corresponding duty) is simply a question of the most apt way of achieving the result.

My second illustration relates to a familiar rule concerning the mitigation of damages. *A* and *B* enter a contract whereby *A* is to construct a specially designed machine for *B* and *B* is to pay $10,000 when the job is completed. After *A* has begun work on the machine, *B* repudiates his contract. There is no question but that *B* is liable for damages, which would include reimbursement to *A* for expenses incurred up to the time of repudiation as well as any profit *A* would have made on the whole job. The crucial issue is whether *A* can disregard *B*'s repudiation, continue work on the machine and, when he has finished, recover the full price. The law is that he cannot charge to *B* any expenses incurred in performing the contract after *B* has repudiated it; whether he continues work or not, the limit of his recovery is set by the amount he would have been entitled to had he quit work after *B*'s repudiation. The courts have commonly expressed this idea by saying that on the repudiation *A* has "a duty to mitigate damages" by ceasing work on the machine, the notion being that he cannot recover for costs incurred in violation of this duty.

This view has been severely criticized as obfuscating the distinction between rules that impose duties and those that grant or take away legal powers. If *A* foolishly continues to work on the machine after *B*'s repudiation of the contract, *B* has no cause of action against *A* to enforce any "duty." The only sanction this misnamed duty has is that if *A* does continue work, he cannot recover the cost of doing so from *B*. Prior to the repudiation *A* had a legal power in that by continuing work day by day he was increasing *B*'s possible obligation to him. Now he has lost that power. The situation is comparable to that produced by the passage of the Statute of Frauds. Prior to the Statute men had the power to create binding contracts orally; after the Statute was enacted this power, as to certain kinds of contracts, was removed. So runs an argument based on the Hohfeldian analysis.[51]

This argument seems quite convincing until we reflect that in cases like that of the machine the courts start with the assumption that A ought to stop work, for by continuing he squanders his and society's resources on something that no longer serves any need. This is what the courts mean by saying A has a duty to mitigate. There is no occasion for B to sue for a breach of this duty; since he doesn't have to pay for the work done after his repudiation, he is not personally injured by A's continued performance. The Statute of Frauds, on the other hand, does not say that men ought to put their contracts in writing; it simply says that if certain contracts are left in oral form they will not be legally enforced. Contracting parties, familiar with the terms of the Statute, may in fact deliberately refrain from executing a written memorandum so as to preserve for their contract the status of a "gentlemen's agreement."

In the cases of the machine and the Statute, what has been called "the sanction of nullity" is employed to effectuate quite different ends. In the one case it is used to make A do what he ought to do, by cutting off his pay, as it were; in the other, it is used to insure that the power to enter binding contracts will be exercised under circumstances that will protect against fraud and mistaken memory.

It is impossible to deal here adequately with the many problems that can arise out of the distinction between rules imposing duties and those conferring powers, particularly when arguments from analogy are involved. Even the sketchy account presented here makes it plain, however, that there are two different standards for applying the distinction. The one inquires into the fundamental legislative intent; the other into the legal mechanics by means of which the aim of the rule is effectuated. A failure to perceive that these are distinct standards has muddied many at-

51. 5 Corbin, *Contracts,* §1039, 205–07 (1951).

tempts to put the Hohfeldian analysis to practical account.[52] On the other hand, if one attempts always to penetrate behind legal forms to underlying intent, the distinction loses much of its appeal and scarcely provides the pervasive illumination that the Hohfeldians expected of it. The disappointing experience with the Hohfeldian analysis, projected against the enthusiasm with which it was originally greeted, inclines me to view with some skepticism the suggestion that the distinction Hart proposes is "a most powerful tool for the analysis of much that has puzzled both the jurist and the political theorist." (*The Concept of Law,* p. 95.)

These doubts approach something like a certitude when it comes to Hart's "rule of recognition." Let me express what I understand this rule to mean by the aid of an illustration of perhaps grotesque simplicity. A small country is ruled by King Rex. Within this country there is unanimous agreement that the highest legal power rests in Rex. To make this abundantly clear we may suppose that every adult citizen signs, with cheerful sincerity, a statement reading, "I recognize in Rex the sole and ultimate source of law in my country."

Now it is apparent that there is in his kingdom an accepted rule according to which Rex has the final say as to what shall be considered law. Hart proposes to call this "the rule of recognition." Certainly there can be no quarrel with this proposal. But Hart goes further and insists that we apply to this rule the distinction between rules that confer powers and those that impose duties. The rule of recognition, he declares, must be regarded as a power-conferring rule. Again, this seems almost a truism.

But Hart seems to read into this characterization the further notion that the rule cannot contain any express or tacit provision to the effect that the authority it confers can be withdrawn for abuses of it. To one concerned to discourage tendencies

52. An outstanding example is Cook, "The Utility of Jurisprudence in the Solution of Legal Problems." This article appears in 5 *Lectures on Legal Topics* 337–90 (1928), published by the Association of the Bar of the City of New York.

toward anarchy something can be said for this and Hobbes in fact had a great deal to say for it. But Hart seems to consider that he is dealing with a necessity of logical thinking. If one is intent on preserving a sharp distinction between rules imposing duties and rules conferring powers, there are reasons for being unhappy about any suggestion that it may be possible to withdraw the lawmaking authority once it has been conferred by the rule of recognition. If Rex began to keep his laws secret from those legally bound to obey them, and had his crown taken away from him for doing so, it would certainly seem foolish to ask whether he was deposed because he violated an implied duty or because, by exceeding the tacit limits of his power, he had worked an automatic forfeiture of his office and thus became subject to "the sanction of nullity." In other words, a rule that confers a power and provides, expressly or by implication, that this power may be revoked for abuses, presents in its proviso a stipulation that straddles ambiguously the distinction between duty-imposing rules and those that grant powers.

It follows then that if Hart is to preserve his key distinction he is compelled to assume that the lawmaking authority cannot be lawfully revoked. In his whole analysis of the rule of recognition it seems to me Hart has fallen into a familiar trap properly dreaded by all of us in the field of jurisprudence. He is applying to the attitudes that bring into being and support a legal system juristic distinctions that can have no meaning in this application. There is no doubt that a legal system derives its ultimate support from a sense of its being "right." However, this sense, deriving as it does from tacit expectations and acceptances, simply cannot be expressed in such terms as obligations and capacities.

Suppose, to borrow a famous example from Wittgenstein, a mother leaving to attend a matinee says to her baby-sitter, "While I'm gone teach my children a game." The baby-sitter teaches the children to throw dice for money or to duel with kitchen knives. Must the mother before passing judgment on this act ask herself whether the baby-sitter has violated a tacit promise or has simply exceeded her authority? I suggest that she would be as little concerned with that question as she would with the one Wittgenstein himself raises: Can she truthfully say, "I did not mean that kind of game," when she never thought of the possibility of such a game being taught to her children? There are some outcomes in human relations too absurd to rise to the level of conscious exclusion. So it would be, in modern times at least, if a parliament should forget that its accepted function is, after all, to make laws and should begin to act as if it had been given the power to save souls or to declare scientific truth. And if the expectations and acceptances that underlie a parliament's power confine it to lawmaking, does not this tacitly entail further limitations? Is it not assumed, for example, that the parliament will not hold a drinking bout with the understanding that those members still on their feet at midnight shall have the power to make the laws? And is it going much further—or even as far—to say that it is tacitly understood that the parliament will not withhold its enactments from the knowledge of those bound to obey them or express its laws in terms deliberately made unintelligible?

Hart is bent on rescuing the concept of law from its identification with coercive power. A legal system, he asserts, is not "the gunman situation writ large." But if the rule of recognition means that anything called law by the accredited lawgiver counts as law, then the plight of the citizen is in some ways worse than that of the gunman's victim. If a gunman says, "Your money or your life," it is certainly expected that if I give him my money, he will spare my life. If he accepts my purse and then shoots me down, I should suppose his conduct would not only be condemned by moralists, but also by right-thinking highwaymen. In this sense not even an "unconditional surrender" is really unconditional, for there must be an expectation on the part of him who surrenders that he is not trading sudden death for slow torture.

Hart's own distinction between the "gunman situation" and a legal system (pp. 20–25) contains no suggestion of any element of tacit reciprocity. Instead, the distinction runs entirely in formal or structural terms. The gunman communicates his threat in a single face-to-face situation; the law expresses itself normally in standing and general orders that may be published, but do not constitute a direct communication between lawgiver and subject. Acting through general rules is "the standard way in which law functions, if only because no society could support the number of officials necessary to secure that every member of the society was officially and separately informed of every act which he was required to do" (p. 21). Every step in the analysis seems almost as if it were designed to exclude the notion that there could be any rightful expectation on the part of the citizen that could be violated by the lawgiver.

I shall not attempt to trace in detail Hart's application of the rule of recognition to a complex, constitutional democracy. Suffice it to say he concedes that in this case there is not one rule of recognition, but a whole complex of rules, practices, and conventions that determine how lawmakers are elected, what the qualifications and jurisdiction of judges shall be, and all the related matters that affect the determination in a given case of what shall count as law and what not (pp. 59, 75, 242, et passim). He also concedes "that a great proportion of ordinary citizens— perhaps a majority—have no general conception of the legal structure or of its criteria of validity" (p. 111). Finally, he concedes that it is not always possible to draw a sharp line of distinction between ordinary rules of law and those rules that grant lawmaking powers (p. 144). Yet he seems to insist that, despite all these concessions, *the* rule of recognition that ascribes legal sovereignty to the Queen in Parliament can in some way summarize and absorb all the little rules that enable lawyers to recognize law in a hundred different special contexts. He seems further to assert that this view of the matter is not a juristic construction imposed from without, nor an expression of confidence in the political power of Parliament to resolve any conceivable conflicts that may arise within the system, but rather something provable empirically in the daily practices of his government.

I have difficulty in seeing how this can be. "Parliament" is, after all, only a name for an institution that has changed its nature drastically over the centuries. The memory of one such change is preserved in the gracious fiction that even today speaks, not of lawmaking by the Parliament, but by "the Queen in Parliament." To speak of *one* rule of recognition as pointing to something constantly changing is, it seems to me, almost like saying that in a given country the rule of recognition has always accorded the supreme lawmaking power to *The Great X,* where *X* in one decade meant an elected official, in the next, the eldest son of the last *X,* and in a third, a triumvirate selected by lot from the Army, the Clergy, and the Laborers' Union.

It thus appears in Hart's account that the pointing finger which the rule of recognition directs toward the source of law can move through a wide arc without losing its target. How wide can that arc become? It is perhaps a matter of political wisdom not to ask for too precise an answer to this question. It is well in surveying the past of one's country to see continuities even where contemporaries saw revolutions. But when the rule of recognition is used as a "powerful tool of analysis" then it becomes essential to know when there is anything toward which it can point and when it has shifted from *A* to a quite distinct *B.*

A basic error of method permeates, I submit, Hart's whole treatment of the rule of recognition. He is throughout attempting with the aid of that rule to give neat juristic answers to questions that are essentially questions of sociological fact. This misapplication of the rule is most apparent in his discussion of what he calls the problem of "the persistence of law" (pp. 60–64).

An absolute monarch, King Rex V, succeeds to the throne on the death of his father, Rex IV. Despite this displacement in the human source of law, the laws enacted by Rex IV are commonly regarded as persisting and as remaining unchanged until Rex V announces some alteration in them. This is the sociological fact Hart seeks to explain. It was described more than a century and a half ago by Portalis in these words: "L'expérience prouve que les hommes changent plus facilement de domination que de lois."[53]

53. "Discours préliminaire," in Locré, *La législation de la France* (1827), p. 251.

Hart's explanation of this fact of experience is to say that the rule of recognition points not to the man, but to the office, and includes within itself the rules of lawful succession. In a similar way we are in a position to explain, Hart suggests, why a law enacted by Parliament in 1735 can still be law in 1944.

But suppose that in our hypothetical case Rex IV is succeeded not by his son, Rex V, but by Brutus I, who ousts Rex IV from the throne without the slightest pretense of title and in open violation of the accepted rules of succession. Are we to say that it is a necessary consequence of this event that all previous laws —including those of property, contract, and marriage—have now lost their force? This is the result demanded by Hart's analysis, yet it violates the experience of history. In this case Hart would have to employ, presumably, some such argument as that Brutus I, by saying nothing about the matter, tacitly re-enacted the previous law—the very argument Hart himself criticizes in Hobbes, Bentham, and Austin and an argument Hart's analysis is intended to render unnecessary.

There is perhaps an irony here in that the old-fashioned, military, non-ideological coup d'état presents the clearest model of a change in "the rule of recognition," yet perhaps constitutes the least threat to "the persistence of law." The modern ideological revolution, insinuating itself into power by a manipulation of legal forms, represents precisely the kind of change most likely to create doubts as to whether previous laws (say, exempting churches from taxation) remain in effect. As an explanation for the persistence of law the rule of recognition weights the balance exactly in the wrong direction.

An equally infelicitous application of the rule of recognition occurs, it seems to me, when Hart attempts to use it to explain how and when a primitive society makes its "step from the pre-legal into the legal world" (p. 41). A society living in the pre-legal world knows only primary rules of obligation, that is, duty-imposing rules (p. 89). Such a system of rules is defective in a number of respects: it provides no machinery for resolving doubts and contradictions, or for effecting deliberate change; its rules depend for their effectiveness on diffuse social pressures (pp. 90–91). A transition to the "legal world" occurs when a society first conceives and applies to its affairs the notion that a rule may confer a power to make or change rules of duty (p. 61). This discovery "is a step forward as important to society as the invention of the wheel" (p. 41).

Now it seems to me that this essentially Austinian conception represents, again, a misapplication of juristic distinctions to a context that will not support them. For one thing, in a society where there is a pervasive belief in magic, and where nature is invoked by a formula, it is apparent that there can be no clear distinction between "natural" and "legal" powers. The charismatic lawgiver is not authorized by any man-made rule of recognition to make the law. Rather, the authority he enjoys in society derives from a belief that he possesses a special capacity to discern and declare the law.[54] If we can speak of the emergence of something like an explicit rule of recognition, this took place over centuries and involved a gradual shift from the notion of powers as an attribute of the person to powers conferred by an assigned social role. Before this transition is complete, we have long since left behind anything that could be called a primitive state of society. Indeed, it may be said that this transition is never secure against a relapse into more primitive notions. The cult of personality remains in some measure with us always.

It is furthermore doubtful whether primitive society was dominated by anything like the modern conception of duty. It is at least arguable that as between power and duty, power represents the more primitive conception. What we would today call "punishment" quite generally took the form in primitive society of an exercise of magical powers over the offender to purge the com-

---

54. See Weber, *Law in Economy and Society,* trans. Shils and Rhein stein (1954), pp. 73–82. The distinction taken in Chinese philosophy between a government by men and a government by laws is also worthy of note, since it can serve to counteract somewhat Weber's insistence on the nonrational character of "charisma." See Escarra, *Le droit chinois* (1936), pp. 7–57.

munity of an uncleanliness. A similar purging was accomplished through the generous use of ostracism. Instead of a generalized notion of duty we encounter acts that are allowed and disallowed, proper and improper, *fas et nefas*. The first legal procedures often took the form, not of a judicial determination of guilt, but of a ritualistic self-help. Every misdeed tended to demand for its cure a distinctive, and specially designed remedy. A generalized conception of duty may perhaps be said to emerge only when we have several remedies for the breach of a single duty, or several duties that may be enforced by a single remedy. So long as the consequences of a misdeed are identified with the formal steps necessary to cure it, it would seem we are confronted with a notion of power, rather than of duty.

It will be useful to test Hart's hypothesis concerning the transition to "the legal world" against the actual experience of a primitive people making that transition in quite modern times. The experience in question is that of the Manus people of the Admiralty Islands as reported by Margaret Mead.[55]

After World War II the Manus people learned from their Australian governors that there was a way of dealing with disputes of which they had no previous knowledge. This was the procedure of adjudication. Their own methods of settling disputes had been most unsatisfactory, consisting as they did of "feuds, raids, and subsequent ephemeral peace-making ceremonies often with payments in expiation." Now they came to see that a dispute could be decided and settled by a submission of it to an impartial arbiter. There followed a veritable fad for adjudication, their own elders being assigned or assuming a quite unfamiliar social role, that of judge. Curiously the justice thus dispensed was a kind of black market commodity since the "judges" who decided their disputes lacked any legal standing with the Australian government; their powers were quite unsupported by any rule of recognition except a very informal and shifting one among the Manus people themselves.

55. *New Lives for Old* (1956). The quotations in the text are taken from pp. 306 and 307.

The attitude of the indigenous people toward this innovation is thus described by Miss Mead:

> to the New Guinea native, newly fired with a desire to keep his society "straight," the whole legal system looks fresh and beautiful. He sees it as a magnificent invention, as wonderful as the airplane, so that far into the interior of New Guinea proper the institution of illegal "courts" is spreading.

If Miss Mead's account is correct, then the rule of recognition among the Manus people ran primarily not toward a human agency empowered by the rule to make law, but toward a procedure. And surely if one is going to speak of an invention comparable to that of the wheel or the airplane, it is appropriate to think of a procedure and not of a mere grant of authority.

Law as a Purposeful Enterprise and Law as a Manifested Fact of Social Power

The many different oppositions of viewpoint that have been examined in this chapter may be said to reflect in shifting contexts a single, underlying disagreement. The nature of this fundamental divergence may be expressed in these terms: I have insisted that law be viewed as a purposeful enterprise, dependent for its success on the energy, insight, intelligence, and conscientiousness of those who conduct it, and fated, because of this dependence, to fall always somewhat short of a full attainment of its goals. In opposition to this view it is insisted that law must be treated as a manifested fact of social authority or power, to be studied for what it is and does, and not for what it is trying to do or become.

In dealing with this fundamental opposition let me begin with a statement of the considerations that seem to me to have led to the view which I oppose. Since I have no authority to speak for the opposition, this statement will have to be hypothetical in form. I shall, however, try to phrase it as persuasively as I can.

Such a statement would begin with a concession that purpose

has a proper role to play in the interpretation of individual legal enactments. A statute is obviously a purposive thing, serving some end or congeries of related ends. What is objected to is not the assignment of purposes to particular laws, but to law as a whole.

Any view that ascribes some purpose or end to a whole institutional complex has, it may be said, very unattractive antecedents in the history of philosophy. It calls to mind the excesses of German and British idealism. It suggests that if we start talking about the purpose of law we may end by talking about the Purpose of the State. Even if we dismiss as unreal the danger that the spirit of Hegel may ride again, the view under consideration has other affinities that are far from reassuring. It recalls, for example, the solemn discussions about the Purpose of Swamps that Thomas Jefferson conducted with his associates in the American Philosophical Society.[56] A naïve teleology, it may be said, has shown itself to be the worst enemy that the scientific pursuit of objective truth can have.

Even if its historic affinities were less disturbing, there is an intrinsic improbability about any theory that attempts to write purpose in a large hand over a whole institution. Institutions are constituted of a multitude of individual human actions. Many of these follow grooves of habit and can hardly be said to be purposive at all. Of those that are purposive, the objectives sought by the actors are of the most diverse nature. Even those who participate in the creation of institutions may have very different views of the purpose or function of the institutions they bring into being.

In answering these criticisms I shall begin by recalling that the purpose I have attributed to the institution of law is a modest and sober one, that of subjecting human conduct to the guidance and control of general rules. Such a purpose scarcely lends itself to Hegelian excesses. The ascription of it to law would, indeed, seem a harmless truism if its implications were not, as I believe

56. Boorstin, *The Lost World of Thomas Jefferson* (1948), pp. 45–47.

I have shown in my second chapter, far from being either self-evident or unimportant.

Before denying ourselves the modest indulgence in teleology I have proposed, we should consider carefully the cost entailed in this denial. The most significant element of that cost lies in the fact that we lose wholly any standard for defining legality. If law is simply a manifested fact of authority or social power, then, though we can still talk about the substantive justice or injustice of particular enactments, we can no longer talk about the degree to which a legal system as a whole achieves the ideal of legality; if we are consistent with our premises we cannot, for example, assert that the legal system of Country X achieves a greater measure of legality than that of Country Y. We can talk about contradictions in the law, but we have no standard for defining what a contradiction is. We may bemoan some kinds of retroactive laws, but we cannot even explain what would be wrong with a system of laws that were wholly retroactive. If we observe that the power of law normally expresses itself in the application of general rules, we can think of no better explanation for this than to say that the supreme legal power can hardly afford to post a subordinate at every street corner to tell people what to do. In short, we can neither formulate nor answer the problems to which my second chapter was devoted.

It may be said that if in truth these problems cannot be formulated in a manner that enables us to answer them then we ought to face that fact courageously and not deceive ourselves with fictions. It is at this point that issue is most sharply joined. The question becomes, not which view is most comforting and reassuring, but which view is right, which view corresponds most faithfully to the reality with which we must deal. In the remainder of this chapter I shall seek to show that the view which pretends to abstract from the purpose of law and to treat law simply as a manifested fact of social power cannot be supported except through a falsification of the reality on which it purports to build.

The view I am criticizing sees the reality of law in the fact of

147

an established lawmaking authority. What this authority determines to be law *is* law. There is in this determination no question of degree; one cannot apply to it the adjectives "successful" or "unsuccessful." This, it seems to me, is the gist of the theory which opposes that underlying these chapters.

Now this theory can seem tenable, I submit, only if we systematically strike from view two elements in the reality it purports to describe. The first of these lies in the fact that the established authority which tells us what is law is itself the product of law.[57] In modern society law is typically created by corporate action. Corporate action—by a parliament, for example —is possible only by adopting and following rules of procedure that will enable a body of men to speak legally with one voice. These rules of procedure may meet shipwreck in all of the eight ways open to any system of law. So when we assert that in the United Kingdom Parliament has the final say as to what law is, we are tacitly assuming some measure of success in at least one legal enterprise, that directed toward giving Parliament the corporate power to "say" things. This assumption of success is normally quite justified in countries with a long parliamentary tradition. But if we are faithful to the reality we purport to describe, we shall recognize that a parliament's ability to enact law is itself an achievement of purposive effort, and not simply a datum of nature.

The second falsification of reality consists in ignoring the fact that a formal structure of authority is itself usually dependent on human effort that is not required by any law or command. Weber points out that all formal social structures—whether embodied in a tradition or a written constitution—are likely to have gaps that do not appear as such because they are filled by appropriate actions taken, often, without any awareness that an alternative is open.[58] Men do not, in other words, generally do absurd things

57. I had occasion to touch on this point in discussing parliamentary supremacy; see p. 115 supra.
58. Weber, *Law in Economy and Society*, pp. 31–33. Weber writes, "It is a fact that the most 'fundamental' questions often are left unregulated by

that would defeat the whole undertaking in which they are engaged, even though the formal directions under which they operate permit these absurdities.

A good example of a gap in formal structure is to be found in the Constitution of the United States. That laws should be promulgated is probably the most obvious demand of legality. It is also the demand that is most readily reduced to a formal constitutional requirement. Yet the Constitution says nothing about the publication of laws. Despite this lack I doubt if it has ever entered the mind of any Congressman that he might curry favor with the taxpayers through a promise to save them money by seeing to it that the laws were left unpublished. One can, of course, argue that a constitutional requirement of publication can be reached by interpretation, since otherwise the provisions against certain retrospective laws would make little sense. But the point is that no such interpretation was in fact engaged in by those who from the first assumed as a matter of course that laws ought to be published.

The scholar may refuse to see law as an enterprise and treat it simply as an emanation of social power. Those whose actions constitute that power, however, see themselves as engaged in an enterprise and they generally do the things essential for its success. To the extent that their actions must be guided by insight rather than by formal rule, degrees in the attainment of success are inevitable.

Hart's problem of "the persistence of law"—how can the law made by Rex IV still be law when Rex V comes to the throne?— is another example of a gap in postulated formal structure that does not appear as such in practice. The need for continuity in law despite changes in government is so obvious that everyone normally assumes this continuity as a matter of course. It becomes a problem only when one attempts to define law as an emanation

---

law even in legal orders which are otherwise thoroughly rationalized." He goes on to say that generally men act so that "the 'absurd' though legally possible situation" does not arise in practice.

of formal authority and excludes from its operations the possible influence of human judgment and insight.

The heavy emphasis theory tends to place on an exact definition of the highest legal power expresses, no doubt, a concern that obscurity on this point may cause the legal system as a whole to disintegrate. Again, it is forgotten that no set of directions emanating from above can ever dispense with the need for intelligent action guided by a sense of purpose. Even the lowly justice of the peace, who cannot make head or tail of the language by which his jurisdiction is limited, will usually have the insight to see that his powers derive from an office forming part of a larger system. He will at least have the judgment to proceed cautiously. Coordination among the elements of a legal system is not something that can simply be imposed; it must be achieved. Fortunately, a proper sense of role, reinforced by a modicum of intelligence, will usually suffice to cure any defaults of the formal system.

There is, I think, a curious irony about any view that refuses to attribute to law as a whole any purpose, however modest or restricted. No school of thought has ever ventured to assert that it could understand reality without discerning in it structure, relatedness, or pattern. If we were surrounded by a formless rain of discrete and unrelated happenings, there would be nothing we could understand or talk about. When we treat law as a "fact," we must assume that it is a special kind of fact, possessing definable qualities that distinguish it from other facts. Indeed, all legal theorists are at great pains to tell us just what kind of fact it is— it is not "the gunman situation writ large," it normally involves the application of general rules to human behavior, etc., etc.

This effort to discover and describe the characteristics that identify law usually meets with a measure of success. Why should this be? The reason is not at all mysterious. It lies in the fact that in nearly all societies men perceive the need for subjecting certain kinds of human conduct to the explicit control of rules. When they embark on the enterprise of accomplishing this subjection, they come to see that this enterprise contains a certain inner logic of its own, that it imposes demands that must be met (sometimes with considerable inconvenience) if its objectives are to be attained. It is because men generally in some measure perceive these demands and respect them, that legal systems display a certain likeness in societies otherwise quite diverse.

It is, then, precisely because law is a purposeful enterprise that it displays structural constancies which the legal theorist can discover and treat as uniformities in the factually given. If he realized on what he built his theory, he might be less inclined to conceive of himself as being like the scientist who discovers a uniformity of inanimate nature. But perhaps in the course of rethinking his subject he might gain a new respect for his own species and come to see that it, too, and not merely the electron, can leave behind a discernible pattern.

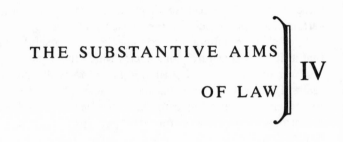

THE SUBSTANTIVE AIMS OF LAW

IV

Yet law-abiding scholars write
Law is neither wrong nor right.—W. H. Auden

We must not expect a good constitution because those who make it are
moral men. Rather it is because of a good constitution that we may expect
a society composed of moral men.—Immanuel Kant

Holmes' legal philosophy had as its central theme the necessity for maintaining a sharp distinction between law and morals. Yet in *The Path of the Law* he wrote:

> I do not say that there is not a wider point of view from which the distinction between law and morals becomes of secondary importance, as all mathematical distinctions vanish in the presence of the infinite.[1]

So it is now time in these investigations—without, to be sure, invoking the infinite—to see whether there are not contexts in which distinctions previously insisted upon may become of

1. 10 *Harvard Law Review* 457–78, at p. 459 (1897).

secondary importance. The two principal distinctions upon which the discussion has so far been built are, it will be recalled, the distinction between the moralities of duty and of aspiration and the distinction between the internal and external moralities of law.

The Neutrality of the Law's Internal Morality toward Substantive Aims

In presenting my analysis of the law's internal morality I have insisted that it is, over a wide range of issues, indifferent toward the substantive aims of law and is ready to serve a variety of such aims with equal efficacy. One moral issue in lively debate today is that of contraception. Now it is quite clear that the principles of legality are themselves incapable of resolving this issue. It is also clear that a legal system might maintain its internal integrity whether its rules were designed to prohibit or to encourage contraception.

But a recognition that the internal morality of law may support and give efficacy to a wide variety of substantive aims should not mislead us into believing that *any* substantive aim may be adopted without compromise of legality. Even the adoption of an objective like the legal suppression of contraception may, under some circumstances, impair legal morality. If, as sometimes seems to be the case, laws prohibiting the sale of contraceptives are kept on the books as a kind of symbolic act, with the knowledge that they will not and cannot be enforced, legal morality is seriously affected. There is no way to quarantine this contagion against a spread to other parts of the legal system. It is unfortunately a familiar political technique to placate one interest by passing a statute, and to appease an opposing interest by leaving the statute largely unenforced.

One of the tasks of the present chapter is to analyze in general terms the manner in which the internal and external moralities of law interact. Before presenting this analysis it will be useful to oppose against it the view expressed by H. L. A. Hart in

The Concept of Law.[2] In his chapter on "Law and Morals" Hart writes:

> If social control [through legal rules] is to function, the rules must satisfy certain conditions: they must be intelligible and within the capacity of most to obey, and in general they must not be retrospective, though exceptionally they may be . . . Plainly these features of control by rule are closely related to the requirements of justice which lawyers term principles of legality. Indeed one critic of positivism has seen in these aspects of control by rules, something amounting to a necessary connexion between law and morality, and suggested that they may be called "the inner morality of law." Again, if this is what the necessary connexion of law and morality means, we may accept it. It is unfortunately compatible with very great iniquity.[3]

Certainly one could not wish for a more explicit denial of any possible interaction between the internal and external moralities of law than that contained in this last sentence. I must confess I am puzzled by it. Does Hart mean merely that it is possible, by stretching the imagination, to conceive the case of an evil monarch who pursues the most iniquitous ends but at all times preserves a genuine respect for the principles of legality? If so, the observation seems out of place in a book that aims at bringing "the concept of law" into closer relation with life. Does Hart mean to assert that history does in fact afford significant examples of regimes that have combined a faithful adherence to the internal morality of law with a brutal indifference to justice and human welfare? If so, one would have been grateful for examples about which some meaningful discussion might turn.

Hart's view that problems of legality deserve no more than casual and passing consideration does not by any means reveal

2. This book has been previously discussed at some length; see pp. 133–45, supra.
3. Ibid., p. 202. The unidentified "critic of positivism" mentioned in the quoted passage is myself.

itself solely in the few sentences I have quoted. It permeates his book as a whole. In his discussion of what he calls "the core of good sense in the doctrine of Natural Law" (pp. 189–95), he concerns himself exclusively with substantive aims, passing over in silence the fine English tradition of "fundamental law," a tradition largely concerned with what may be called the laws of lawfulness.[4] When he comes to treat of "The Pathology of a Legal System" (pp. 114–20), the issues discussed largely reduce themselves in the vernacular to the question, "Who's boss around here anyway?" Finally, the predicament of postwar Germany in attempting to clean up the moral and legal debris left by the Nazis still takes no account of the drastic deterioration in legal morality that occurred under Hitler (p. 204). In short, while Hart recognizes in passing that there exists something that may be called an internal morality of the law, he seems to consider that it has no significant bearing on the more serious concerns of jurisprudence.

Against this view of Hart's—certainly not untypical of modern legal thinking—I shall attempt in what follows to restore the intellectual channels which it seems to me should connect the problem of legality with the other major issues of legal philosophy.

Legality as a Condition of Efficacy

I think I need not repeat here the argument implicit in my whole second chapter that the internal morality of the law is not something added to, or imposed on, the power of law, but is an essential condition of that power itself. If this conclusion is accepted, then the first observation that needs to be made is that law is a precondition of good law. A conscientious carpenter, who has learned his trade well and keeps his tools sharp, might, we may suppose, as well devote himself to building a hangout for thieves as to building an orphans' asylum. But it still remains true that it takes a carpenter, or the help of a carpenter, to build an or-

4. See supra, pp. 99–101.

phans' asylum, and that it will be a better asylum if he is a skill-ful craftsman equipped with tools that have been used with care and kept in proper condition.

If we had no carpenters at all it would be plain that our first need would be, not to draft blueprints for hospitals and asylums or to argue about the principles of good design, but to recruit and train carpenters. It is in this sense that much of the world today needs law more than it does good law.

It is worth recalling that in the indictment set forth in the Declaration of Independence, George III was as much charged with a denial of law as with the imposition of unjust laws.

> He has refused his assent to laws, the most wholesome and necessary for the public good . . . He has forbidden his Governors to pass laws of immediate and pressing impor-tance . . . He has dissolved representative houses repeatedly . . . He has refused for a long time, after such dissolutions to cause others to be elected . . . He has obstructed the administration of justice, by refusing his assent to laws for establishing judiciary powers . . . He has abdicated govern-ment here, by declaring us out of his protection and waging war against us.

When these words were written, Americans were on their way to becoming "decolonized." We were fortunate that we had learned from our British teachers something of the need for law and for preserving its integrity and force. Much of the world today yearns for justice without having undergone a similar tutelage. There was never a time that could reveal more plainly the vacuity of the view that law simply expresses a datum of legitimated social power. Nor was there ever a time when it was more dangerous to take that view seriously.

I should apologize for insisting on so obvious a proposition as that some minimum adherence to legal morality is essential for the practical efficacy of law, were it not that the point is so often passed over precisely in contexts where it needs most to be made explicit. A notable example of this occurs, I believe, in

Hart's treatment (pp. 114–20) of "The Pathology of a Legal System." All the situations he discusses under that heading involve either a conflict of ultimate authority or "the simple breakdown of ordered legal control in the face of anarchy or banditry without political pretensions to govern." Here, as elsewhere in Hart's book, law is conceived entirely in terms of its formal source rather than as a complex undertaking capable of various degrees of success. There is no recognition that there may be a continued public acceptance of a single source of legal power and yet that power may be so ineptly or corruptly exercised that an effective legal system is not achieved. Nor is there any recognition that some degree of "pathology" attends all legal systems, including the most exemplary. Even if one is interested only in shifts from one formal source of legal power to another, no realistic account can be given if problems of legal morality are excluded. In the course of history lawfully established governments have been overthown in the name of law. The threat of lawless revolution can make it difficult to maintain lawfulness in the actions of a government genuinely dedicated to legality. These antinomies dominating the actual drama of history are lost from view in an account content simply to say, in effect, "First there was Act I, then there was Act II."

Legality and Justice

One deep affinity between legality and justice has often been remarked and is in fact explicitly recognized by Hart himself (p. 202). This lies in a quality shared by both, namely, that they act by known rule. The internal morality of the law demands that there be rules, that they be made known, and that they be observed in practice by those charged with their administration. These demands may seem ethically neutral so far as the external aims of law are concerned. Yet, just as law is a precondition for good law, so acting by known rule is a precondition for any meaningful appraisal of the justice of law. "A lawless unlimited power" expressing itself solely in unpredictable and patternless interventions in human affairs could be said to be unjust only in the sense that it does not act by known rule. It would be hard to call it unjust in any more specific sense until one discovered what hidden principle, if any, guided its interventions. It is the virtue of a legal order conscientiously constructed and administered that it exposes to public scrutiny the rules by which it acts.

It is now generally forgotten by what dodges the Nazis avoided that public disclosure. During their regime there appeared in many German shop windows a sign reading "Jüdisches Geschäft." No law was ever passed requiring the display of such signs. They were installed at the "request" of Party members who went about distributing them to the stores where their display was thought appropriate. The explanation of this procedure current among the German citizenry was that the Nazis knew that a formal and published legal enactment would invite foreign criticism. This ruse was in fact partly successful. At times when an influx of foreigners was expected, say, during a commercial fair, the signs were, again at the request of the Party, temporarily removed. In Berlin, where a great many foreign visitors were coming and going at all times, signs were not used at all. Instead stores of Jewish ownership were "requested" by the Party to use a distinctive paint around the frames of their display windows. The casual foreign visitor would be likely to observe the frequency with which this color was used, but generally remained ignorant of its significance and that it had been used in compliance with a rule that was never enacted publicly.

In our own country it is quite common for the practices of governmental agencies to be controlled by unwritten and unpublished rules. Sometimes these rules are quite innocent in substance, though a lack of knowledge of them may handicap the citizen in dealing with the agency. At other times these undeclared rules are far from innocent. A particularly brutal instance of such a rule was revealed recently in Boston. It appears that when an arrested person is detained in jail overnight, it is the practice to require him to sign a paper releasing the police from all civil liability for acts connected with his arrest and detention.

Signing such a paper is a condition of his discharge from custody. No doubt many a police officer, quite unreflective about this practice, has applied it with a sense of conscientiously observing standard operating procedure. It is hard to imagine any lawmaker who would be willing to authorize such a procedure by a published rule.

So far I have spoken as if the affinity between legality and justice consisted simply in the fact that a rule articulated and made known permits the public to judge of its fairness. The affinity has, however, deeper roots. Even if a man is answerable only to his own conscience, he will answer more responsibly if he is compelled to articulate the principles on which he acts. Many persons occupying positions of power betray in their relations with subordinates uniformities of behavior that may be said to constitute unwritten rules. It is not always clear that those who express these rules in their actions are themselves aware of them. It has been said that most of the world's injustices are inflicted, not with the fists, but with the elbows. When we use our fists we use them for a definite purpose, and we are answerable to others and to ourselves for that purpose. Our elbows, we may comfortably suppose, trace a random pattern for which we are not responsible, even though our neighbor may be painfully aware that he is being systematically pushed from his seat. A strong commitment to the principles of legality compels a ruler to answer to himself, not only for his fists, but for his elbows as well.

Legal Morality and Laws Aiming at Alleged Evils That Cannot Be Defined

The simple demand that rules of law be expressed in intelligible terms seems on its face ethically neutral toward the substantive aims law may serve. If any principle of legal morality is, in Hart's words, "compatible with very great iniquity," this would seem to be it. Yet if a legislator is attempting to remove some evil and cannot plainly identify the target at which his statute is directed, it is obvious he will have difficulty in making his laws clear. I have already tried to illustrate this point by a reference to statutes designed to prevent "a return of the old saloon."[5] In that case, however, we have to do with legislative foolishness, rather than with anything touching on iniquity.

It is quite otherwise with laws attempting to make legal rights depend on race. It is common today to think of the government of South Africa as combining a strict observance of legality with the enactment of a body of law that is brutal and inhuman. This view could only arise because of the now inveterate confusion between deference for constituted authority and fidelity to law. An examination of the legislation by which racial discrimination is maintained in South Africa reveals a gross departure from the demands of the internal morality of law.

The following extracts are taken from a careful and objective study of the racial laws enacted by the Union of South Africa:

> The Legislation abounds with anomalies and the same person may, in the result, fall into different racial categories under different statutes . . . the Minister of the Interior on the 22nd March 1957, stated that approximately 100,000 race classification cases were then pending before the Director of Census and Statistics which were regarded as "borderline cases" . . . As the present study has revealed, the absence of uniformity of definition flows primarily from the absence of any uniform or scientific basis of race classification . . . In the final analysis the legislature is attempting to define the indefinable.[6]

Even the South African judge who in his private life shares the prejudices that have shaped the law he is bound to interpret and apply, must, if he respects the ethos of his calling, feel a deep distaste for the arbitrary manipulations this legislation demands of him.

5. See pp. 89–91, supra.
6. Suzman, "Race Classification and Definition in the Legislation of the Union of South Africa, 1910–1960," *Acta Juridica* (1960), pp. 339–67; the extracts quoted in the text are taken from pp. 339, 355, and 367.

It should not be supposed it is only in South Africa that statutes attaching legal consequences to differences in race have given rise to serious difficulties of interpretation. In 1948 in *Perez v. Sharp*[7] the Supreme Court of California held unconstitutional a statute providing that "no license may be issued authorizing the marriage of a white person with a Negro, mulatto, Mongolian or member of the Malay race." The holding that the statute was invalid was rested in part on the ground that it did not meet the constitutional requirement "that a law be definite and its meaning ascertainable by those whose rights and duties are governed thereby."

Our naturalization laws now expressly provide that the "right of a person to become a naturalized citizen . . . shall not be denied . . . because of race."[8] The Supreme Court is thus now safe from the danger of getting itself entangled in its own interpretations as it did in 1922 and 1923. In *Ozawa v. United States*[9] the Court had to give some meaning to a provision restricting naturalization to "white persons." The court observed, "Manifestly, the test afforded by the mere color of the skin of each individual is impracticable as that differs greatly among persons of the same race." In an attempt to achieve something like scientific exactitude the Court declared that "white person" should be interpreted to mean a person of the Caucasian race. In a case argued a few months after this decision, the applicant for citizenship was a high-caste Hindu.[10] His counsel introduced rather convincing proof that among anthropologists employing the term "Caucasian," he would be assigned to that race. The Court observed that the term Caucasian was unknown to those who drafted the statute in 1790, and that "as used in the science of ethnology, the connotation of the word is by no means clear and the use of it in its scientific sense as an equivalent for the words of the statute . . . would simply mean the substitution of one perplexity

7. 32 Cal. 2d 711.
8. USCA, Tit. 8, §1422.
9. 260 U.S. 178 (1922).
10. *United States v. Thind,* 261 U.S. 204 (1923).

for another . . . The words of familiar speech, which were used by the original framers of the law, were intended to include only the type of man whom they knew as white."

Finally, by a bitter irony the Israeli High Court of Justice has encountered well-nigh insoluble problems in trying to give some simple and understandable interpretation to the Law of Return granting citizenship automatically to immigrants who are "Jews." On December 6, 1962, a divided Court held that a Roman Catholic monk was not a Jew for purposes of this law. His counsel argued that, being of Jewish parentage, he was by rabbinical law still a Jew. The Court conceded that this was true, but said that the question was not one of religious law but of the secular law of Israel. By that law he was no longer a Jew because he had embraced the Christian religion.[11]

The View of Man Implicit in Legal Morality

I come now to the most important respect in which an observance of the demands of legal morality can serve the broader aims of human life generally. This lies in the view of man implicit in the internal morality of law. I have repeatedly observed that legal morality can be said to be neutral over a wide range of ethical issues. It cannot be neutral in its view of man himself. To embark on the enterprise of subjecting human conduct to the governance of rules involves of necessity a commitment to the view that man is, or can become, a responsible agent, capable of understanding and following rules, and answerable for his defaults.

Every departure from the principles of the law's inner morality is an affront to man's dignity as a responsible agent. To judge his actions by unpublished or retrospective laws, or to order him to do an act that is impossible, is to convey to him your indifference to his powers of self-determination. Conversely, when the view is accepted that man is incapable of responsible action, legal

11. See the *New York Times* for Dec. 7, 1962, pp. 1 and 15, and Dec. 8, 1962, p. 13.

morality loses its reason for being. To judge his actions by un-published or retrospective laws is no longer an affront, for there is nothing left to affront—indeed, even the verb "to judge" be-comes itself incongruous in this context; we no longer judge a man, we act upon him.

Today a whole complex of attitudes, practices, and theories seems to drive us toward a view which denies that man is, or can meaningfully strive to become, a responsible, self-determin-ing center of action. The causes of this development are of the most varied sort; in their motivation they seem to run the gamut from the basest to the most noble.

One stream of influence comes from science, and more par-ticularly from certain doctrinaire schools of thought in the social sciences. Let me allow the eminent psychologist B. F. Skinner at this point to speak for himself:

> If we are to use the methods of science in the field of human affairs, we must assume that behavior is lawful and determined. We must expect to discover that what a man does is the result of specifiable conditions and that once these conditions have been discovered, we can anticipate and to some extent determine his actions. This possibility is offensive to many people. It is opposed to a tradition of long standing which regards man as a free agent . . . no one who is a product of Western civilization can [accept the scientific view of human behavior] without a struggle.
>
> The conception of a free, responsible individual is em-bedded in our language and pervades our practices, codes, and beliefs. Given an example of human behavior, most people can describe it immediately in terms of such a con-ception. The practice is so natural that it is seldom examined. A scientific formulation, on the other hand, is new and strange.
>
> We do not hold people responsible for their reflexes—for example, for coughing in church. We hold them responsible for their operant behavior—for example, for whispering in

church or remaining in church while coughing. But there are variables which are responsible for whispering as well as coughing, and these may be just as inexorable. When we recognize this, we are likely to drop the notion of responsibility altogether and with it the doctrine of free will as an inner causal agent. This may make a great difference in our practices. The doctrine of personal responsibility is associated with certain techniques of controlling behavior— techniques which generate "a sense of responsibility" or point out "an obligation to society." These techniques are relatively ill-adapted to their purpose.[12]

That views like those just quoted represent an overreaching of "science" and are based on a most naïve epistemology,[13] does not seem seriously to detract from their appeal. Though no one, including Professor Skinner, really believes them to the extent of adopting them as a consistent basis for action, we recognize that they express a partial truth. By overstating that truth and leaving undefined its proper limits, they encourage an attitude of indifference toward the decay of the concept of responsibility implicit in many developments in the law, most of which certainly do not serve the ends for which Professor Skinner has striven so hard.

For in justice to Professor Skinner it should be noted that he does not simply doubt the validity of the concept of responsibility; he proceeds to construct an alternative mode of social control. Stated in very simple terms he proposes that instead of telling men to be good, we condition them to be good. Whatever the merits or faults of this program, it has no affinity with that of the

12. *Science and Human Behavior* (1953); the quotations in the text are taken from pp. 6–7, 10, 115–16.

13. Two themes that run through Skinner's thinking are: (1) that purpose must be excluded from scientific explanation, since it involves a conceived future state as governing the present, whereas it is an accepted tenet of science that the past controls the present; (2) human behavior must, so far as possible, be explained in terms of causes "outside" the organism, rather than operative "within" it.

overworked prosecutor who seeks to simplify his job through laws that will make criminal responsibility independent of any proof of fault or intent.

I have spoken of "noble" impulses as having played a part in confusing the concept of responsibility. An outstanding example lies in abuses of the rehabilitative ideal in the criminal law. As Francis Allen has demonstrated,[14] misapplied this ideal can brutalize the criminal law it sought to make more humane. When, for example, rehabilitation is taken as the exclusive aim of the criminal law, all concern about due process and a clear definition of what is criminal may be lost. If the worst that can happen to the defendant is that he should be given a chance to have himself improved at public expense, why all the worry about a fair trial?

Since Professor Allen published his article the fears he there expressed have received fresh confirmation in the opinion rendered by Mr. Justice Clark in *Robinson v. California*.[15] As most of the court viewed the issue in that case it was whether the condition of being a drug addict—a condition that might come about innocently—could constitutionally be made a crime. The majority of the court held that it could not. In dissenting from this decision Mr. Justice Clark argued that the statute in question might be regarded as a curative measure. Since it is conceded that a state may through civil proceedings commit an addict to the hospital for the purpose of curing him, he saw no reason why it might not also sentence him to six months in jail where, presumably, narcotics would be beyond his reach.

On this view of the criminal law what relevance would the principles of legality have for such a statute as that involved in *Robinson v. California?* Do curative measures need to be limited and controlled by formal rules? Need the nature of these measures and the cases to which they are applicable be promulgated?

14. "Criminal Justice, Legal Values and the Rehabilitative Ideal," 50 *Journal of Criminal Law and Criminology* 226–32 (1959).

15. 370 U.S. 660 at pp. 679–86 (1962); the majority opinion in this case was discussed supra, pp. 105–06.

May not curative measures be applied to conditions arising before they were officially adopted?

There is much reason to believe that our approach to the problem of drug addiction is wrong, and that more would be achieved through medical and rehabilitative measures than through the criminal law. But such a program of reform, if it is to succeed, will have to create the institutions necessary for its realization. It cannot project itself incongruously into institutions created with quite different aims in mind; you cannot make a jail a hospital by calling it that or make a criminal trial a medical examination by pretending that it is.

There are other trends in the law that serve to obscure the citizen's role as a self-determining agent. Not the least of these lies in the increasing use being made of taxation as a sort of legal maid-of-all-work. In recent times taxation has become the means of serving a multitude of oblique ends. Taxes have been imposed to control the business cycle, to identify professional gamblers, to allocate economic resources, to discourage the use of alcohol, to make vendors of cosmetics share with the government a part of the high price women are willing to pay for their unnatural beauty, to discourage travel, to expand federal jurisdiction—and who knows for what other objectives? Meanwhile prosecutors discover that the tax laws provide a convenient means of securing convictions not obtainable on other grounds.

Small wonder, then, that the object and victim of it all should sometimes become perplexed and begin to ask himself what lies ahead. The corpulent citizen, already obsessed by the guilt of overeating, may become concerned lest the government do something about his extra poundage. To be sure, he will probably feel fairly safe in assuming they are not likely to fine him for weighing too much. But can he be certain that tomorrow he may not be the subject of a special tax, justified on the theory that it costs more to transport him over governmentally subsidized air lines, though the fact is he never travels by air? And may he not ask himself what, after all, is the difference between a tax and a fine? His mood of quiet desperation is not likely to be improved if he is unfortunate enough to learn that a famous justice of the Supreme Court of the United States used to insist that there is no difference.

I shall not dwell longer on these incongruities of the modern legal order. I should like instead to recall what we would lose if the concept of responsibility ever disappeared completely from the law. The whole body of the law is permeated by two recurring standards of decision: *fault* and *intent*. Philosophic discussion of these notions has largely concentrated on their role in the criminal law, where they have given rise to the most abstruse arguments, including that concerning freedom of the will. But these twin standards play an equally important role in the law of contracts, torts, and property. Examined closely they turn out to be difficult and elusive conceptions in whatever area of the law they appear. Yet without them we would have no thread to guide us through the labyrinth. When one of them fails, we are apt to reach for the closest approximation of it. When there is no clearly determined intent, we ask what intention the parties would have had had they foreseen the situation that has arisen. When neither party seems chargeable directly with fault, we ask which of them had the best chance to prevent the harm—which, in other words, was closest to being at fault.

Notice what happens when these two tests, and their near relatives, fail completely. This occurs in the law of contracts when performance of an agreement is hampered or its significance is changed by some external event, such as the cancellation of a coronation procession. In the law of property our familiar standards fail when nature intervenes and takes control, as when a river shifts its course, removing twenty acres from A's land and adding twenty-five to B's. In cases like these the litigants do not appear as responsible agents, but as the helpless victims of outside forces. We can no longer ask: Who was to blame? What did they intend? Since our usual standards of justice fail us, we are at a loss to know what justice requires. If we were to lose throughout the law the view of man as a responsible center of action, all legal problems would become like those I have just suggested.

167

The Problem of the Limits of Effective Legal Action

So far in this chapter I have attempted to show that the internal morality of law does indeed deserve to be called a "morality." I hope I have demonstrated that an acceptance of this morality is a necessary, though not a sufficient condition for the realization of justice, that this morality is itself violated when an attempt is made to express blind hatreds through legal rules, and that, finally, the specific morality of law articulates and holds before us a view of man's nature that is indispensable to law and morality alike.

It is now time to turn to the limits of legal morality and to an analysis of the situations in which an application of this morality may be inappropriate and damaging.

But first note must be taken of a confusion that threatens our subject. Let me give an historical instance of this confusion. In his essay *On Liberty* Mill had written:

> The object of this Essay is to assert one simple principle, as entitled to govern absolutely the dealings of society with the individual by way of compulsion and control, whether the means used be physical force in the form of legal penalties, or the moral coercion of public opinion. That principle is, that . . . the only purpose for which power can be rightfully exercised over any member of a civilized community, against his will, is to prevent harm to others. His own good, either physical or moral, is not a sufficient warrant.[16]

In his famous reply to Mill, James Fitzjames Stephen sought to refute Mill's "one simple principle" by pointing out that the British citizen has power exercised over him to extract taxes which go in support of the British Museum, an institution ob-

16. The quoted passage appears in Ch. I.

viously designed, not to protect the citizen from harm, but to improve him.[17]

What is illustrated here is a confusion between law in the usual sense of rules of conduct directed toward the citizen, and governmental action generally. Mill was arguing that "physical force in the form of *legal penalties*" should not itself be used as a direct instrument for improving the citizen. Certainly he did not intend to assert that the government should never use funds raised through taxes—enforced, if necessary, by coercive measures—to provide facilities that will enable the citizen to improve himself.

The confusion Stephen introduced in his controversy with Mill represents a fairly subtle representative of its class. A more thorough piece of obfuscation is found in the following passage from a famous anthropologist:

> Law has been often used as an instrument of legislative omnipotence. There was an attempt to make a whole nation sober by law. It failed. [At this point we may say, so far, so good.] In Nazi Germany a whole nation is being transformed into a gang of bloodthirsty world-bandits through the instrumentality of law, among others. This, we hope, will fail again. The Italian dictator is trying to make his intelligent, cynical, and peace-loving people into courageous heroes. The fundamentalists have tried in some states of this Union to make people God-fearing and bibliolatric by law. A great communistic Union has tried to abolish God, marriage, and the family, again by law.[18]

This identification of law with every conceivable kind of official act has become so common that when one finds an author

17. *Liberty, Equality, Fraternity* (1873), p. 16. "To force an unwilling person to contribute to the support of the British Museum is as distinct a violation of Mr. Mill's principle as religious persecution."
18. Malinowski, "A New Instrument for the Interpretation of Law—Especially Primitive," 51 *Yale Law Journal* 1237–54, at p. 1247 (1942).

about to discuss, in Pound's famous phrase, "the limits of effective legal action," one is not sure whether the subject will be the attempted legal suppression of homosexuality or the failure of the government to convert the power of the tides into electricity at Passamaquoddy.

Legal Morality and the Allocation of Economic Resources

So much by way of an attempt at intellectual prophylaxis. Let me now turn directly to situations in which the internal morality of law reaches beyond its proper domain.

You will recall how in my first chapter I invoked the analogy of a kind of scale, starting at the bottom with the duties most obviously necessary to social existence and ending at the top with the highest and most difficult achievements of which human beings are capable. I also spoke of an invisible pointer as marking the line where the pressure of duty leaves off and the challenge of excellence begins. I regarded the proper location of that pointer as a basic problem of social philosophy. If it is set too low, the notion of duty itself may disintegrate under the influence of modes of thought appropriate only to the higher levels of a morality of aspiration. If the pointer is set too high, the rigidities of duty may reach up to smother the urge toward excellence and substitute for truly effective action a routine of obligatory acts.

This figure of the scale and the pointer is useful, I believe, in surveying the range of governmental action. At the bottom we have government establishing set rules of duty for the control of human conduct. At the other end of the scale we have, for example, the President conducting (with the advice and consent of the Senate) our relations with foreign countries, relations that obviously cannot be set by fixed rules of duty, if for no other reason, because they involve decisions by powers beyond the reach of our law.

In my second chapter I pointed out that the internal morality of the law is itself largely a morality of aspiration. At the same time it takes its peculiar quality from the fact that it has to do with creating and enforcing legal duties. The internal morality of law, in other words, is not and cannot be a morality appropriate for every kind of governmental action. The Army is a creature of law and its officers are, in a sense, officials of the government. Yet certainly it does not follow that every exercise of military command must subject itself to the restraints appropriate, for example, to a discharge of the judicial function.

It is chiefly in the economic field that truisms like those just advanced have commonly been ignored. It will be recalled how in the first chapter I pointed out that private economic activity takes place within a restraining framework set by the law and morality of property and contract. At the same time, this activity cannot and should not be conducted in accordance with anything resembling the internal morality of law. It knows but one general principle, that of obtaining a maximum return from limited resources. This remains true even when the restraints surrounding economic calculation are expanded to include, let us say, the obligation to pay a minimum wage, to provide some form of job security, and to submit discharges to arbitration. Obligations like these serve simply to shrink the framework within which economic calculation takes place; they do not change the essential nature of that calculation.

Nor is the nature of that calculation changed when the government itself engages directly in economic activity. Socialist economies have historically encountered difficulty in developing a meaningful pricing system. Without such a system applications of the marginal utility principle become difficult and conjectural. But the principle itself remains unimpaired, as it must whenever and wherever men seek to make the most effective disposition of the resources at their command. And it is apparent that that principle cannot be realized through set rules of duty.

Now all the considerations I have just outlined are ignored when we attempt, in our mixed economy, to accomplish through adjudicative forms what are essentially tasks of economic allocation. This most notably occurs in the case of the Civil Aeronautics Board and the Federal Communications Commission. By its

171

nature adjudication must act through openly declared rule or principle, and the grounds on which it acts must display some continuity through time. Without this, joinder of argument becomes impossible and all the conventional safeguards that surround decision (such as that proscribing private conferences between the litigant and the arbiter of the dispute) forfeit their meaning.

To act wisely, the economic manager must take into account every circumstance relevant to his decision and must himself assume the initiative in discovering what circumstances are relevant. His decisions must be subject to reversal or change as conditions alter. The judge, on the other hand, acts upon those facts that are in advance deemed relevant under declared principles of decision. His decision does not simply direct resources and energies; it declares rights, and rights to be meaningful must in some measure stand firm through changing circumstances. When, therefore, we attempt to discharge tasks of economic management through adjudicative forms there is a serious mismatch between the procedure adopted and the problem to be solved.

Nowhere is this thought more effectively conveyed than in an illustration suggested by Henry J. Friendly in his Holmes Lectures, *The Federal Administrative Agencies: The Need for Better Definition of Standards.*[19] Judge Friendly speaks of "the frustrating nature" of the task assigned by Congress to the Federal Communications Commission. He continues:

> The job that Congress gave the Commission was somewhat comparable to asking the Board of the Metropolitan Opera Association to decide, after public hearing and with a reasoned opinion, whether the public convenience, interest, or necessity would be served by having the prima donna role on the opening night sung by . . . Tebaldi, Sutherland, or one of several winners of high American awards. Multiply this many hundred fold; add the seemingly capricious element that whoever was selected for the role could assign

19. Harvard University Press, 1962.

it to any of the other qualified applicants; prohibit the board from getting the advice of many best able to help; assume further that the decision-makers know their action is likely to please or displease persons responsible for their continuance in office, who occasionally communicate attitudes while the decision is in progress—and you will have a more sympathetic understanding of the Commission's problem (pp. 55–56).

The "sympathetic understanding" so effectively conveyed in this passage seems to have taken little hold in the remainder of Judge Friendly's lectures. His complaint of the Federal administrative agencies is that they have insufficiently respected what has been called here the internal morality of law. In advancing reasons why the agencies should define clearly the standards on which they act Judge Friendly presents considerations which closely parallel, and in some respects usefully supplement, those I have treated as making up the ingredients of legal morality (pp. 19–26). Yet he extends these considerations indiscriminately over the whole administrative process, making little attempt to distinguish among the kinds of economic tasks that may be assigned to an agency.

The contention I am advancing here is that tasks of economic allocation cannot be effectively performed within the limits set by the internal morality of law. The attempt to accomplish such tasks through adjudicative forms is certain to result in inefficiency, hypocrisy, moral confusion, and frustration.

This contention finds, I believe, an interstitial confirmation in Judge Friendly's lectures. The two targets of his most severe strictures are the Federal Communications Commission and the Civil Aeronautics Board, agencies whose chief tasks are explicitly allocative. He praises the National Labor Relations Board for the clarity with which it has defined unfair labor practices, in other words, for the manner in which it has exercised a jurisdiction closely akin to the criminal law and remote from anything resembling a managerial allocation of resources. Generally it

173

will be found throughout Judge Friendly's lectures that praise and blame trace a path closely adhering to the distinction between allocative and nonallocative functions. Both praise and blame are, however, largely misplaced when they are directed at individuals; they ought instead to be directed to the aptness of the institutional design of the agency to perform the task assigned to it.

In an attempt to alleviate the incongruity between procedure and assignment that afflicts so many administrative agencies, Hector[20] and Redford[21] have, in somewhat different ways, proposed a separation between the function of declaring general policies and the day-to-day decision of particular cases. Redford's proposal is certainly not received with "sympathetic understanding" by Judge Friendly; in fact he rejects it categorically: "Quite simply, I find it hard to think of anything worse" (p. 153). Yet the suggestion that the function of declaring general policies be separately discharged represents a sincere and intelligent attempt to come to grips with the problem of adjusting the institutional design of administrative agencies to the economic tasks assigned to them. One can imagine, for example, a national policy for increasing the production of coal. No one would suppose that such a policy should be arrived at by a judicial process cabined within its normal limits. What such a policy would require in particular contexts would, of course, have to be decided case by case. In this respect the proposals of Hector and Redford make rare economic sense. They have not, however, solved the problem of a mismatch between the institutional design of the allocative agency and the job it has to do. Deciding what a general economic policy requires in particular instances remains an awkward assignment for adjudication. A national policy for increasing the production of coal could not, for example, tell an adjudicative

20. "Problems of the CAB and the Independent Regulatory Commissions," 69 *Yale Law Journal* 931–64 (1960).
21. *The President and the Regulatory Commissions* (1960), a report submitted to the President's Advisory Committee on Government Organization.

agency whether to close down or to subsidize the continued operation of a losing mine. An intelligent determination of that question could only be made after an investigation into alternative uses for the manpower released by the shutdown and into other opportunities for the use of the subsidy.

In stressing the special significance of the allocative function, I do not wish to imply, of course, that there are no gradations in the distinction between allocative and nonallocative tasks. Even a judicial decision declaring a tax unconstitutional may operate to draw investment into the area previously affected by the tax. This allocative side effect is in theory disregarded as irrelevant to the decision. Similarly an administrative tribunal may proceed on standards that ignore the allocative effects of its decisions. This is done by a rate-making agency where it takes as its standard the principle of an adequate return on a particular investment. If, on the other hand, the agency takes as its standard setting a rate that will induce a sufficient flow of capital into the regulated industry as a whole, its allocative function becomes more explicit, but can be muted by an assumption that the industry requires a "normal" inflow of investment, though a wider view of the economy might falsify this assumption. Tasks that were once only incidentally allocative may become more directly so with a change in circumstances. This happened to the Interstate Commerce Commission when the railways came under competition from the truck and the airplane. It is interesting to note that Judge Friendly praises some of the earlier decisions of the ICC (pp. 27–35) and condemns more recent decisions for a lack of "clear standards" (pp. 106–40).

The problem of finding the most apt institutional design for governmental control over the economy has been acute for a long time. In the future this problem is, I think, bound to become more pressing and pervasive. Indispensable facilities, like certain of our railways, will have to be rescued in one way or another from their economic plight, a plight which, in the case of the railways, has in part been brought about by the allocative effects (for which no one assumes explicit responsibility) of subsidies

175

granted to competing forms of transportation. In the labor field, many experienced arbitrators who once unbendingly opposed compulsory arbitration have become more receptive toward it and some even regard it as inevitable. Almost by inadvertence—a multibillion dollar inadvertence—we have developed a new form of mixed economy in that huge segment of industry dependent upon contracts with the armed services. Because this new form of enterprise is classified as "private," it escapes the scrutiny to which direct governmental operation would be subjected. At the same time it is foolish to think of it as being significantly subject to the discipline of the market. When and if our expenditures for armaments are seriously reduced, a great unmeshing of gears will have to take place. Finally, there are the as yet largely unfaced dislocations that will be brought by increasing automation.

If these portents of what lies ahead can be trusted, then it is plain that we shall be faced with problems of institutional design unprecedented in scope and importance. It is inevitable that the legal profession will play a large role in solving these problems. The great danger is that we will unthinkingly carry over to new conditions traditional institutions and procedures that have already demonstrated their faults of design. As lawyers we have a natural inclination to "judicialize" every function of government. Adjudication is a process with which we are familiar and which enables us to show to advantage our special talents. Yet we must face the plain truth that adjudication is an ineffective instrument for economic management and for governmental participation in the allocation of economic resources.

It may be objected that without the guarantees afforded by adjudicative procedures governmental power is subject to grave abuse. This fear may underestimate the sense of trusteeship that goes with being given a job to do that makes sense and being allowed to do it the sensible way. Today greed and the thirst for power most commonly find their outlet in the exploitation of institutional forms no longer animated by any clear sense of purpose. In any event, in the search for institutional safeguards

176

against abuse we need not confine ourselves to adjudicative procedures in the strict sense, but may also consider the models suggested by the French Conseil d'État, the Scandinavian ombudsman, the British Council on Tribunals, and the boards of censors once established by several American states, censors whose function it was not to supervise private morals, but to be alert to detect abuses and deficiencies in government.

Legal Morality and the Problem of Institutional Design

In discussing the limits of legal morality I have so far sought to show that an effective allocation of economic resources cannot be performed within the restraints imposed by that morality. This in turn means that such an allocation cannot be performed satisfactorily through adjudicative processes. It is important to note that the considerations I have advanced in support of these propositions are by no means relevant only to the field of economics in the strict sense. In a broad sense economic calculation is a pervasive part of our lives. No direction of creative human effort can be entirely free from it.

The two fundamental processes of decision that characterize a democratic society are: decision by impartial judges and decision by the vote of an electorate or a representative body. It is important to recall that neither of these processes of decision can by itself solve complex issues involving a wide range of possible solutions. Thus when the faculty of Christ Church College was of many opinions concerning the best design for a new belfry, even the mathematical genius of Charles Dodgson was unable to devise a method of voting that could resolve their differences.[22] Adjudication and majority vote are both dependent in such cases on some preliminary procedure that will narrow the range of

22. Black, *The Theory of Committees and Elections* (1958), Ch. XX, "The Circumstances in which Rev. C. L. Dodgson (Lewis Carroll) Wrote his Three Pamphlets," pp. 189–213. (This fascinating and somewhat Freudian chapter tells how Dodgson was driven to become a pioneer in the mathematical theory of elections by a dislike for his Dean, father of the real-life Alice.)

177

choice. This procedure normally involves a series of accommodations and compromises among those to be affected by the final decision.

The architectural design of legal institutions and procedures obviously cannot be drawn by adjudicative decision. It is for this reason that the Supreme Court has wisely regarded as beyond its competence the enforcement of the constitutional provision guaranteeing to the states a republican form of government. A court acting as such can neither write a constitution nor undertake a general managerial supervision of its administration.

The decision in *Baker v. Carr*[23] represents a gamble that extracurial processes of political adjustment and compromise will produce an issue digestible, as it were, by the Court. In carrying out the commitment it undertook in *Baker v. Carr* the Court will find itself, I believe, compelled to tread a difficult middle course. If, on the one hand, it lays down standards that are too exacting and comprehensive, it will stifle the indispensable preliminary processes of adjustment and compromise. If its standards are too loose, these processes are not likely to produce a solution acceptable to the Court.

Institutional Design as a Problem of Economizing

Implicit in these last remarks, as well as in these essays as a whole, is an assumption that just as man is restricted in what he can do by the limits imposed by physical nature, so also is he limited in the choices open to him in arranging the forms of his social life. Here, as everywhere, he is confronted by scarcity and is compelled to order the resources available to him with skill and prudence.

At the risk of laboring the obvious, let me illustrate the point I am trying to make with a purely hypothetical case. Let us suppose that among the parents of children attending a grammar school dissatisfaction has arisen about the way in which some

23. 82 Sup. Ct. 691 (1962).

pupils are denied promotion and are compelled to repeat a grade. The parents' dissatisfaction is twofold: (1) they are not certain that decisions on this matter are correctly made—there have, in fact, been rumors of favoritism and of carelessness in the study of records; (2) the parents think that in any event too much is made of a failure to be promoted and that a disproportionate stigma attaches to being made to repeat a grade. To meet the first objection the parents demand that all recommendations against promotion by grade teachers be submitted to a board of senior teachers, who in reaching a final decision will follow adjudicative procedures in which the affected parents will be permitted to appear and be given access to all relevant records. To meet the second objection the parents demand that a concerted effort be made to reduce the stigma attaching to a failure to be promoted and that all teachers in discussing cases where a pupil is held back make an effort to minimize the significance of the decision.

Now it is apparent that this program combines elements between which there is a very considerable incompatibility. Skill and tact in administering the program can reduce this clash, but it will still remain generally true that the more effective the procedural guarantees against mistake and favoritism are, the more unambiguously the finger of shame will point to the pupil not promoted. A public trial may protect him against injustice, but it will do so at the cost of depriving him of the consolation of believing that those who held him back did not know what they were doing.

Similar problems of weighing costs run throughout our legal and political life. For example, if the question be asked, "How much effort should be expended to make certain that no innocent man is ever convicted of crime?," the answer is apt to run toward the absolute, and the suggestion may even be made that where fundamental human rights are at stake a question so indecently calculative should not even be raised. Yet when we reflect that in order to make sure that a decision is right we must consume the scarce commodity of time, and that a right decision too long

179

delayed may do more damage to the accused himself than a mistaken decision promptly rendered, the matter assumes a different aspect. We then perceive that even in this case we are compelled to make a calculation that is in the broad sense "economic" even though money costs are completely left out of account.

It is a great mistake to treat questions of the design and administration of our institutions as if the problem were merely one of weighing substantive ends against one another. For institutions have an integrity of their own which must be respected if they are to be effective at all. I have developed this point at great length with respect to the internal morality of the law. In the following passage from Henry M. Hart the point is properly expanded to institutions and procedures generally:

> In the criminal law, as in all law, questions about the action to be taken do not present themselves for decision in an institutional vacuum. They arise rather in the context of some established and specific procedure of decision: in a constitutional convention; in a legislature; in a prosecuting attorney's office; in a court charged with the determination of guilt or innocence; in a sentencing court; before a parole board; and so on. This means that each agency of decision must take account always of its own place in the institutional system and of what is necessary to maintain the integrity and workability of the system as a whole. A complex of institutional ends must be served, in other words, as well as a complex of substantive social ends. It is axiomatic that each agency of decision ought to make those decisions which its position in the institutional structure best fits it to make.[24]

Though Professor Hart speaks with special reference to the criminal law, he makes it clear that the problems he suggests run through government as a whole. I believe, for reasons already

24. "The Aims of Criminal Law," 23 *Law and Contemporary Problems* 401–41, at p. 402 (1958).

outlined, that these problems of the proper design and coordination of our legal institutions are certain to become more pressing in the years ahead. Their solution will require an earnest collaborative effort among those competent to understand them. Something like the spirit of the Federalist Papers will become essential—a spirit at once inquiring and constructive.

Unfortunately this spirit seems to be largely lacking in our present intellectual climate. On the one hand, there are competent scholars who seem to deny the very existence of problems of institutional design. Their program seems to be a maximum exploitation of governmental power—without any inquiry into its moral sources—for whatever ends seem worthy at a given time. On the other hand, there are those who—in the terms of my presentation—assign these problems to the morality of duty rather than to the morality of aspiration. They resist the suggestion that the solution of these problems requires anything like an economic calculation or an application of the principle of marginal utility. From this entrenched position they are likely to regard those who disagree with them, not merely as being mistaken, but as being unprincipled and immoral.

Fortunately, the lines of controversy are not quite so grimly drawn as the account just given might suggest. One hopes that the future will bring a further bridging of extremes, for the capacity to devise institutions and procedures adequate to its problems is perhaps the chief mark of a civilized society. That capacity is in any event the chief instrument by which civilization can hope to survive in a radically changing world.

The Problem of Defining the Moral Community

So far in these pages a basic question has been passed over in silence. This is the question, Who are embraced in the moral community, the community within which men owe duties to one another and can meaningfully share their aspirations? In plain straightforward modern jargon the question is, Who shall count as a member of the in-group?

This is a problem that has bothered all moral philosophers. Within a functioning community, held together by bonds of mutual interest, the task of drafting a moral code is not difficult. It is comparatively easy to discern in this situation certain rules of restraint and cooperation that are essential for satisfactory life within the community and for the success of the community as a whole. But this confidence in moral judgment is bought at a cost, for if there are no rational principles for determining who shall be included in the community, the internal code itself rests on what appears to be an essentially arbitrary premise.

Is there any resolution for this dilemma? If so, it cannot be obtained from the morality of duty for that morality is essentially a morality of the in-group. It presupposes men in living contact with one another, either through an explicit reciprocity or through relations of tacit reciprocity embodied in the forms of an organized society.

A measure of resolution can, however, be obtained from the morality of aspiration. The most eloquent expression of this possibility is found in the Bible. The morality of duty expounded in the Old Testament includes the command: Thou shalt love thy neighbor as thyself. The New Testament tells of an encounter between a lawyer and Jesus that turned on this command. The lawyer, perceiving that the passage contained a point of difficulty, wished to test Jesus' powers of exegesis. He asked, "And who is my neighbor?"

On this occasion Jesus does not answer, "Your neighbor is everyone; you are bound to love all men everywhere, even your enemies." Instead he relates the parable of the Good Samaritan.[25] A certain man had been struck down by thieves and left half dead. Two of his community brothers passed him by without offering aid. Then one of the despised Samaritans—definitely a member of the out-group—bound up his wounds and took him into care. Jesus ends with the question: "Which now of these

25. Luke 10:25–37.

three, thinkest thou, was neighbor unto him that fell among the thieves?"

The meaning of this parable is, I believe, not that we should include everyone in the moral community, but that we should aspire to enlarge that community at every opportunity and to include within it ultimately, if we can, all men of good will.

But this still leaves a certain difficulty. The morality of aspiration speaks, not imperatively, but in terms of praise, good counsel, and encouragement. Is there no firmer basis for deciding the question of the membership of the moral community?

I believe that in one situation there is. I shall put this situation abstractly, though it is far from being hypothetical. Within a given political society there are men commonly described as being of different races. These men have lived together for many years. Each group has enriched the idiom, the thought, the music, the humor, and the artistic life of the other. They have together produced a common culture. Is there no moral principle that can imperatively condemn drawing a line between them, and denying to one group access to the essentials on which a satisfactory and dignified life can be built?

I believe there is. In this case the morality of aspiration speaks in terms fully as imperative as those characteristic of the morality of duty, so that the distinction between the two at this point breaks down. The morality of aspiration is after all a morality of *human* aspiration. It cannot refuse the human quality to human beings without repudiating itself.

In the Talmud there is a passage that reads, "If I am not for myself, who shall be for me? If I am for myself alone, what am I?"[26] If we put this in the plural, we have, "If we are not for ourselves, who shall be for us? If we are for ourselves alone, what are we?" Whatever answer we may give to this last question, it must be predicated on the assumption that we are above all else human beings. If we have to qualify our answer by adding some

26. Aboth, Ch. 1, Mishnah 14.

biological tag line to our own title, then we deny the human quality to ourselves in an effort to justify denying it to others.

The Minimum Content of a Substantive Natural Law

In seeking to know whether it is possible to derive from the morality of aspiration anything more imperative than mere counsel and encouragement, I have then so far concluded that, since the morality of aspiration is necessarily a morality of human aspiration, it cannot deny the human quality to those who possess it without forfeiting its integrity. Can we derive more than this?

The problem may be stated in another form. In my third chapter I treated what I have called the internal morality of law as itself presenting a variety of natural law. It is, however, a procedural or institutional kind of natural law, though, as I have been at pains in this chapter to show, it affects and limits the substantive aims that can be achieved through law. But can we derive from the morality of aspiration itself any proposition of natural law that is substantive, rather than procedural, in quality?

In his *Concept of Law* H. L. A. Hart presents what he calls "the minimum content of natural law" (pp. 189–95). Starting with the single objective of human survival, conceived as operating within certain externally imposed conditions, Hart derives, by a process I would describe as purposive implication, a fairly comprehensive set of rules that may be called those of natural law. What is expounded in his interesting discussion is a kind of minimum morality of duty.

Like every morality of duty this minimum natural law says nothing about the question, Who shall be included in the community which accepts and seeks to realize cooperatively the shared objective of survival? In short, who shall survive? No attempt is made to answer this question. Hart simply observes that "our concern is with social arrangements for continued existence, not with those of a suicide club."

In justifying his starting point of survival Hart advances two

184

kinds of reasons. One amounts to saying that survival is a necessary condition for every other human achievement and satisfaction. With this proposition there can be no quarrel.

But in addition to treating survival as a precondition for every other human good, Hart advances a second set of reasons for his starting point—reasons of a very different order. He asserts that men have properly seen that in "the modest aim of survival" lies "the central indisputable element which gives empirical good sense to the terminology of Natural Law." He asserts further that in the teleological elements that run through all moral and legal thinking there is "the tacit assumption that the proper end of human activity is survival." He observes that "an overwhelming majority of men do wish to live, even at the cost of hideous misery."

In making these assertions Hart is, I submit, treading more dubious ground. For he is no longer claiming for survival that it is a necessary condition for the achievement of other ends, but seems to be saying that it furnishes the core and central element of all human striving. This, I think, cannot be accepted. As Thomas Aquinas remarked long ago, if the highest aim of a captain were to preserve his ship, he would keep it in port forever.[27] As for the proposition that the overwhelming majority of men wish to survive even at the cost of hideous misery, this seems to me of doubtful truth. If it were true, I question whether it would have any particular relevance to moral theory.

Hart's search for a "central indisputable element" in human striving raises the question whether in fact this search can be successful. I believe that if we were forced to select the principle that supports and infuses all human aspiration we would find it in the objective of maintaining communication with our fellows.

In the first place—staying within the limits of Hart's own argument—man has been able to survive up to now because of his capacity for communication. In competition with other crea-

27. *Summa Theologica*, Pt. I–II, Q. 2, Art. 5. "Hence a captain does not intend as a last end, the preservation of the ship entrusted to him, since a ship is ordained to something else as its end, viz., to navigation."

tures, often more powerful than he and sometimes gifted with keener senses, man has so far been the victor. His victory has come about because he can acquire and transmit knowledge and because he can consciously and deliberately effect a coordination of effort with other human beings. If in the future man succeeds in surviving his own powers of self-destruction, it will be because he can communicate and reach understanding with his fellows. Finally, I doubt if most of us would regard as desirable survival into a kind of vegetable existence in which we could make no meaningful contact with other human beings.

Communication is something more than a means of staying alive. It is a way of being alive. It is through communication that we inherit the achievements of past human effort. The possibility of communication can reconcile us to the thought of death by assuring us that what we achieve will enrich the lives of those to come. How and when we accomplish communication with one another can expand or contract the boundaries of life itself. In the words of Wittgenstein, "The limits of my language are the limits of my world."

If I were asked, then, to discern one central indisputable principle of what may be called substantive natural law—Natural Law with capital letters—I would find it in the injunction: Open up, maintain, and preserve the integrity of the channels of communication by which men convey to one another what they perceive, feel, and desire. In this matter the morality of aspiration offers more than good counsel and the challenge of excellence. It here speaks with the imperious voice we are accustomed to hear from the morality of duty. And if men will listen, that voice, unlike that of the morality of duty, can be heard across the boundaries and through the barriers that now separate men from one another.

A REPLY

TO CRITICS

V

In the internal debate that preceded the decision to add this chapter to my book, I was acutely aware of considerations that weighed heavily against my undertaking it. For one thing, it has been my observation that authors generally serve themselves badly when they attempt to defend their books against critical reviews. The reviewer enjoys the advantage of occupying a fairly well understood role. The expectations of his readers make it appropriate for him to assume the part of a vigorous prosecutor; if he is reasonably fair and sticks to the evidence a considerable license of advocacy will gladly be accorded to him and will indeed seem to serve the ultimate cause of truth.

The author defending his work confronts a very different set of expectations. He has published his book, he has already had his day in court and the becoming posture for him may seem to be that of awaiting quietly the verdict of the intelligent and disinterested reader. Furthermore, any reply to critical reviews is apt to become a muddled thing, mixing charges of misinterpretation with rearticulations of what the author claims he meant to say, intermingling awkwardly defense and counteroffensive, and ending with dark intimations that only limitations of space prevent him from demonstrating with devastating finality how completely mistaken his critics are. In general, efforts at self justification are apt to be painful for all concerned; there is, indeed, a saying in my profession that a lawyer never appears to worse advantage than when pleading his own cause.

In the case at hand there was also the consideration that any *Reply to Critics* would mark the continuation of a debate between H. L. A. Hart and myself that has already gone on for more than a decade. It began when Professor Hart published the Holmes Lecture delivered at the Harvard Law School in April 1957.[1] In that lecture he undertook to defend legal positivism against criticisms made by myself and others. The first attempt at counterthrust was my critical commentary on this lecture.[2] Round three was marked by the publication of Hart's *The Concept of Law;* round four occurred when the first edition of the present work was published; round five took place when Hart published his review.[3] One has the feeling that at some point such an exchange must terminate. *Interest reipublicae ut sit finis litium.* As Ernest Nagel remarked in the fourth and final round of a debate we had in 1958 and 1959, "There is, in general, little intellectual nourishment to be found in rebuttals to rejoinders to replies."[4]

A final deterrent lay in the sheer number of reviews and the diversity of opinion expressed in them,[5] not to speak of the contributions to a symposium held on April 2, 1965,[6] or of incidental

1. "Positivism and the Separation of Law and Morals," 71 *Harvard Law Review* 593–629 (1958).

2. "Positivism and Fidelity to Law—A Reply to Professor Hart," 71 *Harvard Law Review* 630–72 (1958).

3. 78 *Harvard Law Review* 1281–96 (1965).

4. "Fact, Value and Human Purpose," 4 *Natural Law Forum* 26–43, at p. 26 (1959).

5. There have been some 46 reviews. See list, pp. 243–44.

6. "The Morality of Law—A Symposium," 10 *Villanova Law Review* 631–78 (1965). Individual contributions were Murray, "Introduction to the Morality of Law," 624–30; Dworkin, "The Elusive Morality of Law," 631–39; Cohen, "Law, Morality and Purpose," 640–54; Fuller, "A Reply to Professors Cohen and Dworkin," 655–66; with comments by John E. Murray, Jr., 667–70; E. Russell Naughton, 671–72; Francis H. Parker, 673–75; and Donald A. Giannella, 676–78.

appraisals of the book contained in articles of a larger scope.[7] To do justice to all of the points raised in these reviews and commentaries would require a very long chapter indeed.

Notwithstanding the misgivings just outlined I have decided to undertake in this new and final chapter, not only a continuation of my debate with Hart, but a reply to certain other critics as well. Several considerations have prompted this decision.

One of these lay in certain statements contained in Hart's review. In his first paragraph he remarks that it may be that "our starting points and interest in jurisprudence are so different" that he and I "are fated never to understand each other's works." As critical reviews of my book came in, I myself became increasingly aware of the extent to which the debate did indeed depend on "starting points"—not on what the disputants said, but on what they considered it unnecessary to say, not on articulated principles but on tacit assumptions. What was needed therefore, it seemed to me, was to bring these tacit assumptions to more adequate expression than either side has so far been able to do.

I was further encouraged to undertake this effort at clarification by the closing words of Hart's review—words that seem to intimate what he himself conceives to be the fundamental difference in our "starting points":

> In conclusion I would say this: the virtues and vices of this book seem to me to spring from the same single source. The author has all his life been in love with the notion of purpose and this passion, like any other can both inspire and blind a man. I have tried to show how it has done both

7. Anastaplo, "Natural Right and the American Lawyer," *Wisconsin Law Review* 322–43 (1965); Dworkin, "Philosophy, Morality, and Law—Observations Prompted by Professor Fuller's Novel Claim," 113 *University of Pennsylvania Law Review* 668–90 (1965); Hughes, *1964 Annual Survey of American Law—Jurisprudence* (1965), New York University, pp. 693–97; King, "The Concept, The Idea, and The Morality of Law," *Cambridge Law Journal* 106–28 (1966); Lewan, "Die Rechtsphilosophie Lon Fullers," *Archiv für Rechts- und Sozialphilosophie,* 377–413 (1966); Sturm, "Lon Fuller's Multidimensional Natural Law Theory," 18 *Stanford Law Review* 612–39 (1966).

to the author. The inspiration is so considerable that I would not wish him to terminate his longstanding union with this *idée maitresse*. But I wish that the high romance would settle down to some cooler form of regard. When this happens, the author's many readers will feel the drop in temperature; but they will be amply compensated by an increase in light.[8]

The amatory figure—though inevitably a little vivid for the taste of its victim—I accept as a legitimate literary device. I take it what Hart is attempting to convey is that I make too much of purpose and that I would do well to play it down in my thinking. In my view Hart makes too little of purpose; he suffers from the positivist delusion that some gain—unstated and unanalyzed —will be realized if only we treat, insofar as we can, purposive arrangements as though they served no purpose.

Another development prompting me toward this *Reply to Critics* occurred in November 1966, when there appeared an article announcing the emergence of a new school of legal philosophy, denominated as that of the New Analytical Jurists.[9] The acknowledged leader of this school of thought is H. L. A. Hart. The school itself is described as being "less positivistic" than its forerunners, though most of its members are said to remain positivists in the sense that their core commitment is to the proposition that "law as it is can be clearly differentiated from law as it ought to be." To the layman this proposition is likely to seem too obvious a truth to justify running up a philosophic banner over it; to the lawyer experienced in issues of interpretation it will suggest a host of problems hardly intimated in Summer's article.

Though at the conclusion of his article Summers asserts that "professional interest in the new analytical jurisprudence grows

8. Supra n. 3, at 1295–96.
9. Summers, "The *New* Analytical Jurists," 41 *New York University Law Review* 861–96 (1966).

each year," he seems throughout to have some difficulty in articulating just what philosophic creed unites this new school of thought. I think I may be able to help him in this. According to Summers the adherents of the New Analytical Jurisprudence include Hart, Ronald Dworkin, and himself. He also considers Marshall Cohen as a philosopher thinking and writing in a vein similar to that of the New Analytical Jurists. These four men have written in all some ninety pages of critical commentary on my book. I can testify to an amazing uniformity in their reactions; whole paragraphs could be transferred from one discussion to another without any perceptible break in continuity of thought. It is apparent that here, too, we are dealing not with explicit theories but with what Hart called "starting points." Perhaps I can in what follows identify those starting points more clearly than the New Analytical Jurists themselves have been able to do.

The Structure of Analytical Legal Positivism

What I shall attempt here is to bring to articulation the basic intellectual commitments underlying analytical legal positivism. By the adjective "analytical" I mean to exclude behavior-pattern positivism of the sort suggested when it was proposed, at the height of the movement called American Legal Realism, to define law as "the behavior patterns of judges and other officials."[10] The term "analytical" is also apt in conveying an intellectual mood that finds more satisfaction in taking things apart than in seeing how they fit and function together; there is, indeed, little interest among analytical positivists in discerning the elements of tacit interrelatedness that infuse—though always somewhat imperfectly—what we call, by no accident, a legal *system*.

The structure of thought I shall try to describe is one generally shared by Austin, Hart, and Kelsen. In presenting it I shall deal only incidentally with intramural debates among adherents of

10. References to behavior-pattern legal realism will be found in my book, *The Law in Quest of Itself* (1940, 1966), pp. 53–57.

the positivist position. Confining myself, then, to the basic "starting points" that shape the positivist creed, I would discern five of these.

First, the analytical positivist sees law as a one-way projection of authority, emanating from an authorized source and imposing itself on the citizen. It does not discern as an essential element in the creation of a legal system any tacit cooperation between lawgiver and citizen; the law is seen as simply acting on the citizen —morally or immorally, justly or unjustly, as the case may be.

Second, the positivist philosophy asks of law not what it is or does, but whence it comes; its basic concern is with the question, *Who* can make law? Intramural disputes within the school of legal positivism relate almost entirely to the problem of defining the principle or principles by which the right to create law is allocated. Thus we have Austin's "sovereign one or many enjoying the habit of obedience," Kelsen's postulated "Grundnorm," and Hart's "empirically" grounded "Rule of Recognition."[11] Positivism may recognize, of course, that the authorized lawgiver may lack the power to enact specific kinds of law, as, for example, where a written constitution proscribes certain exercises of legislative power. But no modern positivist elevates to a central position in his thinking any limitations contained in "the law job" itself, to borrow a phrase that was a favorite of Karl Llewellyn's.

Third, the legal positivist does not in fact view the lawgiver as occupying any distinctive office, role, or function. If we spoke of his performing a role this would imply that his role should

11. I have not attempted here or elsewhere any critical appraisal of Hart's concept of the Rule of Recognition. The interested reader will find such an appraisal in Sartorius, "The Concept of Law," *Archiv für Rechts- und Sozialphilosophie* 161–90 (1966); and Dworkin, "The Model of Rules," 35 *University of Chicago Law Review* 14–46 (1967). These two articles make it clear that the Rule of Recognition is by no means so simple a notion as might appear from Hart's presentation of it. How it is to be "empirically" established, instead of being "postulated" after the manner of Kelsen's Basic Norm, remains largely unexamined and unexplained.

be adjusted to the complementary roles of others, including that of the ordinary citizen. Any such view would compromise the attempt to regard law as a one-way projection of authority.

Fourth, since the lawgiver is not regarded as occupying a distinctive and limited role, nothing that could be called a "role morality" attaches to the performance of his functions. The ordinary lawyer is, of course, subject to a code of ethics governing his conduct toward clients, fellow lawyers, courts, and the public. This code is no mere restatement of the moral principles governing human conduct generally, but sets forth special standards applicable to the discharge of a distinctive social function. There is, however, no room in the positivist philosophy for a similar ethical code governing the lawgiver's role. If the lawgiver enacts what Hart calls "iniquitous" laws, he sins of course against general morality, but there is no special morality applicable to his job itself.

I think I need not labor the point that the four elements of the positivist creed just outlined are interdependent; each in a sense implies the others. They may all be summed up in the observation that the positivist recognizes in the functioning of a legal system nothing that can truly be called a *social dimension.* The positivist sees the law at the point of its dispatch by the lawgiver and again at the point of its impact on the legal subject. He does not see the lawgiver and the citizen in interaction with one another, and by virtue of that failure he fails to see that the creation of an effective interaction between them is an essential ingredient of the law itself.

So far I have left out the *fifth* and most central article of faith in the credo of positivism. This lies in a belief that clear thinking is impossible unless we effect a neat separation between the purposive effort that goes into the making of law and the law that in fact emerges from that effort. This aspect of the positivist philosophy—which is, indeed, what justifies its name—may seem unconnected with the other four. It stands, however, in intimate relation with them.

It is in dealing with human interaction that the positivistic

193

stance toward reality becomes most difficult to maintain. In contrast, whenever human action can plausibly be viewed as unilaterally projected, the embarrassments of a commitment to positivism are reduced to a minimum. If A is attempting to accomplish some purpose by acting upon an inert B, then we can expect to distinguish with some measure of success between A's purpose—what he was trying to achieve—and the result of his action—some change in the external world. If A is a surgeon operating on an anesthetized B, we can say that A is attempting to achieve some specified result and we can ask ourselves meaningfully what result he in fact achieves. To be sure, if I am not myself a surgeon I may not, as I watch the operation, really understand what is going on, except in broad outlines; the specific motions of the surgeon's hands, the instruments used, and other details may not really register themselves on my perception. All of these details would be meaningful to a fellow surgeon witnessing the same operation, simply because he would perceive and be able to participate in the purposive *why* of what was happening. But ignoring this limitation on my comprehension of what was going on, I can still insist that as a layman I had at least a general understanding of the purpose back of the operation and that this was something quite different from its actual outcome, whether that outcome be viewed as a success or as a failure in terms of the purpose pursued by the surgeon.

Suppose, however, that A is not acting upon an inert B, but that A and B are two persons in conscious and lively interaction with one another. A and B may, for example, have entered upon some common undertaking. They have not yet settled on the terms of their collaboration, but as the venture gets under way they begin to negotiate, by words explicitly and by actions tacitly, a kind of constitution regulating their relations with one another. Each is orienting his words, signs, and actions by what he thinks the other seeks and in part also by what he thinks the other thinks *he* seeks. Here there emerges from the parties' interactions no hard factual datum that can be set off against the purposes that brought it into existence. The quality and terms of the parties' emergent relationship—its "laws" if you will—constitute an important social reality, but it is a reality brought into being and kept alive by purposive effort and by the way each of the parties interprets the purposes of the other.

What I have just been trying to convey is brought to eloquent expression in the following passage from a treatise on interactional sociology: "Reality, then, in this distinctively human world, is not a hard immutable thing but is fragile and adjudicated—a thing to be debated, compromised, and legislated."[12]

It is then, I suggest, no accident that the elements of interaction that create and give meaning to the law are pushed to one side and largely ignored by the analytical positivist. If they were not, he would be in serious trouble in maintaining the basic articles of his faith.

The remarks just concluded have not been offered in the belief that they constitute any solution for what is ordinarily called the problem of the fact-value dichotomy. What I have presented here has been intended simply to put that question into relation with the other tenets of positivism. If in this effort I have misrepresented the positivist position generally, or the views of particular positivists, especially those designated as the New Analytical Jurists, I stand ready to be corrected. Spelling out the other fellow's tacit assumptions is a hazardous business, but some attempt at it is sometimes necessary if effective communication is to take place at all.

Before proceeding more directly to my *Reply*, I should like to supplement the account just given by referring to two intellectual influences that have, I believe, impinged upon and helped to shape the thinking of the New Analytical Jurists. One of these is the common-language philosophy associated with the name of J. L. Austin; the other is utilitarianism.

In general the practice of ordinary-language philosophy consists in digging out and clarifying the distinctions embedded in everyday linguistic usage. In whatever field these distinctions are

---

12. McCall and Simmons, *Identities and Interactions* (1966), p. 42.

found, there seems to be a kind of presumption that they will prove valid and useful and that once they have been fully articulated there is no need to go further. An exemplification of the method is offered by Hart's intense interest in the distinction between "being obliged" and "having an obligation." Some useful insights have been derived through this method; there is indeed a lot of tacit and subtle wisdom concealed in the interstices of everyday speech. But the tendency of the practitioners of this method has been to regard as an end in itself what ought to be viewed as a useful adjunct to philosophic thought. As Stuart Hampshire has observed, there seems to be an assumption among linguistic philosophers that distinctions disentangled from ordinary speech have a utility that is independent of the context of any particular problem and that these distinctions can be transferred freely from one problem to another.[13] I agree with Hampshire that this is a serious mistake.

I shall call attention later to some instances in which the assumptions of ordinary-language have, in my opinion, misled certain of my critics. For the time being let me just note one illustrative outcropping of the spirit of this philosophy. On pages 124–29 I suggested that the problems involved in maintaining the integrity of a legal system were characteristic not only of state and national law, but affected also the creation and administration of the internal law of such associational forms as churches, clubs, universities, and labor unions. I declared therefore that for purposes of my analysis the internal regulations of these bodies were "law." Hart calls this assertion "unashamed,"[14] while Summers was so unnerved by it he could find nothing better to say than that it was another instance of what he regards as my life-long intellectual dedication, that is, to an activity he calls

13. "J. L. Austin and Philosophy," 62 *Journal of Philosophy* 511–13 (1965).

14. "This large conception of law, admittedly and unashamedly, includes the rules of clubs, churches, schools 'and a hundred and one other forms of human association.'" Supra n. 3, p. 1281.

"axe-grinding."[15] Surely in a dispassionate analysis one should be permitted to suggest that the ordinary usages of the word "law" may obscure, as well as reveal, essential similarities.

A second major influence on the thinking of the New Analytical Jurists derives from the utilitarian philosophy. It is often considered that the basic fault of utilitarianism is its tendency to trivialize ends. The more basic fault lies, I think, in its falsification of the relation of means and ends—a fault mitigated but certainly not cured by what is called rule-utilitarianism. The utilitarian philosophy encourages us in the intellectually lazy notion that means are a mere matter of expediency and that nothing of general significance can be said of them; it makes us forget that in a legal system, and in the institutional forms of society generally, what is means from one point of view is end from another and that means and ends stand in a relation of pervasive interaction.

Is Some Minimum Respect for the Principles of Legality Essential to the Existence of a Legal System?

In my second chapter I indicated that a sufficiently gross departure from the principles of legality therein set forth would result in something that was not simply bad law, but not law at all. Do my critics agree with this conclusion? It would seem they do.

In his *Concept of Law,* responding in part to points I had made in our exchange of 1958, Hart indicated his acceptance of the proposition that to bring law into existence there must be some minimum respect for what "lawyers term principles of legality."[16] In a similar vein Cohen writes, "Fuller's 'canons' . . . are . . . a tolerable start at producing a set of conditions necessary for the presence of a (modern) legal system. . . . One might argue with Fuller's list, but there can be no doubt that some list of this

---

15. Summers, review listed on p. 244, at p. 22. In this review Professor Summers finds occasion six times to characterize passages in my book as "axe-grinding"; see pp. 15, 18, 19, 20, 22, and 24.
16. P. 202.

sort is correct."[17] Dworkin puts it this way: "I accept Fuller's conclusion that some degree of compliance with his eight canons of law is necessary to produce (or equally as important, to apply) any law, even bad law."[18] Summers is more cautious: "at least some of [Fuller's] opponents would not deny that if we are to have law at all, we must have some compliance with [his] 'principles of legality.' "[19]

My four critics, then, do not embrace the Kelsenian doctrine of the Identity of Law and the State; they do not assert that any-thing—even a grunt or a groan—is law provided only it comes from a source identified by the Rule of Recognition; they share the view that before what emanates from that source can be called law, it must conform to certain standards that will enable it to function meaningfully in men's lives.

On this general issue, then, the agreement between my critics and me seems, in words at least, complete. To what extent this appearance of agreement conceals underlying differences cannot, unfortunately, be answered without some recourse to the for-bidden concept of Purpose; we have to ask, in other words, *to what end* is law being so defined that it cannot "exist" with-out some minimum respect for the principles of legality? I'm afraid that when we pursue that inquiry we shall find that my critics and I have quite different answers to this question of "why." I shall for the moment, however, postpone that inquiry, which will find a more congenial environment in my next section.

Meanwhile, I should like to explore briefly a collateral point raised by Dworkin. This lies in his assertion that the existence of law cannot be a matter of degree; law exists or it does not, it cannot half-exist. "Some concepts are almost always matters of degree (baldness is an example)," but law is not of that class. If we wish to talk about the existence and non-existence of law we must "to some extent calibrate the concept of law" by estab-lishing a kind of "threshold" that will mark the line between law

17. Supra n. 6, at p. 648.
18. See the article cited supra n. 7, at p. 669.
19. See the review listed on p. 244, at p. 25.

and non-law.[20] When, through a deterioration in governmental respect for legality, law passes that threshold it ceases all at once to exist; in other words, law does not just fade away, but goes out with a bang.

Dworkin makes no attempt to explain why this should be so— why, in his view, a man can be half-bald, but a country cannot be ruled by a system that is half-law. I suspect that the distinction taken by Dworkin is tacitly drawn from the usages of ordinary language. In ordinary speech the word "law" is indeed an either-or word; it stands in this respect in contrast with even so close a cousin as the word "justice." Consider, for example, these two statements: "The act you propose would be a little bit unjust." "The act you propose would be a little bit illegal." The second sentence is infected with an inevitable flavor of irony, which is not present, or not present to the same degree, in the first. We are accustomed to thinking of justice as something that may be difficult to define; we do not cringe at an open recognition that its boundaries may be shaded and uncertain. The word "law," on the other hand, contains a built-in bias toward the black-and-white. Since law is a man-made thing, we assume—and the assumption shapes our use of words—that if we but put enough effort into the task, we shall be able to define with exactitude what is lawful and what is not. The usages of language in effect express a resolution not to relax in that effort. We may know perfectly well that a particular statute is so vaguely drawn that it is impossible to determine just where its boundaries lie, but our modes of speaking about the matter will normally continue to run in either-or terms. And this is so not only of the lawfulness or un-lawfulness of acts but of the "existence" of a legal system as a whole.

In fairness to Dworkin I should say that he seems not to take his own point with great seriousness, though he does not hesitate to accuse me of a "mistake" in not recognizing the essential difference between baldness and legality. In any event, neither the

20. Supra n. 7, at pp. 677–78.

dictates of ordinary language nor the insistences of the New Analytical Jurisprudence need cause any serious inconvenience; if one wishes to avoid saying that the law of *Country A* is more truly law than that of *Country B,* one can simply affirm that the government of *A* displays a greater respect for the principles of legality than does the government of *B.* If one is addressing an audience that has had its tolerance for metaphor and oxymoron reduced through exposure to ordinary-language philosophy, the course of prudence will be to choose the second and more routine form of expression.

Do the Principles of Legality Constitute an "Internal Morality of Law"?

The title of my second chapter, *The Morality that Makes Law Possible,* represents a thesis my four reviewers find thoroughly unacceptable. In attempting a response to their criticisms I shall strive to avoid any escalation of polemics, for the level I confront on this issue is already uncomfortably high. "Axe-grinding," "absurd," "bizarre," "grotesque"—these are some of the terms my critics find necessary in characterizing my thesis that there is such a thing as an internal morality of law.

According to my four critics the notion of an internal morality of law betrays a basic confusion between efficacy and morality. Some respect for the eight principles of legality is essential if law is to be effective, but that does not mean that these principles are moral in nature, any more than holding a nail straight in order to hit it right is a matter of morality. You won't drive the nail properly if you don't hold it straight and so also you won't achieve an effective system of law unless you give some heed to what I have called principles of legality. Neither of these exercises of common prudence has anything to do with morality.

So runs the argument of my critics. They are not content, however, with any such prosaic comparison as that offered by the driving of nails. Instead, they assert that if there is such a thing as an internal morality of law-making and law-administering, then there must also be an internal morality of even the most disreputable and censurable of human activities. Cohen asks whether there is a lapse in morality when a would-be assassin forgets to load his gun;[21] Dworkin raises a similar question about an inept attempt at blackmail.[22] As usual, Hart is at once the most eloquent and most explicit of my critics:

> the author's insistence on classifying these principles of legality as a "morality" is a source of confusion both for him and his readers . . . the crucial objection to the designation of these principles of good legal craftsmanship as morality, in spite of the qualification "inner," is that it perpetrates a confusion between two notions that it is vital to hold apart: the notions of purposive activity and morality. Poisoning is no doubt a purposive activity, and reflections on its purpose may show that it has its internal principles. ("Avoid poisons however lethal if they cause the victim to vomit," or "Avoid poisons however lethal if their shape, color, or size is likely to attract notice.") But to call these principles of the poisoner's art "the morality of poisoning" would simply blur the distinction between the notion of efficiency for a purpose and those final judgments about activities and purposes with which morality in its various forms is concerned.[23]

I must confess that this line of argument struck me at first as being so bizarre, and even perverse, as not to deserve an answer. Reflection has, however, convinced me that I was mistaken in this. As I now view the matter no issue in the exchange between me and my critics reveals more clearly the tacit presuppositions that each side brings to the debate; taking seriously this argument that the alleged internal morality of law is merely a matter of efficacy has helped me to clarify not only the unarticulated "starting points" of my critics, but my own as well.

21. Supra n. 6, at p. 651.
22. Supra n. 6, at p. 634.
23. Supra n. 3, at pp. 1285–86.

That something is here involved more basic than any mere quibble about the word "morality" becomes apparent when we note the fundamental obscurity of my critics' position. Just what do they have in mind when they speak of efficacy? It is not hard to see what is meant by efficacy when you are trying to kill a man with poison; if he ends up dead, you have succeeded; if he is still alive and able to strike back, you have failed. But how do we apply the notion of efficacy to the creation and administration of a thing as complex as a whole legal system? Let me offer an example drawn from the recent history of the Soviet Union that will suggest some of the difficulties involved in answering that question.

At the beginning of the 1960s the problem of economic crimes (including illegal transactions in foreign currencies) had apparently reached such proportions in Russia that the Soviet authorities decided drastic countermeasures were in order. Accordingly in May and July of 1961 statutes were passed subjecting such crimes to the death penalty. These statutes were then applied retrospectively and convicted men were put to death for acts which, while not lawful when committed, were not then subject to the death penalty.

The purpose of the Soviet authorities was obviously to make people quit stealing from the state. Was a retrospective application of the death penalty "inefficacious" for this purpose? One of the problems of criminal law is to convey to the prospective criminal that you are not engaged in a game of idle threats, that you mean what you say. Is there any more effective way of conveying that message than the restrospective application of a criminal penalty? The very fact that it marks a drastic departure from ordinary practice is, in effect, a pledge of the earnestness of the lawgiver. Yet there were Russians who were disturbed by this action of the authorities, as my colleague Harold Berman reports in the following passage:

> I asked a leading Soviet jurist if he could explain the decision of the Supreme Court of the Russian Republic applying the

July law retroactively—in clear violation, it seemed to me, of the 1958 Fundamental Principles of Criminal Procedure. He replied, "We lawyers didn't like that"—a statement as interesting for the "we lawyers" as for the "didn't like that."[24]

Now it is reasonable to suppose, I think, that the Soviet lawyer was not asserting that the action of the authorities was an ineffective measure for combating economic crime. He was saying that it involved a compromise of principle, an impairment of the integrity of the law. As Berman remarks with reference to this conversation: "it is the lawyers who understand best of all, perhaps, the integrity of law, the universality of legal standards— in other words, the threat to legality *in general* which is posed by any *particular* infringement of legality."[25]

At this point I can imagine my critics pulling at my sleeve: "Ah, but you have misunderstood what we meant by efficacy. We did not have in mind short-run efficacy in meeting some passing emergency. The Soviet action impaired the efficacy of law because it tended to undermine public confidence in legal rules generally and reduced the incentive to obey them. It achieved an immediate gain at a cost in the damage done to the institution of law generally." But plainly if my critics begin to expand the notion of efficacy in this direction, they will soon find themselves drifting across the boundary they have so painstakingly set up to distinguish morality from efficacy. They are likely to get themselves into the predicament of those who try to convert all morality into enlightened selfishness and who end up with so much enlightenment, and so little selfishness, that they might have saved themselves a good deal of trouble by simply talking about morality in the first place.

I do not think, therefore, that in discussing problems of legality any useful joinder of issue is achieved by opposing ef-

24. Berman, "The Struggle of Soviet Jurists Against a Return to Stalinist Terror," 22 *Slavic Review* 314–20, at p. 315 (1963).
25. Ibid., p. 320.

ficacy to morality; certainly nothing is attained that justifies treating the use of the word "morality" in this connection as an exercise in obfuscation. In truth, the appeal of "efficacy" does not lie in any definiteness of its meaning, but in the tough-sounding, positivistic flavor of the word; it suggests an observer clear-eyed and result-oriented, not easily misled by fuzzy concepts of purpose. In other words, my critics' preference for "efficacy" over "morality" reflects the influence of deep-seated and largely unarticulated resolutions of the mind, rather than any reasoned-out conclusion about a specific issue.

I confront therefore the most unwelcome task of demonstrating that my critics' rejection of an internal morality of law rests on premises they have not themselves brought to expression in their writings. Let me make it clear, however, that I do not purport to explore unavowed emotional biases; my efforts lie in the realm of the intellect, in the exploration of an implicit structure that shapes my critics' thought processes. If their conclusions do not imply the premises I ascribe to them, they are at liberty to set me straight.

Proceeding then to the task at hand, I perceive *two* assumptions underlying my critics' rejection of "the internal morality of law." The *first* of these is a belief that the existence or nonexistence of law is, from a moral point of view, a matter of indifference. The *second* is an assumption I have already described as characteristic of legal positivism generally. This is the assumption that law should be viewed not as the product of an interplay of purposive orientations between the citizen and his government but as a one-way projection of authority, originating with government and imposing itself upon the citizen.

In the literature of legal positivism it is of course standard practice to examine at length the relations of law and morals. With respect to the influence of morals on law it is common to point out that moral conceptions may guide legislation, furnish standards for the criticism of existing law, and may properly be taken into account in the interpretation of law. The treatment of the converse influence—that of law on morality—is generally more meager, being confined chiefly to the observation that legal rules long established tend, through a kind of cultural conditioning, to be regarded as morally right.

What is generally missing in these accounts is any recognition of the role legal rules play in making possible an effective realization of morality in the actual behavior of human beings. Moral principles cannot function in a social vacuum or in a war of all against all. To live the good life requires something more than good intentions, even if they are generally shared; it requires the support of firm base lines for human interaction, something that —in modern society at least—only a sound legal system can supply.

"Do not take what belongs to another" is about as trite an example of a moral precept as can be found in the books. But how do we decide what belongs to another? To answer that question we resort not to morals but to law. In some contexts we can, of course, talk meaningfully of a person's being morally entitled to some object of property. For example, an ailing mother has two daughters. One of them foregoes marriage and devotes herself for many years to looking after the invalid parent; the other selfishly refuses to go near her mother or to contribute anything to her care. On the mother's death it is found that she left no will; under the law the two daughters succeed equally to their mother's meager estate. Here we may say that the faithful daughter is morally entitled to the whole estate, even though the law apportions it equally. Indeed, in court decisions involving situations such as I have described, a strain in the judicial process can often be plainly discerned and doubtful interpretations of fact and of law are sometimes indulged in to give the deserving daughter what she ought to have. At the same time, it is perfectly clear that no society could function on the basis of the principle, "Let all property be apportioned in accordance with moral desert." So it is that the moral precept, "Do not take what belongs to another," must of necessity rest on standards borrowed from the law; without that support it could not achieve reality in the conduct of human affairs.

205

Again, all would agree, I suppose, that the institution of marriage has moral implications—indeed, many of them. But this institution can scarcely function—morally or legally—without some fairly definite rule that will enable us to know when the marital state exists. An illustration drawn from Hoebel's chapter, "The Eskimo: Rudimentary Law in a Primitive Anarchy," may be instructive here.[26] It appears that among the Eskimos the concept of marriage exists, but there are lacking clear signposts "which might demarcate the beginning and the end of a marital relationship." The result is that what one man views as a fair contest for the lady's favors, the other may see as an adulterous invasion of his home; in Hoebel's words there are "no cultural devices signalizing marriage in such a way as to keep out trespassers." In consequence Eskimo society is beset by an inordinate number of violent quarrels arising out of sexual jealousy and these quarrels in turn produce a high rate of homicide. Plainly the remedy here is not to be found in preaching, but in some explicit legislative measure that will define and set visible boundaries around the marital relation. The Eskimos simply lack the social machinery needed to accomplish this task; the consequent non-existence of needed law may be said to impoverish seriously the quality of their lives.

So when we speak of "the moral neutrality of law" we cannot mean that the existence and conscientious administration of a legal system are unrelated to a realization of moral objectives in the affairs of life. If respect for the principles of legality is essential to produce such a system, then certainly it does not seem absurd to suggest that those principles constitute a special morality of role attaching to the office of law-maker and law-administrator. In any event the responsibilities of that office deserve some more flattering comparison than that offered by the practices of the thoughtful and conscientious poisoner who never forgets to tear the chemist's label off before he hands the bottle to his victim.

26. *The Law of Primitive Man,* Ch. 5, at pp. 83–85 (1954).

To regard as morally indifferent the existence or non-existence of law is to assume that moral precepts retain the same meaning regardless of the social context into which they are projected. It thus illustrates what I have previously described as an abstraction from the social dimension; it brings to expression a distaste for phenomena of interaction characteristic of positivistic thought. This bent of mind comes openly to the fore in the second assumption underlying my critics' rejection of the notion of an internal morality of law. This is the assumption that the essential reality of law is perceived when we picture it as a one-way projection of authority originating with government and imposing itself upon the citizen. Since this assumption is shared by unreflective common sense, and finds tacit recognition in the ordinary usages of language, it will be well to examine in some detail what is wrong with it.

Let me begin by putting in opposition to one another two forms of social ordering that are often confounded. One of these is *managerial direction,* the other is *law*. Both involve the direction and control of human activity; both imply subordination to authority. An extensive vocabulary is shared by the two forms: "authority," "orders," "control," "jurisdiction," "obedience," "compliance," "legitimacy,"—these are but a few of the terms whose double residence is a source of confusion.

A general and summary statement of the distinction between the two forms of social ordering might run somewhat as follows: The directives issued in a managerial context are *applied* by the subordinate in order to serve a purpose set by his superior. The law-abiding citizen, on the other hand, does not *apply* legal rules to serve specific ends set by the lawgiver, but rather *follows* them in the conduct of his own affairs, the interests he is presumed to serve in following legal rules being those of society generally. The directives of a managerial system regulate primarily the relations between the subordinate and his superior and only collaterally the relations of the subordinate with third persons. The rules of a legal system, on the other hand, normally serve the primary purpose of setting the citizen's relations with other citizens and only in a collateral manner his relations with the seat of authority from which the rules proceed. (Though we sometimes think of the criminal law as defining the citizen's duties toward his government, its primary function is to provide a sound and stable framework for the interactions of citizens with one another.)

The account just given could stand much expansion and qualification; the two forms of social ordering present themselves in actual life in many mixed, ambiguous, and distorted forms. For our present purposes, however, we shall attempt to clarify the essential difference between them by presupposing what may be called "ideal types." We shall proceed by inquiring what implications the eight principles of legality (or analogues thereof) have for a system of managerial direction as compared with their implications for a legal order.

Now five of the eight principles are quite at home in a managerial context. If the superior is to secure what he wants through the instrumentality of the subordinate he must, first of all, communicate his wishes, or "promulgate" them by giving the subordinate a chance to know what they are, for example, by posting them on a bulletin board. His directives must also be reasonably clear, free from contradiction, possible of execution and not changed so often as to frustrate the efforts of the subordinate to act on them. Carelessness in these matters may seriously impair the "efficacy" of the managerial enterprise.

What of the other three principles? With respect to the requirement of generality, this becomes, in a managerial context, simply a matter of expediency. In actual practice managerial control is normally achieved by standing orders that will relieve the superior from having to give a step-by-step direction to his subordinate's performance. But the subordinate has no justification for complaint if, in a particular case, the superior directs him to depart from the procedures prescribed by some general order. This means, in turn, that in a managerial relation there is no room for a formal principle demanding that the actions of the superior conform to the rules he has himself announced; in this context the principle of "congruence between official action and declared rule" loses its relevance. As for the principle against restrospectivity, the problem simply does not arise; no manager retaining a semblance of sanity would direct his subordinate today to do something on his behalf yesterday.

From the brief analysis just presented it is apparent that the managerial relation fits quite comfortably the picture of a one-way projection of authority. Insofar as the principles of legality (or, perhaps I should say, their managerial analogues) are here applicable they are indeed "principles of efficacy"; they are instruments for the achievement of the superior's ends. This does not mean that elements of interaction or reciprocity are ever wholly absent in a managerial relation. If the superior habitually overburdens those under his direction, confuses them by switching signals too frequently, or falsely accuses them of departing from instructions they have in fact faithfully followed, the morale of his subordinates will suffer and they may not do a good job for him; indeed, if his inconsiderateness goes too far, they may end by deserting his employ or turning against him in open revolt. But this tacit reciprocity of reasonableness and restraint is something collateral to the basic relation of order-giver and order-executor.

With a legal system the matter stands quite otherwise, for here the existence of a relatively stable reciprocity of expectations between lawgiver and subject is part of the very idea of a functioning legal order. To see why and in what sense this is true it is essential to continue our examination of the implications of the eight principles, turning now to their implications for a system of law. Though the principles of legality are in large measure interdependent, in distinguishing law from managerial direction the key principle is that I have described as "congruence between official action and declared rule."

Surely the very essence of the Rule of Law is that in acting upon the citizen (by putting him in jail, for example, or declaring invalid a deed under which he claims title to property) a government will faithfully apply rules previously declared as those to be followed by the citizen and as being determinative of his rights and duties. If the Rule of Law does not mean this, it means nothing. Applying rules faithfully implies, in turn, that rules will take the form of general declarations; it would make little sense, for example, if the government were today to enact a special law whereby Jones should be put in jail and then tomorrow were "faithfully" to follow this "rule" by actually putting him in jail. Furthermore, if the law is intended to permit a man to conduct his own affairs subject to an obligation to observe certain restraints imposed by superior authority, this implies that he will not be told at each turn what to do; law furnishes a baseline for self-directed action, not a detailed set of instructions for accomplishing specific objectives.

The twin principles of generality and of faithful adherence by government to its own declared rules cannot be viewed as offering mere counsels of expediency. This follows from the basic difference between law and managerial direction; law is not, like management, a matter of directing other persons how to accomplish tasks set by a superior, but is basically a matter of providing the citizenry with a sound and stable framework for their interactions with one another, the role of government being that of standing as a guardian of the integrity of this system.

I have previously said that the principle against retrospective rule-making is without significance in a context of managerial direction simply because no manager in his right mind would be tempted to direct his subordinate today to do something yesterday. Why do things stand differently with a legal system? The answer is, I believe, both somewhat complex and at the same time useful for the light it sheds on the differences between managerial direction and law.

The first ingredient of the explanation lies in the concept of legitimation. If A purports to give orders to B, or to lay down rules for his conduct, B may demand to know by what title A claims the power to exercise a direction over the conduct of other persons. This is the kind of problem Hart had in mind in formulating his Rule of Recognition. It is a problem shared by lawmaking and managerial direction alike, and may be said to involve a principle of *external* legitimation. But the Rule of Law demands of a government that it also legitimate its actions toward citizens by a second and *internal* standard. This standard requires that within the general area covered by law acts of government toward the citizen be in accordance with (that is, be authorized or validated by) general rules previously declared by government itself. Thus, a lawful government may be said to accomplish an internal validation of its acts by an exercise of its own legislative power. If a prior exercise of that power can effect this validation, it is easy to slip into the belief that the same validation can be accomplished retrospectively.

What has just been said may explain why retrospective legislation is not rejected out of hand as utterly nonsensical. It does not, however, explain why retrospective law-making can in some instances actually serve the cause of legality. To see why this is so we need to recall that under the Rule of Law control over the citizen's actions is accomplished, not by specific directions, but by *general* rules expressing the principle that like cases should be given like treatment. Now abuses and mishaps in the operations of a legal system may impair this principle and require as a cure retrospective legislation. The retrospective statute cannot serve as a baseline for the interactions of citizens with one another, but it can serve to heal infringements of the principle that like cases should receive like treatment. I have given illustrations of this in my second chapter. As a further example one may imagine a situation in which a new statute, changing the law, is enacted and notice of this statute is conveyed to all the courts in the country except those in *Province X,* where through some failure of communication the courts remain uninformed of the change. The courts of this province continue to apply the old law; those in the remaining portions of the country decide cases by the new law. The principle that like cases should be given like treatment is seriously infringed, and the only cure (at best involving a choice of evils) may lie in retrospective legislation.[27] Plainly problems

27. In *Anatomy of the Law* (1968), pp. 14–15, I have given an historical example of retroactive (and "special") legislation designed to cure a judicial departure from legality.

of this sort cannot arise in a managerial context, since managerial direction is not in principle required to act by general rule and has no occasion to legitimate specific orders by showing that they conform to previously announced general rules.

We have already observed that in a managerial context it is difficult to perceive anything beyond counsels of expediency in the remaining principles of legality—those requiring that rules or orders be promulgated, clear in meaning, noncontradictory, possible of observance, and not subject to too frequent change. One who thinks of law in terms of the managerial model will assume as a matter of course that these five principles retain the same significance for law. This is particularly apt to be true of the desideratum of clarity. What possible motive, one may ask, other than sheer slovenliness, would prompt a legislator to leave his enactments vague and indefinite in their coverage?

The answer is that there are quite understandable motives moving him in that direction. A government wants its laws to be clear enough to be obeyed, but it also wants to preserve its freedom to deal with situations not readily foreseeable when the laws are enacted. By publishing a criminal statute government does not merely issue a directive to the citizen; it also imposes on itself a charter delimiting its powers to deal with a particular area of human conduct. The loosely phrased criminal statute may reduce the citizens' chance to know what is expected of him, but it expands the powers of government to deal with forms of misbehavior which could not be anticipated in advance. If one looks at the matter purely in terms of "efficacy" in the achievement of governmental aims, one might speak of a kind of optimum position between a definiteness of coverage that is unduly restrictive of governmental discretion and a vagueness so pronounced that it will not only fail to frighten the citizen away from a general area of conduct deemed undesirable, but may also rob the statute of its power to lend a meaningful legitimation to action taken pursuant to it.

Opposing motivations of this sort become most visible in a bureaucratic context where men deal, in some measure, face to face. Often managerial direction is accompanied by, and inter-twined with miniature legal systems affecting such matters as dis-cipline and special privileges. In such a context it is a common-place of sociological observation that those occupying posts of authority will often resist not only the clarification of rules, but even their effective publication. Knowledge of the rules, and free-dom to interpret them to fit the case at hand, are important sources of power. One student in this field has even concluded that the "toleration of illicit practices actually enhances the con-trolling power of superiors, paradoxical as it may seem."[28] It enhances the superior's power, of course, by affording him the opportunity to obtain gratitude and loyalty through the grant of absolutions, at the same time leaving him free to visit the full rigor of the law on those he considers in need of being brought into line. This welcome freedom of action would not be his if he could not point to rules as giving significance to his actions; one cannot, for example, forgive the violation of a rule unless there is a rule to violate. This does not mean, however, that the rule has to be free from obscurity, or widely publicized, or consistently en-forced. Indeed, any of these conditions may curtail the discretion of the man in control—a discretion from which he may derive not only a sense of personal power but also a sense, perhaps not wholly perverse, of serving well the enterprise of which he is a part.

It may seem that in the broader, more impersonal processes of a national or state legal system there would be lacking any im-pulse toward deformations or accommodations of the sort just suggested. This is far from being the case. It should be remem-bered, for example, that in drafting almost any statute, par-ticularly in the fields of criminal law and economic regulation, there is likely to occur a struggle between those who want to preserve for government a broad freedom of action and those whose primary concern is to let the citizen know in advance where he stands. In confronting this kind of problem there is room in

28. Blau, *The Dynamics of Bureaucracy* (2d ed. 1963), p. 215.

close cases for honest differences of opinion, but there can also arise acute problems of conscience touching the basic integrity of legal processes. Over wide areas of governmental action a still more fundamental question can be raised: whether there is not a damaging and corrosive hypocrisy in pretending to act in accordance with preestablished rules when in reality the functions exercised are essentially managerial and for that reason demand —and on close inspection are seen to exhibit—a rule-free response to changing conditions.

What has just been said can offer only a fleeting glimpse of the responsibilities, dilemmas, and temptations that confront those concerned with the making and administering of laws. These problems are shared by legislators, judges, prosecutors, commissioners, probation officers, building inspectors, and a host of other officials, including—above all—the patrolman on his beat. To attempt to reduce these problems to issues of "efficacy" is to trivialize them beyond recognition.

Why, then, are my critics so intent on maintaining the view that the principles of legality represent nothing more than maxims of efficiency for the attainment of governmental aims? The answer is simple. The main ingredients of their analysis are not taken from law at all, but from what has here been called managerial direction. One searches in vain in their writings for any recognition of the basic principle of the Rule of Law—that the acts of a legal authority toward the citizen must be legitimated by being brought within the terms of a previous declaration of general rules.

This omission is conspicuous throughout Hart's *Concept of Law*. His only extended treatment of the principle of generality, for example, seems plainly inspired by the managerial model:

> Even in a complex large society, like that of a modern state, there are occasions when an official, face to face with an individual, orders him to do something. A policeman orders a particular motorist to stop or a particular beggar to move on. But these simple situations are not, and could not be,

the standard way in which law functions, if only because no society could support the number of officials necessary to secure that every member of society was officially and separately informed of every act which he was required to do. Instead such particularized forms of control are either exceptional or reinforcements of general forms of directions which do not name, and are not addressed to, particular individuals, and do not indicate a particular act to be done. (Pp. 20–21.)

Other comments by Hart on the principle of generality, while less explicit, in no way qualify the statement just quoted. (See pp. 38, 121, 202, 236.) All run in terms of providing "instruments of social control" and of enabling "social control to function."

With respect to what I have called the principle requiring "congruence between official action and declared rule," Hart's comments again relate to the problem of achieving "effective control" over the citizen's actions; failure of this control is said to be illustrated when the criminal law is so laxly enforced that the public ends by ignoring it. (See pp. 23, 82, 141.) The only departure from what may be called the managerial frame of reference is found in some remarks (pp. 156, 202) about an abstract affinity between the ideal of justice and an efficiently run legal system; both are said to respect the principle that like cases should be given like treatment. Thus "we have, in the bare notion of applying a general rule of law, the germ at least of justice." There is no intimation that a government has toward the citizen any obligation to realize this "germ of justice" in the way it makes and administers laws; the point seems to be simply that if we happen to observe a well-run legal system in operation we shall discover in it a certain formal resemblance to justice.

Thus, it will be seen that Hart's concept of law, being based essentially on the managerial model,[29] contains no element in-

29. It may be well at this point to mention briefly one possible source of misunderstanding. A reader generally familiar with Hart's *Concept of Law* may recall that he explicitly rejects Austin's "command theory of law." To one who does not have in mind just what this rejection implies, it may seem

consistent with the view that law is a one-way projection of authority. This does not mean, of course, that the lawgiver can bring a legal system into existence by himself; like the manager he requires the acquiescence and cooperation of those subject to his direction. This is recognized quite explicitly and with his usual aptness of phrasing by Hart himself:

> if a system of rules is to be imposed by force on any, there must be a sufficient number who accept it voluntarily. Without their voluntary cooperation, thus creating *authority,* the coercive power of law and government cannot be established. (P. 196.)

There is no suggestion here that the citizen's voluntary cooperation must be matched by a corresponding cooperative effort on the part of government. There is no recognition in Hart's analysis that maintaining a legal system in existence depends upon the discharge of interlocking responsibilities—of government toward the citizen and of the citizen toward government.

If we assume, as I do here, that an element of commitment by the lawgiver is implicit in the concept of law, then it will be well to attempt to spell out briefly in what form this commitment manifests itself. In a passage headed by his translator "Interaction in the Idea of Law," Simmel suggests that underlying a legal system

---

that in disapproving of the command theory Hart is also rejecting what I have here described as a managerial theory of law. This would, however, be to misunderstand Hart's argument. Hart rejects the command theory chiefly on two grounds: (1) it sees the force of law as residing in the threat of sanctions, rather than in an acceptance of authority; (2) Austin's theory presupposes direct communication between lawgiver and legal subject. But, plainly, effective managerial direction rests, much more obviously than does law, on a willingness to accept authoritative direction. Furthermore, managerial directions need not be conveyed in a face-to-face manner; they are in fact commonly embodied in something like a manual of operations or may be set forth on a bulletin board. The crucial point in distinguishing law from managerial direction lies in a commitment by the legal authority to abide by its own announced rules in judging the actions of the legal subject. I can find no recognition of this basic notion in *The Concept of Law.*

is a contract between lawgiver and subject.[30] By enacting laws government says to the citizen, "These are the rules we ask you to follow. If you will obey them, you have our promise that they are the rules we will apply to your conduct." Certainly such a construction contains at least this much truth: if the citizen knew in advance that in dealing with him government would pay no attention to its own declared rules, he would have little incentive himself to abide by them. The publication of rules plainly carries with it the "social meaning" that the rulemaker will himself abide by his own rules. On the other hand, any attempt to conceive of a legal system as resting on a contract between lawgiver and subject not only stirs inconvenient historical associations, but has a certain incongruity about it, especially when we recall that in a democratic society the same citizen may be both lawgiver and legal subject.

There is an old-fashioned legal term that may offer an escape from our predicament. This is the word "intendment." Our institutions and our formalized interactions with one another are accompanied by certain interlocking expectations that may be called intendments, even though there is seldom occasion to bring these underlying expectations across the threshold of consciousness. In a very real sense when I cast my vote in an election my conduct is directed and conditioned by an anticipation that my ballot will be counted in favor of the candidate I actually vote for. This is true even though the possibility that my ballot will be thrown in the wastebasket, or counted for the wrong man, may never enter my mind as an object of conscious attention. In this sense the institution of elections may be said to contain an intendment that the votes cast will be faithfully tallied, though I might hesitate to say, except in a mood of rhetoric, that the election authorities had entered a contract with me to count my vote as I had cast it.

A passage from Lilburne quoted at the head of my second chapter is eloquently in point on this matter of institutional

30. See the references supra pp. 39–40.

intendments. This is the passage in which Lilburne demands to know "whether ever the Commonwealth, when they chose the Parliament, gave them a lawless and unlimited power, and at their pleasure to walk contrary to their own laws and ordinances before they have repealed them?" Lilburne is suggesting that underlying the institution of parliamentary government there is an intendment—that is, a generally shared tacit expectation—that parliament will act toward the citizen in accordance with its own laws so long as those laws remain unrepealed. A tacit commitment by parliament to that effect is so taken for granted that, except when things go wrong, there is no occasion to talk or even to think about it.

It is, I am aware, quite unfashionable today to say such things as that institutions have or contain intendments. One might cast about for some linguistic cover more acceptable to modern taste; one might, for example, speak of the "role expectations" that accompany the assumption of legislative powers. But by whatever name we call it, we must not ignore the reality of the commitment implied in lawmaking, nor forget that it finds expression in empirically observable social processes; it is not something projected on those processes by a moralistic outside observer.

Silent testimony to the force of this commitment can be found in the strenuous efforts men often make to escape its grip. When we hear someone say he is going to "lay down the law" to someone else, we tend to think of him as claiming a relatively unfettered right to tell others what they ought to do. It is therefore interesting to observe what pains men will often take *not* to "lay down law." When a person in a position of authority is asked to make some concession in a particular case he will not infrequently insist on an understanding that his action shall not be taken "to set a precedent." What he dreads and seeks to escape is the commitment contained in the Rule of Law: to conform his actions toward those under his direction to general rules that he has explicitly or tacitly communicated to them. That the stipulation against setting a precedent often turns out in practice to be ineffective simply provides further evidence of the force of the commitment men tend to read into the acts of those having authority over them.

A similar struggle over the meaning to be attributed to exercises of authority is a familiar accompaniment of the managerial allocation of duties among subordinates. An employer, for example, directs A to perform certain tasks, at the same time assigning a different set of tasks to B. If this division of labor continues for some time any reallocation of functions may arouse resentment and a sense of injury. An employee may resist the assignment of new duties to him, saying, "That's not my job." Conversely, he may oppose the assignment to anyone else of tasks he is accustomed to perform on the ground that these tasks fall within his "jurisdiction." Here the employer thinks of himself as discharging a purely managerial function, free from the restraints that attach to a legislative role. The employees, on the other hand, are apt to read into the employer's actions an element of juristic commitment; they attempt to bring his decisions within the Rule of Law.

The commitment implied in lawmaking is not, then, simply an element in someone's "conceptual model"; it is a part of social reality. I have been emphasizing that obedience to rules loses its point if the man subject to them knows that the rulemaker will not himself pay any attention to his own enactments. The converse of this proposition must also be kept in mind, namely, that the rulemaker will lack any incentive to accept for himself the restraints of the Rule of Law if he knows that his subjects have no disposition, or lack the capacity, to abide by his rules; it would serve little purpose, for example, to attempt a juristic ordering of relations among the inmates of a lunatic asylum. It is in this sense that the functioning of a legal system depends upon a cooperative effort—an effective and responsible interaction—between lawgiver and subject.

A complete failure in this interaction is so remote from ordinary experience that the significance of the interaction itself tends to be lost from our intellectual perspective. Yet in numberless instances, all about us, we can perceive the ways in which the success of law depends on a voluntary collaboration between the citizen and his government, as well as upon a coordination of effort among the various agencies of government concerned with the making and enforcing of law.

In the regulation of traffic the dependence of law on voluntary cooperation often becomes painfully visible. The example I am about to give is by no means entirely hypothetical. In a university city located on the Atlantic seaboard traffic congestion has during the last thirty years presented an increasing problem; at one street intersection in particular the situation has for some time approached a state of crisis. At this intersection there were until recently no stop-and-go signals addressed to pedestrians, and the common law of the situation—as understood by police and pedestrians alike—was that the pedestrian was free to take his own chances in crossing against the flow of vehicular traffic, though if he were particularly foolhardy he might receive a verbal dressing-down from the officer in charge. About three years ago a reform took place; pedestrian signals were installed and signs were posted warning "jaywalkers" that they would be arrested and fined.

For a short time this measure brought an improvement in the situation. Soon, however, a deterioration commenced as pedestrians, discovering that during the slack hours of vehicular traffic no officer was present, began during those hours to disregard the stop signals addressed to them. This disregard then spread into the hours of heavy traffic, quickly reaching such a volume that any police action to restrain it, according even a minimum respect to the principle of "equal justice under law," would have required arrests on such a scale as to have overwhelmed the traffic courts. Despite this epidemic of pedestrian law-breaking, motorists continued for a period to observe the signals directed to them. In time, however, the deterioration progressed to the point where the motorist, held up by trespassing pedestrians while the light was in his favor, often found his first opportunity to cross just as the red light turned against him; this opportunity he began increasingly to embrace. Finally, the law-abiding pedestrian, intent on his own bodily integrity, might discover that the only safe course for him was to join a phalanx of stalwart law-breakers, instead of waiting timidly for the signal legalizing a crossing he would have to negotiate alone, unprotected, and perhaps against a flood of delayed motorists seizing their first opportunity to cross.

When a system of legal controls has suffered this degree of breakdown it is often difficult to allocate blame or to discern what curative measures will be effective. Each human element involved will contend that any mending of its own ways would be rendered pointless by a failure in the performance of complementary roles. And it should be noted that in the case of the intersection just described the roster of those implicated may extend much beyond those already mentioned. It may be that the basic difficulty arises from an unwise routing of traffic through the city as a whole, or from a failure of the taxpayers to finance a police force adequate to its task in numbers and training, or from the action of a transportation authority in relocating a bus stand in such a manner as to render inappropriate the existing disposition of traffic signals. Even the performance of the city electrician may enter into the account. If he fails to keep the automatic traffic lights functioning properly, and as a result they operate erratically, then pedestrians, motorists, and the police may all lose any incentive to act in accordance with the signals; conversely, if the electrician knows that the signals will be ignored even if they are in perfect order, doing his job right will lose its point.

It is unfortunate that the interdependencies involved in the successful operation of a legal system are by no means generally so visible as they are in the regulation of traffic. If we could come to accept what may be called broadly an interactional view of law, many things would become clear that are now obscured by the prevailing conception of law as a one-way projection of authority. It would become clear, for example, that a disregard of the principles of legality may inflict damage on the institution of law itself, even though no immediate harm is done to any individual. This point, along with some others, is ignored in a rhetorical question posed by Dworkin in refutation of my sugges-

221

tion that legal morality embraces a principle against contradictory laws: "A legislature adopts a statute with an overlooked
inconsistency so fundamental as to make the statute an empty
form. Where is the immorality, or lapse of moral ideal?"[31]

Now in the first place even to imagine a case such as Dworkin
supposes requires a fantastic set of assumptions. Suppose, for
example, a statute is passed affecting the validity of foreign divorces; as applied to a particular situation of the fact the statute
seems in one paragraph to say that A is married to Y, while by
the terms of another provision it would appear that he is still
married to X. To make a harmless blank cartridge of such a
statute we would have to suppose that any layman could see,
without having to pay a lawyer to tell him, that the statute was
self-cancelling, that he could confidently foresee that no judicial
ingenuity would suffice to rescue it from nullity, and that with the
dead corpse of the statute removed from the scene the true legal
situation would become immediately obvious. But let us, in favor
of Dworkin's point, indulge ourselves in all these exercises in
whimsy. The case then becomes like that of a man who tells me
a reckless falsehood, but leaves me uninjured because before I
act on what he told me I happen to learn the truth for myself. In
such a case though I may not have suffered any immediate injury,
damage has certainly been done to my relations with the man who
told me the falsehood and my trust of him in any future dealings
will have been impaired.

If we view the law as providing guideposts for human interaction, we shall be able to see that any infringement of the demands of legality tends to undermine men's confidence in, and
their respect for, law generally. It is worth recalling in this connection that there is an ancient crime of disturbing boundary
markers and a very modern crime of moving, destroying, or de-
facing official highway signs. Neither of these crimes requires that
the perpetrator's action inflict any direct injury on anyone. Part
of the basis for such laws is that if the physical pointers by which

31. Supra n. 7, at p. 675.

men guide their actions toward one another are sufficiently tampered with, those that remain intact will lose their meaning and men will no longer feel secure in relying on them. If this is true when men tamper with well-placed markers, what shall we say of the engineer who puts the signs up in the wrong places to start with, or of the legislator who bungles the job of laying out the vital written paragraphs by which men's rights and duties toward one another are defined?

My colleague Henry M. Hart offers us a refreshing reorientation in our usual ways of thinking and talking about law when he reminds us that law may be regarded as a *facility* enabling men to live a satisfactory life in common.[32] If this facility is to serve its intended beneficiaries, they must use it well. But those whose task it is to design and install the facility itself have an even heavier responsibility, which is that of doing their job right in the first place. It is this onerous and often complex responsibility that I have tried to describe by the phrase, "the internal morality of law."

That such a morality could have any intelligible meaning at all is an idea that is emphatically—not to say, vehemently—rejected by my critics. I have tried to show that our differences on this issue stem from a basic disagreement about law itself. This disagreement I have attempted to express by contrasting a view of law that sees it as an interactional process and one that sees in it only a unidirectional exercise of authority. My reviewers have, of course, criticized a number of positions on specific issues taken in my book that I have left unmentioned and undefended here. I believe that most, though not all, of these disagreements on subsidiary matters have their origin in the same fundamental divergence in starting points that I have just examined at length. This is particularly true of my critics' rejection of the suggestion that governmental respect for the internal morality of law will generally be conducive toward a respect for what may be called

32. "The Relations between State and Federal Law," 54 *Columbia Law Review* 489, 490 (1954).

the substantive or external morality of law. The interested reader will find a defense of my position on this issue in a paper I presented in April 1965.[33]

Some Implications of the Debate

In conclusion I should like to explore briefly certain issues that have not been directly raised in the criticisms aimed at my book by the New Analytical Jurists. My reason for going into these issues is that I believe an exploration of them will serve to clarify further the basic differences in viewpoint that underlie our whole debate. The first problem I propose to discuss is that of *interpretation*.[34]

This is a subject treated at some length in my second chapter, where I viewed it as an aspect of the task of maintaining "congruence between official action and declared rule." At the conclusion of my discussion (page 91) I wrote: "With all its subtleties, the problem of interpretation occupies a sensitive, central position in the internal morality of the law. It reveals, as no other problem can, the cooperative nature of the task of maintaining legality."

Despite the basic significance of interpretation for every aspect of the legal enterprise, it has never been a subject with which analytical positivism has felt comfortable. This is precisely be-

33. Supra n. 6, pp. 661–66.
34. Three recent publications deal helpfully with the problem of interpretation: Dworkin, "The Model of Rules," 35 *University of Chicago Law Review* 14–46 (1967); Gottlieb, *The Logic of Choice* (1968); and Hughes, "Rules, Policy and Decision Making," 77 *Yale Law Journal* 411–39 (1968).

There is one vital problem affecting interpretation that I have not attempted to deal with here and that is not mentioned in the articles by Dworkin and Hughes. This is the problem interactional sociologists call "defining the situation." (See, for example, McHugh, *Defining the Situation*, 1968.) When a court applies a rule or a set of rules to the decision of a case one can distinguish two operations: (1) determining the relevant facts; (2) determining the meaning of the relevant rules for these facts. We tend to think that it is our knowledge of the rules that enables us to sift out irrelevancies and to determine what are the legally operative facts. In reality, however, our definition of the situation is generally conditioned by a host

cause it brings to open expression "the cooperative nature of the task of maintaining legality." Close attention to problems of interpretation is something that comports awkwardly with any attempt to conceive of law as a unidirectional exercise of control over human behavior.

It will be instructive to note briefly how writers in the positivistic mood have dealt with the problem of interpretation and have sought to redefine it in terms congenial to their intellectual commitment. In his 1957[35] lecture Hart seemed to assert that in the ordinary run of cases the application of a statute is controlled in a more or less frictionless manner by the common or dictionary meaning of its words. In these usual or normal cases there is no occasion to engage in any conjecture concerning the policies sought to be promoted by the statute or the intentions of its draftsmen. It is only in an occasional borderline or "penumbral" situation that any attempt to fathom legislative purpose becomes necessary. In this lecture Hart inveighed against a disease of jurisprudential thinking which he called "preoccupation with the penumbra." His thesis seemed to be that we should build our edifice of legal philosophy on the routine or run-of-the-mine case and pass over, as irrelevant for the basic analysis of legal phenomena, the occasional difficulties presented in "penumbral" situations. In *The Concept of Law* the word "interpretation" is not to be found in the index, though the thoughts of the Holmes lecture are repeated with some modification on pages 120–32 and 200–01; the viewpoint differs from that expressed in the lecture chiefly in being somewhat less explicit.

Like Hart, his great predecessor, John Austin, largely excluded interpretation from the basic structure of his theory. Unlike Hart, however, when Austin came finally to deal with the subject his

---

of tacit assumptions that do not appear in the explicit rules at all. Gottlieb's book has some valuable observations on this point in Chapter IV, "The Facts," particularly on pages 56–57, where he remarks that "non-legal standards are infused at a crucial step [that is, in defining the relevant facts] in the process of applying legal rules."

35. Supra n. 1, pp. 606–15.

treatment was complex and beset with internal stresses. He distinguished the interpretation of statutory law from the method of "induction" used in applying "judiciary law."[36] At no point did he argue that a statute can or should be applied without reference to legislative purpose, though he asserted that the "literal meaning" of a statute should be taken as the "primary index" of legislative intention.[37] So far from abandoning a purposive interpretation he wrote: "If the causes of laws and of the rights and obligations which they create be not assigned, the laws themselves are unintelligible."[38]

In *The Pure Theory of Law*[39] Kelsen devotes a few concluding pages to the subject of interpretation, asserting in effect that except as a particular result may be excluded by the logical structure of a statute, judicial interpretation is simply a form of legislation, the motives which shape legislation by judges being as irrelevant for analytical positivism as those that move a legislature to pass one kind of statute instead of another. For Kelsen interpretation is, in short, not a part of juristic analysis at all, but belongs rather to politics and sociology.

A different tack in dealing with the embarrassment of interpretation was taken by Gray and some of the American Legal Realists. Since a statute only becomes "hard law" after its meaning has been judicially determined, Gray proposed that we treat statutes as not being law at all, but only sources of law.[40] By this device the definition of law was intended to be moved downward so as to coincide with its application to human affairs. Gray's realism was marred, however, by the fact that much law is applied by bureaucrats, sheriffs, patrolmen, and others acting without judicial guidance. Accordingly, some of the Realists pro-

36. II *Lectures on Jurisprudence* (1879), pp. 648–51.
37. Ibid., pp. 644–45.
38. Ibid., p. 1113.
39. (1967), Ch. VIII, pp. 348–56. (This is a translation of the second German edition.)
40. *Nature and Sources of the Law* (2d ed. 1921), Ch. IV, pp. 300–25 et passim.

posed that we define law as "the behavior patterns of judges and other public officials."[41] This conceit represented the final default, since it left to the onlooker to decide for himself by what standards he should discern and interpret the "behavior patterns" that constitute the ultimate reality of law.

These diverse ways of confronting a shared predicament suggest that there is something fundamentally wrong with the premises that serve to define the problem. I suggest that the difficulty arises because all of the writers whose views have just been summarized start with the assumption that law must be regarded as a one-way projection of authority, instead of being conceived as a collaborative enterprise. If we discern, as a basic element of law, a commitment by government to abide by its own law in judging the acts of its subjects, then interpretation will occupy in theory the central place it has always occupied in our everyday thinking about law. This emphatically does not mean that the problem will become simple; on the contrary its hidden complexities will come to light and we shall no longer be able to pretend that it is a peripheral matter to be left to unreflective common sense.

In seeking a more fruitful approach to interpretation, it may be well to begin with some observations about language itself. The first of these observations is that among human activities language represents the interactional phenomenon par excellence; its forms arise out of and live by interaction. Communication by words is not a matter of shipping packages of meaning from one head to another; it involves an effort to initiate in another mind perceptual processes that will as closely as possible match those taking place in the mind of the communicating party. If I direct words toward you in a situation where some precision in communication is demanded, I shall have to ask myself what precisely I mean by the words I am using, what you would mean if you were using the same words, and what you would suppose I would

41. See the reference supra, n. 10.

be likely to mean by them in the context of our relationship—not to speak of even more complex lines of reciprocating expectations.

Writers in the positivist mood have generally sought escape from complexities of the sort just intimated by adopting a simplistic view of language which I have described (page 84) as "a pointer theory of meaning." For present purposes it will be useful to disregard, for the moment, the complications caused by the intervention of language and consider how the problem of interpretation appears when the task is to discern the meaning, not of words, but of actions.

Suppose for example that in some area of commercial practice certain kinds of dealings have for a long time been directed by tacitly accepted and complementary expectations, each participant guiding his conduct toward the other by these expectations. A somewhat unusual situation arises and a dispute develops between the parties as to the implications of established practice for their respective rights. An arbitrator or judge is called upon to decide the dispute. His task is to interpret the meaning of established practice for a special situation of fact which had not previously been directly operative in shaping the expectations of the transacting parties.

Now it is plain that in such a case the chief guide for the arbiter's decision would be found in a principle hardly intimated in positivistic discussions of interpretation, namely, that the result reached should be such as to fit harmoniously into the system of complementary expectations expressed in past dealings. The problem would not be one of "logical" consistency, but of what might be called purposive compatibility; the question asked would be, What decision will serve best to keep the established practices "a playable game?" To impose a result incongruent with established expectations would be to disrupt a functioning and accepted system which served to regulate the parties' relations with one another. Plainly, in order to reach a satisfactory resolution of the dispute the arbitrator must be able to perceive and comprehend the implications contained in existing practice; his decision cannot be a just and fitting one if he lacks the imagination necessary to put himself in the place of those whose past conduct toward one another he is interpreting.

In the situation just discussed a good decision would, then, exemplify two interrelated qualities; a respect for systematic structure and an understanding of the social context. Now I submit that these desiderata are also applicable to the interpretation of written law. To be sure, if we think of a statute after the analogy of a military order, as being aimed at controlling the actions of one not admitted to the larger strategy, then the task of the interpreter will be to discern as best he can the desires of the high command. On the other hand, if the function of law is to create an orderly interaction among citizens and to furnish dependable guideposts for self-directed action, the problem assumes a different aspect and the principles governing the interpretation of words will not be seen as radically different from those applicable to the interpretation of interactive behavior. In particular, a respect for systematic structure, and a capacity to perceive the needs of the situation, will both be seen as essential for the wise interpretation of written law.

It may be objected that a concealed bias must inevitably infect any analysis which begins, like that just concluded, with an example drawn from commercial practice. It may seem perverse to suggest that the law against murder is intended, except in a remote and largely irrelevant sense, to provide "dependable guideposts for human interaction." Certainly it is true, as I have throughout insisted, that the proper solution to problems of interpretation depends on context. But even in the case of murder, the crucial issues for interpretation are likely to relate to such matters as the plea of self-defense. Any statutory language governing that issue is apt to be vague and general. Those who interpret the law (which in this case will in reality include both judge and jury) must, if they are to do their job well, put themselves in the position in which the accused found himself and ask what can reasonably be expected of a human being so placed. A knowledge of life, a capacity for empathy, and a sense of what kind of rule will provide a workable guide to action, are all essential for a proper decision.

In my second chapter I dealt at some length with the "antinomies" that may confront those responsible for maintaining legality. Frequently some miscarriage in the legal enterprise will create a situation in which it is impossible to escape some compromise of legality, so that the essential task is to reduce the dimensions of that compromise. The most obvious example of this predicament is presented by situations in which a resort to retrospective legislation will seem the lesser of two evils.

In subtle ways interpretation is permeated with problems of this sort. Suppose, for example, that a statute is passed for the purpose of putting in better order some area of human relations. On its face, we may suppose, the enactment is reasonably clear, but it suffers from the fundamental defect that it is based on a misconception of the situation it is intended to correct, the legislature being in this respect like a physician who prescribes a course of treatment for one disease when the patient is in fact suffering from another. By what standards should a court construe such a statute? A tolerably literal application of its terms may be said to carry out the legislative intent as it actually was, though not as it would have been had the legislature known what it was doing. Furthermore, the interpreter must consider the interest of the occasional citizen who, being an outsider to the situation regulated, may take the statute at its face value, experiencing no qualms in doing so precisely because he is as ignorant as the legislature was of the real nature of the situation addressed by the statute. On the other hand, those who are the primary addressees of the statute, that is, those who actually live in and with the situation the statute is intended to correct, may be able to see in it only obscurity, confusion, and perversity. Reading the statute in the light of their more perceptive definition of the situation which is a part of their own lives, they may regard the statute as a kind of non-law. Here there is no easy way out for the court.

Cases of the sort just supposed provide only one illustration of the perplexities presented when a court has to ask itself how far it is free to correct the mistakes of the legislature. An obvious misprint may present no difficulty. But deciding what the legislature would have said if it had been able to express its intention more precisely, or if it had not overlooked the interaction of its statute with other laws already on the books, or if it had realized that the supreme court was about to reverse a relevant precedent—these and other like questions can remind us that there is something more to the task of interpreting statutes than simply "carrying out the intention of the legislature."

The remarks just concluded may seem to suggest that what is demanded of an interpreting agency is simply that it achieve a balance of restraint and initiative in correcting the errors and oversights of superior authority. But, of course, the problem is more complex. The interpreting agency must recall, for example, that its perceived standards of interpretation are likely to create expectations among those affected by them and that sudden shifts in those standards may impair the collaborative effort essential for achieving and maintaining legality. Let us suppose, for example, that the courts of a given jurisdiction have traditionally interpreted statutes in a narrow and restrictively literal manner. An anticipation that this practice will continue is almost certain to enter into the calculations of the legislature; the draftsman will be likely to phrase his statute so that it will, as it were, come out right after having had its scope reduced by restrictive judicial interpretation. A sudden shift by the courts toward freer standards of interpretation may alter the meaning of legislation in a way contrary to the intention of those who enacted it and perhaps in a way that will be confusing for all concerned.

Similarly when a court has occasion to apply the law of a foreign jurisdiction, it is not enough to know the text of the law; that text must be read as it would be read by native jurists, that is, as it would be understood by those sharing the tacit assumptions that enter into the functioning of the legal system of which it is a part. This consideration was brought to unaccustomed explicitness in a decision of the United States District Court sitting in Massachusetts. The disposition of the case required the application not of Federal but of Massachusetts law. Several precedents of the Massachusetts Supreme Judicial Court were in point, and the question was whether that court, if the controversy were before it, would qualify the language of its precedents and make an exception for the case at hand. In answering that question in the negative, Judge Charles Wyzanski considered it essential to look not simply to the language of the Massachusetts decisions but to the general spirit in which those decisions would be approached by the court that rendered them:

> Subtle variations and blurred lines are not characteristic of [the Massachusetts Supreme Judicial Court]. Principles are announced and adhered to in broad magisterial terms. The emphasis is on precedent and adherence to the older ways, not on creating new causes of action or encouraging the use of novel judicial remedies that have sprung up in less conservative communities.[42]

This exercise in applied anthropology is not the sort of thing one ordinarily encounters in judicial opinions. It can serve to remind us, however, how much of our written law is in reality unwritten; it can help us to see that an understanding of the law in the books requires an understanding of the shared assumptions that enter into the making and interpreting of it.[43]

The mention of anthropology offers an easy transition to my next general topic, which has to do with *customary law* and *international law*. Like the problem of interpretation, neither of these subjects has ever found a comfortable haven in positivist theory. As with interpretation, legal positivists in their attitude toward these forms of law waver between icy rejection and acceptance in a bone-crushing embrace. For Austin customary law and international law were simply not law at all, but a kind of pseudo-law that should properly be called positive morality. Kelsen takes the op-

42. *Pomerantz v. Clark,* 101 F. Supp. 341, at p. 346 (1951).
43. In *Anatomy of the Law* (1968) I have tried to trace some of the interactions between what I have there called "made law" and "implicit law." (See especially pp. 43–84.)

posite tack of reshaping these two forms of law so that they can be accommodated to his theory, though at the cost of so distorting their premises that the subjects themselves become largely unrecognizable.

Plainly the conception of law as a unidirectional assertion of control over human behavior is not a view that can easily be applied to customary and international law. These two manifestations of law have been described as *horizontal* forms of order, while the law that a state imposes on its citizens we tend to think of as having only a *vertical* dimension. Stated in another way, the difficulty of conceiving of customary and international law as being properly law arises from the notion that the concept of law involves at the very minimum three elements: a lawgiver and at least two subjects whose relations are put in order by rules imposed on them by the law-making authority. The question that gives trouble is, How can a person, a family, a tribe, or a nation impose law on itself that will control its relations with other persons, families, tribes, or nations? Unlike morality, law cannot be a thing self-imposed; it must proceed from some higher authority.

Now I suggest that all these questions would require radical redefinition if we were to recognize one simple, basic reality, namely, that enacted law itself presupposes a commitment by the governing authority to abide by its own rules in dealing with its subjects. There is, in this sense, a horizontal element in what positivism views as vertically imposed law. If this basic principle of law-making and law-administering were accepted, then most of the embarrassments that beset discussions of international and customary law would be seen as also affecting "real" law. For example, does the governmental obligation to abide by its own rules rest on a "legal" or a "moral" commitment? If the commitment is said to be "legal" then the question will arise, How can the authority that makes and unmakes law bind itself by law? If the commitment is "moral" in nature, then we shall face a different kind of embarrassment. It will then appear that the crucial quality that serves to distinguish law from managerial direction, or military command, or sheer power, is itself infected with a moral element so that the essential distinction between law and morality is fatally compromised.

If, however, we disregard these conceptual tangles and allow our minds to participate vicariously in the responsibilities involved in maintaining the Rule of Law within a modern state, we shall see that meeting those responsibilities requires a complex, collaborative effort, not different in kind from that demanded by systems of customary and international law. We shall also find ourselves forced to deal with the role of custom in systems of law that purport to be wholly enacted. This role becomes obvious where custom is explicitly made a standard of decision, as it is in this country in the frequent references to commercial usage in the Uniform Commercial Code. But customary law (by which we mean primarily the tacit commitments that develop out of interaction) plays an important, though usually silent role, not only in the interpretation of written law, but in helping to supply the gaps that will always be perceived in any body of enacted law.

Among the different systems of enacted law the generally inconspicuous role of custom will vary considerably, but it is safe to say that the tacit expectations that make up customary law will always enter into any practical realization of the ideal of legality. Fidelity to the Rule of Law demands not only that a government abide by its verbalized and publicized rules, but also that it respect the justified expectations created by its treatment of situations not controlled by explicitly announced rules. Even more plainly it requires that government apply written rules in accordance with any generally accepted gloss written into those rules in the course of their administration. Taking all these complications into account will, of course, embarrass the construction of neat juristic theories. But it will ease the transition of legal thought from state-imposed codes to the somewhat messier seeming manifestations of law exemplified in international and customary law.

In today's world customary law is no longer merely a matter of theoretical interest. The newly emerging nations in Africa, Asia, and elsewhere are engaged in a painful and often hazardous transition from tribal and customary law to national systems of

234

enacted law. Legal experts from the western nations, particularly from the United States, are playing an important role as advisers in facilitating this transition. Those who have performed this function have often regretted that they were not more adequately prepared for it by a deeper understanding of legal anthropology. If they had had a better training in that subject, they believe that they would have had a better comprehension of the meaning of customary law for those who live by it.

I would suggest that equally needed is a more adequate anthropology of our own legal system. In my second chapter I speak repeatedly of law as an "enterprise" and I realize that this expression has grated on some ears. But for those who have never attempted to create or live by a system of explicitly enacted rules, law is indeed an enterprise and a very hazardous one. In such a context the neat geometry of legal positivism is not merely largely irrelevant, but becomes positively dangerous.

It should not be supposed that theories about law play no role in the practical business of assisting tribal peoples to subject themselves to a regime of enacted law. Plainly they require some definition of the goal toward which to work. Recently there has been published a symposium under the title *Africa and Law— Developing Legal Systems in African Commonwealth Nations*.[44] The leading article in this collection contains the following statement on its first page:

> Professor Harvey has defined law as "a specific technique of social ordering, deriving its essential character from its reliance upon the prestige, authority, and ultimately the reserved monopoly of force of politically organized society." It is a value-neutral tool. In this view, law has no moral authority merely because it is law; rather, it embraces every aspect of state power. Indeed, as Hans Kelsen has pointed out, there is no difference between the state and law; they are

44. T. W. Hutchinson, ed., 1968. The quotation is from p. 3 of the article by Robert B. Seidman.

235

merely different sides of the same coin. Every state institution is a manifestation of state power and can be viewed either institutionally or legally.

The precise role played by this conception of law in its author's thinking is not clear; he ultimately reaches the conclusion that neither customary law nor the received English law is adequate to the needs of the new African nations. At the same time, I have to say that I cannot imagine a more inappropriate context for the conception of law conveyed in the words just quoted. (I am quite aware that my critics among the New Analytical Jurists do not explicitly embrace the doctrine of the identity of law and the state. But I ask in all seriousness, what tenet of their philosophy, what principle or standard enunciated by them, offers a stopping place short of this ultimate reductio ad absurdum of the positivist point of view?)

Among those concerned in this country with programs for world peace there appears to have developed a certain polarity of viewpoints. One side opts for the earliest possible realization of something like a world legal order, "vertical style." The opposing view is advanced by those who recommend, as the surest route to peace, efforts toward achieving reciprocal accommodations among nations, accommodations that may take the form of explicit treaties, but that may also develop through tacit adjustments that will gradually harden into law. Insofar as this difference in strategies is based on a candid and realistic appraisal of alternatives, it is useful and the debate about it should be continued. I cannot escape the conclusion, however, that at least some of those who are content with nothing short of a world legal authority are influenced not by political and sociological realities but by an impulse toward conceptual neatness, by a conviction that nothing counts as law that does not fit our accustomed definitions of domestic law. A reexamination of those definitions might put the problem of international order in a different light and soften somewhat the present opposition of viewpoints.

It would be inappropriate to leave the twin subjects of international law and customary law without calling attention to a recent book by Michael Barkun, *Law without Sanctions: Order in Primitive Societies and the World Community* (1968). Barkun has many perceptive things to say about the damage done to thinking in the fields of his concern by simplistic theories about law in general. He calls particular attention to the dangers involved when sociologists and anthropologists base their definitions of law on those that have become current in dealing with domestic law:

> Despite the social scientist's abhorrence of mixtures of fact and value, he has tended to look at stateless societies, both international and primitive, from the received perspective of domestic law. Domestic law is unavoidably a highly visible part of his environment. We have here a kind of unconscious cultural bias in which the theoretical framework of the legal profession, which appears to cover law adequately (as we normally see it), has been unquestioningly imported into social science. But once we accept the premise that theories are constructed and not discovered in a sphere of Platonic archetypes, there is little to justify this kind of uncritical appropriation. (P. 11.)

So far I have been discussing the implications of my debate with the New Analytical Jurists for problems that arise within a framework that is largely "legal" in nature. I should like now to turn briefly to the implications of that debate for *the concept of morality*.

In the opening portions of this *Reply* I suggested that analytical legal positivism "lacks a social dimension." As a cure for this defect I have recommended "an interactional theory of law." I am convinced that the concept of morality adopted by my critics suffers, in some measure at least, from the same defect and would profit from the same correction.

In rejecting my notion of an internal morality of law, Hart seems at one point to suggest that the utilitarian principle is itself largely capable of taking over all the functions I have assigned to

237

the eight principles of legality. These principles should be valued, Hart asserts, "so far only as they contribute to human happiness and other substantive moral aims of the law."[45] In the same passage he indicates that retroactive laws are generally to be condemned simply because they "make no contribution to human happiness" and, if they result in punishment, "inflict useless misery." In commenting on these assertions I would remark that even if we were willing to accept the utilitarian principle as the ultimate test of goodness, any meaningful application of that principle must presuppose some stability of interactional processes within a society and this stability is in turn heavily dependent upon the guidelines furnished by a conscientiously administered legal system. One cannot trace the consequences of a particular action through the fabric of society unless that fabric itself preserves some measure of integrity.

A neglect of the interactional dimensions of morality is generally to be found, I think, in my critics' treatment of what I have called the internal morality of law. None of them seems willing to pass an adverse moral judgment on the legislator who, through indifference to the demands of his role, confuses or misplaces the legal guideposts by which men coordinate their actions. Cohen asserts, for example, that there is nothing

> morally outrageous about passing contradictory laws. This is not to say, of course, that such laws might not be passed for reasons that would make them immoral or that a situation inadvertently created might not be abused in an immoral way.[46]

In the same vein Dworkin condemns the legislator who departs from the principles of legality in order to achieve the "deliberate entrapment" of some innocent victim,[47] but is unwilling to censure the legislator who through a neglect of his job brings about a

45. Supra n. 3, p. 1291.
46. Supra n. 6, p. 652.
47. Supra n. 6, p. 637.

condition of legal uncertainty that may give someone else an opportunity to do the entrapping.

Dorothy Emmet has done a great service to ethical philosophy in her book, *Rules, Roles and Relations* (1966), by reintroducing in a cogently argued and perceptive way the ancient concept of social role. Role morality is patently a morality of interaction. But the modes of analysis appropriate to problems of role morality are also relevant to moral problems which do not involve the performance of roles that have been recognized as such. It is for this reason that I believe a study of the complex demands of the internal morality of law would deepen our insight into moral problems generally.

In particular, a close study of the problems encountered in trying to achieve and maintain legality would confront us in an unmistakable way with the problem I have referred to as that of "antinomies," that is, with the sort of dilemma we face when it is necessary to depart from one principle of legal morality to save another. In my second chapter my illustrations of this phenomenon have chiefly to do with cases where the correction of some mishap or oversight requires a departure from the normal practices of legality, as by demanding curative legislation which is by necessity retrospective.

That ethical philosophers are not universally prepared to deal with this kind of dilemma is shown when Cohen raises the question whether I do not "give my case away" when I "admit" that under some circumstances retrospective legislation may be beneficial.[48] Had I said that in my opinion telling lies is immoral, but that an exception should be made when a lie is told to save an innocent life, I don't think Cohen would have said that in recognizing this exception I had "given away my case" against lying. In both cases the qualification derives from a special social context. The difference is that in one case the demands of this context are highly visible and easily understood—one can imagine a lunatic erupting on the scene and demanding to know where his

48. Supra n. 5, p. 652.

intended victim is hiding—while in the other case the social context is complex and the interactions involved are indirect and inconspicuous.

If Cohen has difficulty with my "admission" that retrospective statutes curing past departures from legality may, on net balance, be beneficial, he has even more difficulty in absorbing the notion that antinomies among the principles of legal morality may be encountered in the design of legal institutions. After dealing with the "admission" involved in my comments on curative statutes, Cohen continues:

> But Fuller's concessions go further. He concedes that whenever a judge decides a case for which the standards are unclear he makes law retroactively. This strain of legal realism is unexpected in Fuller, and is not wholly consistent with his sound claim that unless the judge decides such cases "he fails in his duty to settle disputes arising out of an existing body of law."[49]

The statement just quoted could hardly come from one able to visualize a context in which two litigants, in an argument over the significance of a statute for their respective rights, take their dispute to a judge and ask him to resolve it. Would Cohen have the judge say, "You gentlemen have performed a public service in calling attention to a serious ambiguity in this statute. Though the arguments are about equally balanced, I hereby resolve your dispute about the meaning of the statute in favor of the contention made by A. Since, however, I do not wish to make retrospective law, this interpretation shall be effective only for situations that may arise in the future. As for the specific controversy between you two, I leave that undecided." A soliloquizing ethics will, of course, have little occasion to recognize or deal with problems of this sort; a morality concerned with social interaction will inevitably confront them and solve them as best it can, which means that it will often be forced to weigh the advantages and disadvan-

49. Ibid.

tages of one course of action, or of one institutional design, against those of another.[50]

I come now finally, and with a measure of reluctance, to some brief mention of the issue of *positivism v. natural law*. If the present controversy had arisen thirty years ago, this issue would probably have been seen as central to the whole debate. There was a time, certainly within living memory, when to speak disrespectfully of legal positivism was to open oneself up to the suspicion of being an adherent of some darkly conceived, darkly motivated, metaphysical, and probably ecclesiastical version of natural law.

Fortunately, the winds of doctrine seem to have changed their direction. Positivism is now coming under attack on many fronts, notably in linguistics and in the philosophies of science and of art. In sociology and legal anthropology there is a discernible trend away from structural theories and toward a study of interactional processes; I am told a similar shift has taken place during the last fifteen years in psychiatry and psychoanalysis. As for the law, one of the most uncompromising of my critics, Ronald Dworkin, has recently published what he himself describes as an "attack on positivism."[51] In this new climate of opinion there is no longer any need to apologize for being critical of positivism, nor does one run any serious risk that a rejection of positivism will be taken to imply a pretension that one has established contact with Absolute Truth.

In the reorientation that seems to be taking place, one hopes that there will develop a little more tolerance for, and interest in, the great tradition embodied in the literature of natural law. One will find in this literature much foolishness and much that is unacceptable to modern intellectual tastes; one will also find in it practical wisdom applied to problems that may broadly be called those of social architecture. St. Thomas Aquinas stands for many as a kind of symbol of all that is dogmatic and theological in the

50. In *Anatomy of the Law* (1968), pp. 84–112, I have attempted a comparison in these terms between the Anglo-American common law and systems based on comprehensive codifications.
51. Supra n. 34.

tradition of natural law. Yet as one writer has recently pointed out,[52] Aquinas in some measure recognized and dealt with all eight of the principles of legality discussed in my second chapter. I know of no writer in the positivist vein who has concerned himself in more than a perfunctory way with the general problem of achieving and maintaining legality.

In the philosophy of science the reorientation associated with the names of Michael Polanyi and Thomas Kuhn has been marked by a shift of interest away from the conceptualization and logical analysis of scientific verification and toward a study of the actual processes by which scientific discoveries are made. Perhaps in time legal philosophers will cease to be preoccupied with building "conceptual models" to represent legal phenomena, will give up their endless debates about definitions, and will turn instead to an analysis of the social processes that constitute the reality of law.

52. Lewis, "The High Court: Final . . . but Fallible," 19 *Western Reserve Law Review* 528–643, at p. 565 (1968). (It may be stretching things a bit to say that Aquinas recognized the principle of congruity between official action and declared rule.)

REVIEWS OF *THE MORALITY OF LAW*

Andrews, 89 *Library Journal* 3012 (1964).

Bartholomew, 58 *American Political Science Review* 984 (1964).

Baum, 10 *St. Louis University Law Journal* 435–41 (1966).

Bedau, *The Nation* (April 12, 1965), pp. 398–401.

Berns, *The National Review* (August 11, 1964), pp. 690–91.

Binkley, 1965 *Duke Law Journal* 668–70 (1965).

Blackshield, *Reading Guide of the University of Virginia Law School,* (Feb. 1965), pp. 11–16.

Boyé, *Revue Historique de Droit Français et Étranger* (July-Sept. 1965), pp. 504–05.

Brady, 43 *Texas Law Review* 258–59 (1964).

Braybrooke, 3 *Dialogue* 441–44 (1965).

Burrus, 17 *Hastings Law Journal* 861–64 (1966).

Campbell, 28 *Modern Law Review* 370–73 (1965).

Denonn, 50 *American Bar Association Journal* 1077 (1964).

Dias, 1965 *Cambridge Law Journal* 157–59 (1965).

Dowrick, 81 *Law Quarterly Review* 602–03 (1965).

Golding, 76 *Ethics* 225–28 (1966).

Gross, 40 *New York University Law Review* 1220–29 (1965).

Grunbaum, *Church & State* 473–75 (1966?).

Hanft, 43 *North Carolina Law Review* 238–44 (1964).

Hart, 78 *Harvard Law Review* 1281–96 (1965).

Hosking, 40 *California State Bar Journal* 90–94 (1965).

Hughes, 17 *Stanford Law Review* 547–59 (1965).

Jacobs, F. G., 10 *N.S., Juridical Review* 92–93 (Edinburgh, 1965).

Jacobs, Francis, 75 *N.S. Mind* 605–07 (1966).

Johnson, 33 *Tennessee Law Review* 563–65 (1966).

129 *Justice of the Peace and Local Government Review* 44 (London, Jan. 16, 1965).

Kurczewski, *Studia Filozoficzne* 274–80 (Warsaw, 1967).

235 *Law Times* 502 (London, Sept. 4, 1964).

Lewis, 17 *Western Reserve Law Review* 349–57 (1965).

McDowell, 44 *Boston University Law Review* 587–90 (1964).

Mandelbaum, 10 *New York Law Forum* 648–50 (1964).

Meyer, 10 *McGill Law Journal* 380–83 (1964).

Montrose, 16 *University of Toronto Law Journal* 451–55 (1966).

Morison, 5 *Sydney Law Review* 181–85 (1965).

Perelman, 10 *Natural Law Forum* 242–45 (1965).

Review of Metaphysics, p. 367 (December 1966).

Rose, 39 *Tulane Law Review* 387–95 (1965).

Savarese, 53 *Georgetown Law Journal* 250–58 (1964).

Schwartz, 359 *Annals of the American Academy of Political and Social Sciences* 190 (1965).

Selznick, 30 *American Sociological Review* 947–48 (1965).

Summers, 18 *Journal of Legal Education* 1–27 (1965).

Tucker, 40 *Indiana Law Journal* 270–79 (1965).

Tunc, 3 *Revue Internationale de Droit Comparé* 519–21 (1965).

Wasserstrom, 19 *Rutgers Law Review* 581–86 (1965).

Woozley, 16 *Philosophical Quarterly* 89–90 (St. Andrews Univ., 1966).

Wróblewski, *Ruch Prawniczy, Ekonomiczny i Socjologiczny* 224–30 (Poznań, 1966).

APPENDIX: THE PROBLEM OF

THE GRUDGE INFORMER

By a narrow margin you have been elected Minister of Justice of your country, a nation of some twenty million inhabitants. At the outset of your term of office you are confronted by a serious problem that will be described below. But first the background of this problem must be presented.

For many decades your country enjoyed a peaceful, constitutional and democratic government. However, some time ago it came upon bad times. Normal relations were disrupted by a deepening economic depression and by an increasing antagonism among various factional groups, formed along economic, political, and religious lines. The proverbial man on horseback appeared in the form of the Headman of a political party or society that called itself the Purple Shirts.

In a national election attended by much disorder the Headman was elected President of the Republic and his party obtained a majority of the seats in the General Assembly. The success of the party at the polls was partly brought about by a campaign of reckless promises and ingenious falsifications, and partly by the physical intimidation of night-riding Purple Shirts who frightened many people away from the polls who would have voted against the party.

When the Purple Shirts arrived in power they took no steps to repeal the ancient Constitution or any of its provisions. They also left intact the Civil and Criminal Codes and the Code of Procedure. No official action was taken to dismiss any government official or to remove any judge from the bench. Elections continued to be held at intervals and ballots were counted with apparent honesty. Nevertheless, the country lived under a reign of terror.

Judges who rendered decisions contrary to the wishes of the party were beaten and murdered. The accepted meaning of the Criminal Code was perverted to place political opponents in jail. Secret statutes were passed, the contents of which were known only to the upper levels of the party hierarchy. Retroactive statutes were enacted which made acts criminal that were legally innocent when committed. No attention was paid by the government to the restraints of the Constitution, of antecedent laws, or even of its own laws. All opposing political parties were disbanded. Thousands of political opponents were put to death, either methodically in prisons or in sporadic night forays of terror. A general amnesty was declared in favor of persons under sentence for acts "committed in defending the fatherland against subversion." Under this amnesty a general liberation of all prisoners who were members of the Purple Shirt party was effected. No one not a member of the party was released under the amnesty.

The Purple Shirts as a matter of deliberate policy preserved an element of flexibility in their operations by acting at times through the party "in the streets," and by acting at other times through the apparatus of the state which they controlled. Choice between the two methods of proceeding was purely a matter of expediency. For example, when the inner circle of the party decided to ruin all the former Socialist-Republicans (whose party put up a last-ditch resistance to the new regime), a dispute arose as to the best way of confiscating their property. One faction, perhaps still influenced by prerevolutionary conceptions, wanted to accomplish this by a statute declaring their goods forfeited for criminal acts. Another wanted to do it by compelling the owners to deed their property over at the point of a bayonet. This group argued against the proposed statute on the ground that it would attract unfavorable comment abroad. The Headman decided in favor of direct action through the party to be followed by a secret statute ratifying the party's action and confirming the titles obtained by threats of physical violence.

The Purple Shirts have now been overthrown and a democratic and constitutional government restored. Some difficult problems have, however, been left behind by the deposed regime. These you and your associates in the new government must find some way of solving. One of these problems is that of the "grudge informer."

During the Purple Shirt regime a great many people worked off grudges by reporting their enemies to the party or to the government authorities. The activities reported were such things as the private expression of views critical of the government, listening to foreign radio broadcasts, associating with known wreckers and hooligans, hoarding more than the permitted amount of dried eggs, failing to report a loss of identification papers within five days, etc. As things then stood with the administration of justice, any of these acts, if proved, could lead to a sentence of death. In some cases this sentence was authorized by "emergency" statutes; in others it was imposed without statutory warrant, though by judges duly appointed to their offices.

After the overthrow of the Purple Shirts, a strong public demand grew up that these grudge informers be punished. The interim government, which preceded that with which you are associated, temporized on this matter. Meanwhile it has become a burning issue and a decision concerning it can no longer be postponed. Accordingly, your first act as Minister of Justice has been to address yourself to it. You have asked your five Deputies to give thought to the matter and to bring their recommendations to conference. At the conference the five Deputies speak in turn as follows:

FIRST DEPUTY. "It is perfectly clear to me that we can do nothing about these so-called grudge informers. The acts they reported were unlawful according to the rules of the government then in actual control of the nation's affairs. The sentences imposed on their victims were rendered in accordance with principles of law then obtaining. These principles differed from those familiar to us in ways that we consider detestable. Nevertheless they were then the law of the land. One of the principal differences between that law and our own lies in the much wider discretion it accorded to the judge in criminal matters. This rule and its consequences are as much entitled to respect by us as the reform which the Purple Shirts introduced into the law of wills, whereby only two witnesses were required instead of three. It is immaterial that the rule granting the judge a more or less uncontrolled discretion in criminal cases was never formally enacted but was a matter of tacit acceptance. Exactly the same thing can be said of the opposite rule which we accept that restricts the judge's discretion narrowly. The difference between ourselves and the Purple Shirts is not that theirs was an unlawful government—a contradiction in terms—but lies rather in the field of ideology. No one has a greater abhorrence than I for Purple Shirtism. Yet the fundamental difference between our philosophy and theirs is that we permit and tolerate differences in viewpoint, while they attempted to impose their monolithic code on everyone. Our whole system of government assumes that law is a flexible thing, capable of expressing and effectuating many different aims. The cardinal point of our creed is that when an objective has been duly incorporated into a law or judicial decree it must be provisionally accepted even by those that hate it, who must await their chance at the polls, or in another litigation, to secure a legal recognition for their own aims. The Purple Shirts, on the other hand, simply disregarded laws that incorporated objectives of which they did not approve, not even considering it worth the effort involved to repeal them. If we now seek to unscramble the acts of the Purple Shirt regime, declaring this judgment invalid, that statute void, this sentence excessive, we shall be doing exactly the thing we most condemn in them. I recognize that it will take courage to carry through with the program I recommend and we shall have to resist strong pressures of public opinion. We shall also have to be prepared to prevent the people from taking the law into their own hands. In the long run, however, I believe the course I recommend is the only one that will insure the triumph of the conceptions of law and government in which we believe."

SECOND DEPUTY. "Curiously, I arrive at the same conclusion as my colleague, by an exactly opposite route. To me it seems absurd to call the Purple Shirt regime a lawful government. A legal system does not exist simply because policemen continue to patrol the streets and wear uniforms or because a constitution and code are left on the shelf unrepealed. A legal system presupposes laws that are known, or can be known, by those subject to them. It presupposes some uniformity of action and that like cases will be given like treatment. It presupposes the absence of some lawless power, like the Purple Shirt Party, standing above the government and able at any time to interfere with the administration of justice whenever it does not function according to the whims of that power. All of these presuppositions enter into the very conception of an order of law and have nothing to do with political and economic ideologies. In my opinion law in any ordinary sense of the word ceased to exist when the Purple Shirts came to power. During their regime we had, in effect, an interregnum in the rule of law. Instead of a government of laws we had a war of all against all conducted behind barred doors, in dark alleyways, in palace intrigues, and prison-yard conspiracies. The acts of these so-called grudge informers were just one phase of that war. For us to condemn these acts as criminal would involve as much incongruity as if we were to attempt to apply juristic conceptions to the struggle for existence that goes on in the jungle or beneath the surface of the sea. We must put

249

this whole dark, lawless chapter of our history behind us like a bad dream. If we stir among its hatreds, we shall bring upon ourselves something of its evil spirit and risk infection from its miasmas. I therefore say with my colleague, let bygones be bygones. Let us do nothing about the so-called grudge informers. What they did do was neither lawful nor contrary to law, for they lived, not under a regime of law, but under one of anarchy and terror."

THIRD DEPUTY. "I have a profound suspicion of any kind of reasoning that proceeds by an 'either-or' alternative. I do not think we need to assume either, on the one hand, that in some manner the whole of the Purple Shirt regime was outside the realm of law, or, on the other, that all of its doings are entitled to full credence as the acts of a lawful government. My two colleagues have unwittingly delivered powerful arguments against these extreme assumptions by demonstrating that both of them lead to the same absurd conclusion, a conclusion that is ethically and politically impossible. If one reflects about the matter without emotion it becomes clear that we did not have during the Purple Shirt regime a 'war of all against all.' Under the surface much of what we call normal human life went on—marriages were contracted, goods were sold, wills were drafted and executed. This life was attended by the usual dislocations—automobile accidents, bankruptcies, unwitnessed wills, defamatory misprints in the newspapers. Much of this normal life and most of these equally normal dislocations of it were unaffected by the Purple Shirt ideology. The legal questions that arose in this area were handled by the courts much as they had been formerly and much as they are being handled today. It would invite an intolerable chaos if we were to declare everything that happened under the Purple Shirts to be without legal basis. On the other hand, we certainly cannot say that the murders committed in the streets by members of the party acting under orders from the Headman were lawful simply because the party had achieved control of the government and its chief had become President of the Republic. If we must condemn the criminal acts of the party and its members, it would seem absurd to uphold every act which happened to be canalized through the apparatus of a government that had become, in effect, the alter ego of the Purple Shirt Party. We must therefore, in this situation, as in most human affairs, discriminate. Where the Purple Shirt philosophy intruded itself and perverted the administration of justice from its normal aims and uses, there we must interfere. Among these perversions of justice I would count, for example, the case of a man who was in love with another man's wife and brought about the death of the husband by informing against him for a wholly trivial offense, that is, for not reporting a loss of his identification papers within five days. This informer was a murderer under the Criminal Code which was in effect at the time of his act and which the Purple Shirts had not repealed. He encompassed the death of one who stood in the way of his illicit passions and utilized the courts for the realization of his murderous intent. He knew that the courts were themselves the pliant instruments of whatever policy the Purple Shirts might for the moment consider expedient. There are other cases that are equally clear. I admit that there are also some that are less clear. We shall be embarrassed, for example, by the cases of mere busybodies who reported to the authorities everything that looked suspect. Some of these persons acted not from desire to get rid of those they accused, but with a desire to curry favor with the party, to divert suspicions (perhaps ill-founded) raised against themselves, or through sheer officiousness. I don't know how these cases should be handled, and make no recommendation with regard to them. But the fact that these troublesome cases exist should not deter us from acting at once in the cases that are clear, of which there are far too many to permit us to disregard them."

FOURTH DEPUTY. "Like my colleague I too distrust 'either-or' reasoning, but I think we need to reflect more than he has about where we are headed. This proposal to pick and choose among the acts of the deposed regime is thoroughly objectionable. It is, in fact, Purple Shirtism itself, pure and simple. We like this law, so let us enforce it. We like this judgment, let it stand. This law we don't like, therefore it never was a law at all. This governmental act we disapprove, let it be deemed a nullity. If we proceed this way, we take toward the laws and acts of the Purple Shirt government precisely the unprincipled attitude they took toward the laws and acts of the government they supplanted. We shall have chaos, with every judge and every prosecuting attorney a law unto himself. Instead of ending the abuses of the Purple Shirt regime, my colleague's proposal would perpetuate them. There is only one way of dealing with this problem that is compatible with our philosophy of law and government and that is to deal with it by duly enacted law, I mean, by a special statute directed toward it. Let us study this whole problem of the grudge informer, get all the relevant facts, and draft a comprehensive law dealing with it. We shall not then be twisting old laws to purposes for which they were never intended. We shall furthermore provide penalties appropriate to the offense and not treat every informer as a murderer simply because the one he informed against was ultimately executed. I admit that we shall encounter some difficult problems of draftsmanship. Among other things, we shall have to assign a definite legal meaning to 'grudge' and that will not be easy. We should not be deterred by these difficulties, however, from adopting the only course that will lead us out of a condition of lawless, personal rule."

FIFTH DEPUTY. "I find a considerable irony in the last proposal. It speaks of putting a definite end to the abuses of the Purple Shirtism, yet it proposes to do this by resorting to one of the most hated devices of the Purple Shirt regime, the ex post facto criminal statute. My colleague dreads the confusion that will result if we attempt without a statute to undo and redress 'wrong' acts of the departed order, while we uphold and enforce its 'right' acts. Yet he seems not to realize that his proposed statute is a wholly specious cure for this uncertainty. It is easy to make a plausible argument for an undrafted statute; we all agree it would be nice to have things down in black and white on paper. But just what would this statute provide? One of my colleagues speaks of someone who had failed for five days to report a loss of his identification papers. My colleague implies that the judicial sentence imposed for that offense, namely death, was so utterly disproportionate as to be clearly wrong. But we must remember that at that time the underground movement against the Purple Shirts was mounting in intensity and that the Purple Shirts were being harassed constantly by people with false identification papers. From their point of view they had a real problem, and the only objection we can make to their solution of it (other than the fact that we didn't want them to solve it) was that they acted with somewhat more rigor than the occasion seemed to demand. How will my colleague deal with this case in his statute, and with all of its cousins and second cousins? Will he deny the existence of any need for law and order under the Purple Shirt regime? I will not go further into the difficulties involved in drafting this proposed statute, since they are evident enough to anyone who reflects. I shall instead turn to my own solution. It has been said on very respectable authority that the main purpose of the criminal law is to give an outlet to the human instinct for revenge. There are times, and I believe this is one of them, when we should allow that instinct to express itself directly without the intervention of forms of law. This matter of the grudge informers is already in process of straightening itself out. One reads almost every day that a former lackey of the Purple Shirt regime has met his just reward in some unguarded spot. The people are quietly handling this thing in their own way and if we leave them alone, and instruct our public prosecutors to do the same, there will soon be no problem left for us to solve. There will be some disorders, of course, and a few innocent heads will be broken. But our government and our legal system will not be involved in the affair and we shall not find ourselves hopelessly bogged down in an attempt to unscramble all the deeds and misdeeds of the Purple Shirts."

As Minister of Justice which of these recommendations would you adopt?

INDEX

Absolute liability. *See* Strict liability

Adams, Brooks, 73 n.

Adamson v. California, 102 n.

Adjudication: not indispensable to a legal system, 55–56; legal system may take its start in, 130–31, 144–45; not suited to allocative tasks, 46, 171–75; not suited to problems of institutional design, 177–81

Aigler, R. W., 63 n.

Allen, Francis A., 165

American Arbitration Association, 113

Anastaplo, George, 189 n.

Aquinas, St. Thomas, 18–19, 98, 185, 241

Aristotle, 5, 19, 64, 94

Arnold, Thurman, 50

Ash v. Abdy, 86 n.

Aspiration. *See* Morality of

Associations, voluntary: as administering their own legal systems, 124–29; their decisions subject to judicial review, 125–29; law concerning such review a branch of constitutional law, 128–29

Attainder, bills of, 52 n.

Auden, W. H., 152

Austin, J. L., 195–97

Austin, John, 48–49, 53 n., 63 n., 97, 110, 192, 215–16 n., 225–26

Baker v. Carr, 178

Barkun, Michael, 237

Barnard, Chester, 29 n.

Barth, Karl, 3

Baseball, rewards and censures in, 31

Beatification procedures of Catholic church, 32

Bentham, Jeremy, 6, 7, 18, 63 n., 65 n.

Bergler, Edmund, 8 n.

Berman, Harold, 202–03

Black, Duncan, 177 n.

Black, Hugo, 102 n.

Blau, Peter M., 213

255

INDEX

Bonham's Case, 99–101
Boorstin, D. J., 146 n.
Brandt, R. B., 5 n.
Bridgman, P. W., 119
Brown, Jethro, 49 n.

Caligula, 93
Campbell, Lord, 86 n.
Censors, boards of, in early American history, 177
Chafee, Zechariah, 129
Civil Aeronautics Board, 46, 171–75
Clarity of laws, 36, 43, 45, 63–65, 92, 102–03, 107, 115; as affecting managerial direction, 208; as presenting moral issue in administration of a legal system, 212–14
Clark, Tom, 165
Cohen, Marshall, 191, 197, 201, 238, 239–40
Coke, Sir Edward, 83 n., 99–101
Colleges, judicial review of disciplinary action by, 125–27
Commodity Exchange Theory of Law, 25–26
Conant, J. B., 120
Congruence of official action with declared rule, 38, 39–40, 45, 48, 56, 81–91, 92, 99, 115, 188–89, 190, 191, 193, 194; as affecting managerial direction, 208; as essential to Rule of Law, 209–10; as implying commitment by lawgiver, 216–18; as involved in interpretation of laws, 224, 230–31
Conseil d'État, 177
Constancy of the law through time, 37, 45, 79–81, 92; as affecting managerial orders, 208
Constitution, U.S., 51, 92, 101–03, 149
Constitutional law: and internal

morality of law, 102–06; judicial review of disciplinary action in private associations as a branch of, 128–29
Constitutions, virtues and defects of written, 114–15
Contraception and the law, 153
Contradictions in the law, 36, 65–70, 92, 99, 101–02, 111–13, 115, 130; between institutions, 100–01; as affecting managerial orders, 208; whether presenting moral issue, 238
Cook, W. W., 137 n.
Corbin, A. L., 134 n., 136 n.
Council on Tribunals, 177
Criminal law: and retroactivity, 59; strict liability under, 77–78; and human responsibility, 163–67; abuses of rehabilitative ideal in, 165
Cruel and unusual punishment, 105
Customary law, interpretation of, 227–28; nature of, 233–36; as an ingredient of "made" law, 232, 234; problems of transition from, to enacted law, 234–36

Declaration of Independence, 156
Del Vecchio, G., 23 n.
Devlin, P. A., 132 n.
Dicey, A. V., on parliamentary sovereignty, 115–17
Dispute settlement not exclusive aim of law, 55
Dodgson, Charles, 177
Due process, 81, 105–06
Duties: rules imposing, contrasted with rules conferring powers, 93, 134–37; economic allocation cannot be organized by, 170–76; scope of community within which duties are meaningful, 181–82

256

Duty, concept of, among Greeks, 5; in primitive society, 143–44. *See also* Morality of duty

Dworkin, Ronald, 189, 190, 192, 198–99, 201, 221–22, 224 n., 238–39, 241

Economics: definitions of, 15–17; parallels with morality, 17–30; adjudication an inept means for solving task of, 170–76. *See also* Exchange; Marginal Utility; Reciprocity

Ellesmere, Lord, 68 n.

Emmet, Dorothy, 239

Escarra, Jean, 143 n.

Exchange, economics of, compared with morality of duty, 19–27, 28. *See also* Marginal Utility; Reciprocity

Expulsions from clubs, schools, and associations as subject to judicial review, 124–29

Federal Communications Commission, 46, 171–75

Federalist, The, 80, 101

Fidelity to law, obligation of, 39–41

Findlay, J. M., 5 n.

Force, sanction of, as distinguishing law from morality, 108–10

Frankfurter, Felix, 102 n.

Friedmann, W., 107

Friendly, H. J., 172–75

Fuller, L. L., 18 n., 25 n., 40 n., 46 n., 84 n., 92 n., 232 n., 241 n.

Gambling, 6–9

Generality of law, 34, 46–49; constitutional prohibitions of special and private laws, 47; bills of attainder, 52 n., 97–98, 110, 131; relation to justice, 157–59, 165, 193–95; as affecting managerial direction, 209; as essential to Rule of Law, 209–10

George III, 156

Golden Rule, 20–21

Good Samaritan, 182–83

Gottlieb, Gidon, 224 n.

Gough, J. W., 99

Graham v. Goodcell, 55 n.

Gray, J. C., 49 n., 52 n., 83–84, 97, 112, 226

Greeks, conception of morality among, 5, 13–15

Hale, R. L., 52 n., 103 n.

Hall, J., 78 n.

Hamilton, Alexander, 101

Hampshire, Stuart, 196

Harrod, R. F., 16 n.

Hart, H. L. A., 5 n.; on defeasible concepts, 29–30, 95 n.; on legislating morals, 132 n.; "the rule of recognition," 133–44, 192; rules imposing duties distinguished from rules conferring powers, 134–37; distinction between a legal system and "the gunman situation writ large," 139–40; problem of the persistence of law, 141–42, 149–50; transition from primitive society to "the legal world," 142–44; on the significance of the internal morality of law, 153–55, 197; "the pathology of a legal system," 155, 157; a minimum natural law, 155, 184–86; criticisms of this book, 188, 189–91, 196, 201; his analysis of law based on managerial model, 214–16, 225, 237–38

Hart, Henry M., 50 n., 78 n., 180, 223

Hayek, F. A., 24, 64–65

Hector, L., 174

Heydon's Case, 82–83

Hitler, German law under, 40–41, 54–55, 62, 107, 123, 155, 158

Hochman, C. B., 52 n.

Hoebel, A., 108, 206

Hohfeldian analysis, 134, 136–37

Holmes, O. W., 29, 106, 119, 152

Holt, Lord, 88–89

Honors. *See* Rewards

Hughes, Graham, 189 n., 224 n.

Impossibility, laws commanding an, 36–37, 45, 53–54, 70–79; liability founded on fault, 71–72; liability founded on a wrongful intent, 72–73; liability based on unjust enrichment, 73–74; strict civil liability, 75–77; strict criminal liability, 77–78; not always distinguishable from laws imposing severe hardship, 79; laws requiring political or religious belief, 79, 92, 99, 100; impossibility of obedience as affecting managerial orders, 208

Intention of laws, to whom ascribed, 86–87

Interaction, as an element in law, 39–40, 191, 193–95, 220–24, 233–34

Internal morality of law: primarily a morality of aspiration, 41–44; whether reducible to fewer than eight principles, 70 n.; as applied to secret legislative orders, 91–92; departures from, tend to become cumulative, 92; its demands relaxed when laws correspond to common views of right and wrong, 50, 92–93; demands vary with branch of law, 93; includes both simple and complex respon-

sibilities, 93–94; as expressed in the natural-law tradition, 96–106; treatment of, by positivists, 97; special attention during 17th century, 99–101; as clarifying relation of law and morality, 131–32; meaningless when law is abstracted from any general purpose, 147–48; interaction with substantive aims, 153–67; relation to efficacy of law, 155–57; relation to substantive justice, 157–59; necessarily infringed by laws directed toward undefinable evils, 159–62; requires view of man as responsible agent, 162–67; whether entitled to be called "morality," 200–23; as affecting managerial direction, 208–09. *See also* Clarity of laws; Congruence of official action with declared rule; Constancy of the law through time; Contradictions in the law; Generality of law; Impossibility, laws commanding an; Promulgation; Retroactive laws

Internal morality of science, 120–21

International law, 232–34, 236–37

Interpretation: as an aspect of maintaining congruence between official action and declared rule, 82–91; as demanding creative role of the judge, 87; of the Statute of Frauds, 88–89; of laws designed to prevent a "return of the old saloon," 89–91; theories of, implied in dispute with critics, 224–32; of custom, 228–29; as affected by antinomies among principles of legality, 230–31; as affected by reciprocal expectations within legal system, 231–32

Interstate Commerce Commission, 175

Israeli Law of Return, 162

Jefferson, Thomas, 79, 146

Jhering, Rudolph von, 66 n.

Jones, J. W., 5 n.

Judge-made law, problem of maintaining congruence with declared rule, 82. *See also* Adjudication

Judicial office, law does not in all cases require, 55–56. *See also* Adjudication

Jurisdiction over jobs in industrial management, 219

Kant, Immanuel, 20, 152; Pashukanis' view of, 25–26

Kelsen, Hans, 49 n., 52 n., 65 n., 110–12, 119, 191–92, 198, 227

King, B. E., 189 n.

Kingston v. Preston, 87 n.

Kuhn, Thomas, 242

Lamont, W. D., 5 n., 12 n.

Lange, Oskar, 24 n.

Language, theories of, involved in interpretation of law, 84, 227–28

Law: meaning of, for internal morality of law, 91–92; existence of, a matter of degree, 122–23; multiple systems of, 123–29; distinguished from morality, 130–33; limits of its efficacy, 168–70; whether existence of is a matter of indifference from a moral point of view, 204–07

definitions of: as a prediction of state action, 106–07; as public order, 107, 118; as rules sanctioned by force, 108, 118; as a

hierarchic ordering of command, 110–13, 118, 148–49

Legal morality. *See* Internal morality of law

Legality, principles of, some respect for essential for existence of law, 197–200. *See also* Internal morality of law

Lewan, Kenneth M., 189 n.

Lewis, Ovid, 242 n.

Lilburne, John, 33, 70, 217–18

Lindsay, A. D., 5 n.

Liquor laws, 89–91

Llewellyn, Karl, 192

Lloyd, D., 127 n.

Macbeath, A., 5 n.

McCall, George J., 195

McHugh, Peter, 224 n.

Madison, James, 80

Malinowski, B., 169 n.

Managerial direction, distinguished from law, 207–10, 212–13; juristic aspects of managerial systems, 212–13

Mansfield, Lord, 87

Marginal utility, principle of: as defining scope of economic science, 16; economic counterpart to morality of aspiration, 17–19, 27–29; affects realization of internal morality of law, 44–46; as making adjudicative processes unsuited to allocation of economic resources, 170–77; affects design of institutions, 177–81. *See also* Economics; Exchange; Reciprocity

Marx, Karl, alienation theme in, 26

Marxism. *See* Pashukanis

Mays, Willie, 31

Mead, Margaret, 144–45

Military organization compared with legal hierarchy, 113

Mill, J. S., 18, 168–69

Miscegenation, 161

Mitigation of damages, 135–36

Model Penal Code, 78 n.

Moral community, 181–83

Moral scale. *See* Pointer dividing moralities of duty and of aspiration

Morality: distinguished from law, 6–7, 9, 130–33; vocabulary of, confusing moralities of aspiration and of duty, 13–15; its principles compared with those of economics, 15–30; implications of debate with critics for, 237–41

Morality of aspiration, 5; its view of gambling, 8–9; not concerned exclusively with individual values, 12–13; not subject to discursive demonstration, 14; counterpart of marginal utility economics, 17–19, 28; governs internal morality of law, 41–44; requires affirmative acts, 42–43; implied in constitutional law, 104. *See also* Marginal utility

Morality of duty, 5–6; its view of gambling, 6–8; relation to reciprocity and economic exchange, 19–28; achieves highest expression in a society of traders, 22–24; involves restraints rather than creative acts, 42. *See also* Reciprocity

Nagel, E., 18 n., 188

National Labor Relations Board, 173

Natural law: and the internal morality of law, 96–106; procedural and substantive distinguished, 96–97; special quality of, during 17th century, 99–101; in U.S. Constitution and its interpretation, 99, 102–06; H. L. A. Hart's conception of, 155, 184–86; maintenance of communication basic principle of substantive natural law, 185–86; as an issue in debate with critics, 241–42

Nazi law. *See* Hitler

Newton, N. T., 14 n.

Nietzsche, F., 95

Nottingham, Lord, 86 n.

Ochoa v. Hernandez y Morales, 81 n.

Ombudsman, 82, 177

One-way projection of authority, law viewed as, 191–95

Ordinary-language philosophy, 195–97, 199. *See also* J. L. Austin

Ozawa v. United States, 161

Pappe, H. O., 40 n.

Parliamentary sovereignty, 113–17; political merits, compared with written constitution, 114–15; dependent upon successful functioning of laws of procedure, 115, 148; legal theory of, 115–17

Pashukanis, Eugene, 24–26, 113

Patterson, E. W., 49 n.

Penalties, standards for imposing, 30–32

Perelman, C., 69 n.

Perez v. Sharp, 161

Perfection: departure from, as a test of evil, 10–12; ideal of, in relation to allotment of rewards and penalties, 32; in realization of the internal morality of law, 41–44

Plato, 5, 10, 11, 14–15

Pointer dividing moralities of duty

and of aspiration, 9–13, 27–28; its counterpart, dividing economics of exchange and of marginal utility, 28; as applied to internal morality of law, 42–44; as applied to the range of governmental action, 170–71

Polanyi, M., 29, 118–21, 242

Police lawlessness: inadequacy of courts to control, 81–82; example of, 158–59

Pomerantz v. Clark, 42

Portalis, J. E. M., 141

Positivistic theories of law, 106–18, 145–51

Pound, Roscoe, 95, 170

Powers, legal rules conferring, distinguished from those imposing duties, 134–37; inapplicability of distinction to basic premises of a legal system, 138–40

Precedent, force of, as expressing commitment by lawgiver to apply declared law, 218–19

Private laws. *See* Generality of law

Promotions, arbitration of, 31

Promulgation of laws, 34–35, 43–44, 49–51; whether necessary for rules of internal governmental procedure, 50, 54, 92, 98, 105–06, 139–40, 165, 188, 189, 191; as affecting managerial direction, 208

Punishment. *See* Penalties

Purposive view of law: objections to, 145–46; costs of rejecting, 147–51; Hart's attitude toward, 189–90

Racial discrimination and the law, 159–62, 183–84

Realism, American Legal, 226–27

Reciprocity: and the morality of duty, 19–27; moral force of reciprocity enhanced by equality, 23, and by possibility of a reversal of roles, 23–24; between lawgiver and subject, 39–40, 48, 61–62, 137–40. *See also* Interaction; Morality of duty

Redford, E. S., 174

Reichenbach, Hans, 119 n.

Retroactive laws, 35, 44, 51–62; constitutional provisions regarding, 51 n., 52 n.; curative laws, 53–55, 239–40; as involved in judicial lawmaking, 55–58, 239–40; what constitute, 59–62; compared with laws correcting effects of inadvertence, 74; relation to problem of constancy of laws through time, 80–81, 92, 100; laws enhancing the obligation of contract, 103; Dicey on, 116; as applied to rehabilitative measures, 165–66, 188, 194–95; use of, by Soviet Russia, 202–03; as affecting managerial orders, 209; affecting realization of the Rule of Law, 210–12

Reviews of this book, 187 n., 188 n., 243–44

Rewards, standards for granting, 30–32

Richards, I. A., 14 n.

Right: Greek concept of, 5 n.; as tending toward absolute, 29

Robbins, Lionel, 16 n.

Robinson v. California, 105–06, 165

Role, concept of social, 192–93, 218, 239

Rousseau, J. J., 23 n.

Samuelson, P. A., 16 n.

Sartorius, Rolfe E., 192

261

Science: theories of, compared with theories of law, 118–21; defined as ability to predict and control, 119; as hierarchic ordering of knowledge of nature, 119; reforms of education in, 120; internal morality of, 120–21

Secession of the Plebs, 49

Secret legislative measures, 91–92

Seidman, Robert B., 235

Selective enforcement of laws, 8, 78, 92

Sermon on the Mount, 20

Sidgwick, H., 15

Simmel, Georg, 39, 61, 216–17

Simmons, J. L., 195

Sins, deadly, 15

Skinner, B. F., 163–64

Smith, Adam, 6

Smith v. Westfall, 89 n.

Social dimension, lack of, in positivist theories of law, 193

Somló, Felix, 49 n., 53 n.; on retroactive laws, 97 n., 111 n., 112 n.

South African racial laws, 160

Special laws. See Generality of law

"Standing" to raise constitutional issues, 81

Statute of Frauds, 88–89, 135–36

Statute of Westminster (1931), 129

Stephen, J. F., 168–69

Strict liability: and laws commanding the impossible, 72, 75–78; cannot become a general principle, 76, 167

Sturm, Douglas, 189 n.

Summers, R. C., on "The New Analytical Jurists," 190–91; agreement on need for minimum respect for principles of legality, 198

Suzman, A., 160 n.

Talmud, 183

Teleology. See Purposive view of law

Thorne, S. E., 68 n., 100 n.

Tot v. United States, 62 n.

Traffic regulation as illustrating collaborative nature of legal enterprise, 220–21

Trustee, right to reimbursement, 134–35

Tucker, Robert C., 26

United States v. Cardiff, 67–68

United States v. Thind, 161 n.

Utilitarian philosophy, 197; and retrospective laws, 237–38

"Value judgment," 13

Vaughan, C. J., 33

"Virtue," 15

Weber, Max, 143 n., 148–49

Wechsler, Herbert, 48 n.

Wicksteed, P. H., 26–27

Wittgenstein, L., 138, 186

Workmen's Compensation Law, 76

Written constitutions, 114–15

Wynne's Lessee v. Wynne, 54 n.

Wyzanski, C. E., 129 n., 232